MW00332886

Golden Cities & The Masters of Shamballa

The I AM America Teachings

ALSO BY LORI TOYE

A Teacher Appears

Sisters of the Flame

Fields of Light

The Ever Present Now

New World Wisdom Series

I AM America Atlas

Points of Perception

Light of Awakening

Divine Destiny

Sacred Energies

Temples of Consciousness

Awaken the Master Within

Building the Seamless Garment

Freedom Star Book

I AM America Map

Freedom Star Map

6-Map Scenario

US Golden City Map

GOLDEN CITIES *and the*
Masters *of* Shamballa

the I AM America Teachings
Lori Adaile Toye

AMERICA

I AM AMERICA PUBLISHING & DISTRIBUTING
P.O. Box 2511, Payson, Arizona, 85547, USA.
www.iamamerica.com

© (Copyright) 2019 by Lori Adaile Toye. All rights reserved. ISBN: 978-1-880050-33-0. All rights exclusively reserved, including under the Berne Convention and the Universal Copyright Convention. No part of this book may be reproduced or translated in any language or utilized in any form or by any means, electronic or mechanical, including photocopying, recording, or by any information storage and retrieval system, without written permission from the publisher. Published in 2019 by I AM America Seventh Ray Publishing International, P.O. Box 2511, Payson, Arizona, 85547, United States of America.

I AM America Maps and Books have been marketed since 1989 by I AM America Seventh Ray Publishing and Distributing, through workshops, conferences, and numerous bookstores in the United States and internationally. If you are interested in obtaining information on available releases please write or call: I AM America, P.O. Box 2511, Payson, Arizona, 85547, USA. (928) 978-6435, or visit:
www.iamamerica.com
www.loritoye.com

Graphic Design and Typography by Lori Toye
Host and Questions by Lenard Toye
Guest-student Questions: Rosalie Mashtalier
Editing by Betsy Robinson

Love, in service, breathes the breath for all!
Print On Demand Version
10 9 8 7 6 5 4 3 2 1

Cover Illustration: *Dwarka: Lord Krishna in the Golden City.* Wikimedia Commons, 10 Jan. 2012, commons.wikimedia.org/wiki/File:Dwarka.jpg. "The Lord Krishna in the Golden City from the *Harivamsha*, (Genealogy of Vishnu). Opaque watercolor and gold on paper, India. The painting represents the mythical City of Dwarka, where the blue-skinned Krishna, an incarnation of the Hindu God Vishnu, is enthroned on a golden palace and surrounded by his kinsmen. A pastoral scene in the foreground evokes a familiar village setting and a sense that the gods are present in everyday life. This manuscript was painted for the Mughal emperor Akbar (r. 1556–1605) who was quite interested in other religions. Akbar had translations made of major Hindu texts, including the Sanskrit epic the *Mahabharata–Great Story of the Bharatas*, known in its Persian translation as *Razmnama* (Book of Wars). This image is from a section appended to the *Razmnama* known as the *Harivamsa* (Genealogy of Vishnu), which narrates of the life of Krishna. Circa 1600, Mughal Dynasty, Reign of Emperor Akbar."

"In my Father's house are many mansions;
if it were not so, I would have told you.
I go to prepare a place for you."

~ Jesus Christ

JOHN 14:2

Contents

CHAPTER THREE
Acceleration • 51

CHAPTER FOUR

Leveraging Consciousness • 67

CHAPTER FIVE

A Great Love • 75

CHAPTER SIX

Human to HU-man • 83

CHAPTER SEVEN

The Golden Orb • 91

CHAPTER EIGHT

The Guiding Light • 107

CHAPTER ELEVEN

One-thousand Eighty-eight • 139

CHAPTER TWELVE

Tipping Point • 147

CHAPTER THIRTEEN

Activation • 157

CHAPTER FOURTEEN

Great Awakening • 169

CHAPTER FIFTEEN

The Aquamarine Ray • 181

CHAPTER SIXTEEN

Golden Age of Co-creation • 189

Foreword

This book is your next step on the spiritual path of Ascension with the *I AM America* knowledge from the Ascended Masters, through Lori Toye. Before I met Lori, I had the opportunity to observe other famous mystics and channels. I was on a spiritual journey and experiencing a full-blown Spiritual Awakening. My awakening had been prompted by my own experiences, as I could see and hear the Divine Beings who often visit and bless us with spiritual knowledge and wisdom. I had witnessed trance mediums who were fifty to sixty percent accurate, but I was impressed when I met Lori. She was sitting at Sherry Takala's kitchen table and relaying the Spiritual Masters' information with above ninety-five percent accuracy.

In this book, the Masters of Shamballa concentrate their efforts to explain and demonstrate the consciousness-expanding dynamic of Group Mind. This comprehensive technique is detailed throughout the lessons. The Masters' system is simple and straight forward for the reader and ensures the next valuable step in the Ascension Process. Remember, we are at the mere beginning of the Golden Age of Kali Yuga and you are fortunate and privileged to learn this soul-freeing wisdom.

What many of you may not know is that in March of 2010, Lori withdrew from trance channeling. When she resumed in August of 2018, she was instantly flooded with a surge of spiritual guidance from not only Saint Germain, El Morya, Kuthumi, and Lord Sananda, but also Lady Nada, Mother Mary, Hercules, Amazonia, TronXR, Elohim Siene, Viseeah, Lady Nala, and Serapis Bey. Each of these Ascended Beings contributed to a tremendous momentum of expanding consciousness that is represented in the teachings of this book.

This book precedes its two important forerunners from the *Golden City Series*, *Temples of Consciousness*, and *Awaken the Master Within*. The teachings in these books were received nearly fifteen years ago, and were purposely held back by the Masters and not published until the first of this year, (January 2019). *Golden Cities and the Masters of Shamballa* is the next sequential building block for consciousness development and contains the next phase of Ascension teachings from the Ascended Masters. A significant element of the Ascension Process is the prominent concept of the ONE, also known as Unana. This precept evolves into the practice of the Golden Orb Meditation, a precursor to Group Mind—a key to Ascension.

Ascension is not myth and many souls are still reaching their liberation. In fact, Saint Germain informed us during the Shamballa Season of 2018-

2019 that actually 1,088 Ascensions transpired in the previous year, and most were achieved through devotion to a specific religion and spiritual practice. Because of the significant opportunity of this teaching, and during this critical *Time of Change* and *Great Awakening*, we rushed to get this book to you as soon as possible. I must add that the bulk of this spiritual knowledge came to us during soul-inspiring spiritual pilgrimages, the last one completed in July 2019.

Each page in this book is filled with the knowledge intended to free you from the nonstop rounds of reincarnation and the Wheel of Karma. May your freedom be realized in this lifetime and may your soul's victory continue onward into the Fourth, Fifth, and Sixth layers of Divine Consciousness.

Blessings in the Light of God that Never Fails,

Lenard Toye
August 2019

Preface

The Ascended Masters contact us in a variety of ways. Sometimes it is dramatic, similar to Saint Germain's unmistakable first physical appearance to me at the foot of my bed. There are many accounts of Spiritual Masters appearing to aspirants and chelas, alike. They have materialized in redwood forests, at the edge of a shimmering mountain stream, in unassuming bookstores, and often in disguise—young, old, a homeless beggar, a well attired gentleman, or an average Joe sipping a cup of coffee at a café counter.

Yet, more often, these majestic beings of light communicate or let us know they are present in refined and subtle ways. Sometimes it is a sudden flash of light, a movement caught from the corner of the eye, a fresh breeze of air on a humid, balmy day, or a whisper brushing consciousness in meditation. Throughout the years I've learned how to catch these delicate nuances that may lead to insightful guidance or even detailed discourses with not only one, but maybe two or three Master Teachers. At one time in my channeling career, that now spans more than thirty years, I would see a faint figure of light hovering in the corner of my bedroom. I would then receive a telepathic message, "time to receive information," or "there will be a message tomorrow." This signaled the need for a channeling session that I and my husband, Len, would dutifully follow up the next morning.

Along the way, somehow I began to lose interest. It was not that the precious signals were absent, but to be honest I had become distracted with the pressures of everyday life. Plus, I was working on a sizeable backlog of transcripts. If you've been following our work with *I AM America*, you may have noticed that we've been releasing one or two new titles almost every year. This, of course, takes tremendous time with detailed effort, and often the mere thought of even adding another ounce to this stack of unpublished texts is a bit overwhelming. Plus, I'd been mentoring a small, selected group of students in these teachings for the last five years, and our sessions together were a couple days a week. My life was rich, complex, imperfect *and* perfect, sometimes harried, and inordinately blessed.

My students' mentoring had reached an impasse that could only be solved through one-on-one instruction. It was time to temporarily lay the books and lofty, spiritual philosophy aside. Now we were compelled to learn about the physical energies of Golden Cities, how to identify them from topographical maps and boots-on-the-ground physical assessment, observe their unique landforms and geological characteristics, and of course layer this with our own personal psychic insight. The final step was to ably interface this knowledge for spiritual development alongside the Masters' instruction on the Ascension Process. So with guidance from Saint Germain, we trekked to the rivers and valleys of Idaho and Montana, in the spiritual sanction of the Southern Door of Shalahah. It was here that Len and I hoped to share our years of integrated knowledge regarding our experience with the Ascended Masters, with the assistance of the energy-calibrating Adjutant Points, lei-lines, and metaphysical anomalies of a real-life Golden City.

We arrived at the first point after driving more than a thousand miles, the *Abundance Adjutant Point of the Southern Door of Shalahah*, (Red Door). The location was marked on my map, nestled near a canyon, next to an outcrop of soaring mountains that stood before a lush tapestry of meadows, grasslands, and an occasional field of barley. We passed by a pioneer cemetery and turned north to travel uphill on a gravel road. After several miles our vehicle started vibrating—we had a flat tire! Len was fastidious with our vehicles, and before we had left on our journey had new tires placed on the car. I peered over the map again and asked myself the obvious question, "Is this the right location?"

I hopped out of the car and two students joined me as we walked toward a grove of trees, about a quarter of a mile away. "Looks like we've been intentionally stopped," I stated after we'd walked a few feet together. We headed toward the grove and then noticed a beautiful irrigation ditch, hiding in the tall grass that meandered toward the trees. The waters turned west to ramble onward and perfectly outline a cascading series of meadows. While listening to the soft trickle of the bubbling waters, I paused to observe the mountains, the nearby canyon, and the flowing meadows framed by trees and water. The scene held an almost perfect *ming tang*, a Feng Shui formation also known as a *bright hall*. This type of landform captures and holds benefic energies. We had literally been stopped in our journey, with a flat tire, to find this sublime Adjutant Point.

We signaled to Len and to another student helping him with the tire. The sun was setting, and the five of us gathered near the stream and formed a circle to recite the Violet Flame for the Sunset. Our prayers resounded through the soft air of dusk and we were greeted by a western sky painted with blue, yellow, golden oranges, and hues of violet.

We continued our journey for several days through the mountains of Montana to Lolo Pass near the Apex or Star of Shalahah, then drove down the highway following the Lochsa and Clearwater Rivers, and up the river valley, following the Sevenmile Creek to the Camas Prairie.

The central Idaho prairies were magical and enchanting, with abandoned orchards laden with ripened apples or plums, fields of unending soon-to-be harvested golden wheat, and sweeping horizons filled with the promise of Shalahah's abundance, prosperity, and healing. Though happy to be home again in the countryside of my youth, (I was born and raised on an Idaho farm), fatigue was setting in. Of course I wanted to give all that I could to my students, but there were moments when I couldn't hide my low energy.

Undoubtedly, I had underestimated my physical condition. Just eighteen months prior I had received a nightmarish call from my physician with a cancer diagnosis, and during the next year endured three surgeries. I rallied with loving support from both my family and students. However, Len was uncertain if I was ready for a trip of this length and expenditure, both mentally and physically.

We spent several more days in Shalahah's Southern Door in McCall, Idaho, where Len taught auric energy techniques for healing. This was a specific request from Saint Germain, where he claimed the over-lighting of the Christ Consciousness would begin for the students. Remember, Shalahah is Lord Sananda's Vortex of the Green Ray of Healing.

Venturing onward to the Western Door of Shalahah (Yellow Door), our group traveled to the mouth of Hell's Canyon, near Lewiston, Idaho, and Clarkston, Washington. Invigorated by my return to the Snake River Valley, affectionate memories flooded over me as we drove out to Asotin, where in my early thirties I first began trance channeling. As we drove along the river I could trace almost every turn, twist, and bump of the bike path that mirrored my spiritual path at that time. When we arrived in Asotin, we stopped in front of the small white house where Sherry Takala, my spiritual mentor had once lived and where I had met Len for the first time. For a brief time-compacted moment it felt like 1990 again, and I sensed the spirits of the beloved *Sisters of the Flame*—Sherry, Glenda, and Priscilla—guiding this passage with me for my students.

Just below Sherry's home lies *Chief Looking Glass Park* and hidden off to the park's side is the *Secret Beach*. Primarily known to locals, this was our family's favorite white sandy beach where I spent many hours with my young children when we lived along the banks of this beautiful river. Today, however, I would share this special location with my students, and initiate them into the healing waters of the Cup Ceremony.

The Cup in Ascended Master teaching is a symbol of neutrality. In fact, it is claimed that the Angels of Heaven introduced the Holy Grail specifically to counteract extreme polarities and to defuse conflict. Indeed, it has this quality, but the Cup is also activating and benevolent. Its waters symbolize our emotional body in need of healing, and a focused water ceremony with a Cup can imbue positive, remedial energies for miles. If you perform a Cup Ceremony at a power point or Adjutant Point, this can increase its efficiency exponentially. However, before one can begin to focus the energies of the Mental Body, the chela must claim Mastery over their emotions. This, of course, disciplines our actions, and is the distinctive dividing line between the lower, animal self and the Higher Self.

Water symbolizes the separation between the dimensions. Before a child is born into this world, a bag of waters must break. Psychics and mystics claim that a river or torrent of water-like energy separates Third and Fourth Dimension and that a similar but more refined ether divides the spiritual energies of Fourth and Fifth Dimension. A proficient Cup Bearer can literally open the Fourth and Fifth Dimensions at a ceremonial site to receive the blessings of the Nature Kingdoms and the spiritual heavens. But at the simplest level, water is perhaps one of the most humble and modest gifts we can offer Mother Earth, and once the water in the Cup is infused with our prayer and intention, it is offered as a drink to Babajeran. This paraphrased passage from the Bhagavad Gita reiterates this spiritual wisdom: "Whoever offers me with devotion a leaf, a flower, a fruit, or water, I accept that gift of the pure-hearted man."

In the *I AM America Teachings*, a Cup is often presented to chelas who have proved themselves spiritually ready and encompassing the maturity to share the Ascended Masters' teachings and traditions with others. In many ways, this water ceremony is similar to Christian Baptism, a ceremony of spiritual recognition or admission; or, like the Abhishekam ceremony—the Hindu custom of purification, through the bathing or cleansing of karmas. Receiving the Cup purifies the Emotional Body, and its waters metaphorically and metaphysically cleanse the chela's mind, in this case through their surrender to the principle of love and utmost devotion to Christ Consciousness. As each student stepped from the sandy shore of the Secret Beach into the knee deep water of the Snake River, I literally poured water from my Cup into a new Cup that I had given to each of them. As we performed our Cup Ceremony, the beach seemed inordinately private. However, off to the side a group of young boys played in the water as if our group was entirely invisible. They reminded me of the *Four Youthful Kumaras*, the renowned yogis and sages of the Puranic texts of India.

The next day we rose early and headed northeast from the river valley to the Clearwater Mountains in the soothing trees of the Saint Joe National Forest. In my beginning days of trance channeling, Saint Germain had identified this location as an ancient Atlantean Healing Point. Saint Germain's historical account of this particular time in Atlantean history alleges that in this prescient civilization crime was almost nonexistent. However, with the rare case, criminals were immediately isolated thousands of miles away from civilization. Here, in areas that were minimally affected by the Collective Consciousness, is where true rehabilitation could ensue. Apparently, in another lifetime I had lived and worked in this isolated camp, and assisted

Atlantean patients to recover emotionally and mentally through curative water therapies, and harmonizing energy technologies that balanced body, mind, and soul.

Len and I always enjoyed visiting the site and found it to be genuinely restoring. Throughout the years we had picnicked there, panned for gold in the stream, and hiked throughout its valley of soaring firs, cedars, and peace-instilling energy. After decades of research we determined that the site is filled with glacium, a naturally occurring monatomic element that Saint Germain claims to transconduct energies interdimensionally and initiate the Ascension Process. A small creek winds through the site, and since water can disperse glacium, the stream's waters are inordinately restorative and healing. In fact, several years ago I had spent time at the site, and after several days in the water began to notice that all sorts of aches and pains disappeared.

Upon arrival, I anxiously dipped my feet into the water and in about ten minutes, the glacium began to work its miracle. My students seemed to enjoy the mountain stream, too. Even though the waters were frigid, several had donned bathing suits to lie in the invigorating, restorative current. I perched myself at the creek's grassy edge, and at times I could hear the voices of the Masters whispering, as if to burst out in an impromtu metanarrative of Ascension Valley and Ancient Atlantis. At one point one of my students declared, "I think Lori should tell us stories about the Masters and this site." Undeniably, she must have heard the interdimensional conversation as the waters lifted her consciousness into the spiritual planes. After a full day at Saint Germain's healing site, we left rested and spiritually fortified. That evening I quickly fell into a deep sleep and dream state with spiritual physicians working to restructure and heal my energy fields.

The next morning we woke to hazy, smoky skies from nearby forest fires. After meeting for coffee, our group decided to take the morning off and reschedule our work for late afternoon, in hopes that the smoke would dissipate. Our older students readily agreed, but I sensed that the younger students, eager for the vital experience that comes from studying with a seasoned physical guru, were a bit disappointed. Surprisingly, several hours later, the sky began to clear, so I texted my students and asked them to meet us at the next Adjutant Point, near Kamiak Butte. Upon arrival, the students were obviously excited. Amy was the first to explain, "We decided that it was time for us to take action. So we met and performed Cup Ceremony with *our* Cups . . . and the skies cleared!" There is no doubt in my mind that their Cup Ceremony diffused the smoke.

As we gathered in our circle, it was obvious that more metaphysical intervention was needed for the forest fires. I vividly recalled a memory from years ago when Len and I had sponsored a team of Zuni Grandmothers to dance for the Rodeo-Chediski fire.

The fire had been epic, and one of the worst in Arizona's history. After it had burned hundreds of thousands of acres, with still no end in sight, the grandmothers traveled to Mount Shasta, California, where they collected a special, alchemical water from a stream for use in a unique rain dance to drown the fire. We agreed to meet the grandmothers, their driver, and interpreter at the casino in Payson; it was pitch-black dark, and nearly nine p.m. Following in our car, we drove to the edge of the fire about twenty miles east. After locating an auspicious grove of trees, I was invited to join the ceremony while Len waited in the car. The grandmothers' interpreter explained that we needed to sprinkle the sacred water on the trees, and that this would enable the trees to communicate with one another. She demonstrated the dance, and how to move my hands while sprinkling the water. The grandmothers began to sing, and their shrill yet hearty voices penetrated and echoed throughout the forest's darkness, rimmed with an eerie glow from the forest fire. Suddenly, a flashing light appeared, literally seconds after we finished the ceremony. Apparently we had crossed a yellow fire tape to get close enough to the trees. While flashlights brazenly shone on all of us, we were instructed to stand still, and not move. A radio sounded in the background with deep, official sounding, but garbled words. I would later discover that we were all waiting while federal agents were deciding if they should press charges against me. Fortunately, it was determined that the Zuni Grandmothers had every right to practice their religion in the forest, but the agents were uncertain about me. Certainly, I was *not* Native. They concluded that since the grandmothers had *invited* me to participate, I could legally be there, too. Whew . . .

Before we left, one of the agents walked up to one of the grandmothers, reached for her hand and kissed it—a sign of gratitude and respect. In the next twenty-four hours, the fire was miraculously contained.

After filling my Cup with some of the water students had bottled from the Healing Site, I dipped my fingers into its calming essence to demonstrate for my students the Zuni Grandmother technique. Soon, with the many Cups held by the students, the blessed water was copiously sprinkled on the ground throughout our circle. Now, it could telepathically find the trees. We completed our prayers in about twenty minutes, and within one hour, it began to rain.

The next day we awoke to clearer skies, and drove to our final point, the *Charity Adjutant Point of the Western Door of Shalahah*, (Yellow Door). Once we identified a location for our spiritual circle, we began our prayers and decrees. Again, we passed a Cup, and when it was my time to speak, I could hardly form words let alone make much sense. Many of the familiar faces of the group's students were melting and morphing in front of me. I could see and somewhat understand their many lifetimes—past and future images blending without order or intelligence, name or personal identification. The experience was mentally paralyzing. I seemed to be literally holo-leaping between dimensions. After we completed our circle, I apologized to my students. They, too, had noticed my lapse of reality, and one commented, "It was like you faded . . ."

Later that evening in meditation, I asked Saint Germain about what had happened. He clearly explained that this indeed was yet another sign from him to get my attention, and it was time again for further work. Also, he requested that I invite our students to meet the next day and said that he would reveal information regarding the past lives with meaning and spiritual context.

So we met in the morning at a beautiful park, an arboretum and botanical garden maintained by the nearby university. One student brought an old tape recorder with a cassette. After strolling through meandering trails, we found a private bench where we sat and I prepared myself to receive Saint Germain's guidance. I was a bit uncertain if I could even still trance, since it had been nearly eight years since I had received messages in a formal session. I breathed deeply, and after our decrees of purification, closed my eyes. My consciousness immediately traversed to the spiritual planes. Soon after Saint Germain announced his presence, we were all delightfully surprised to understand that this was not just a private, personal reading for a few students. This was a full-blown instructive channeling, and if we were willing, there would likely be more. In fact, the pages of this book feature sixteen lessons of timely spiritual instruction from Saint Germain, Lord Sananda, Master Kuthumi, El Morya, Lady Nada, and many other Ascended Beings who aspire for humanity's freedom.

Golden Cities and the Masters of Shamballa begins with this first lesson received in the arboretum on that sunny, August morning. In reality, this is the metaphoric garden of self where we cultivate comradery with the I AM Presence; we hoe and tend to its innate perfection through careful toil, precise fertilization, and diligent weeding. This, of course, takes not only our willingness, but also the Divine Intervention of the Christed Beings of Light, the great ones, our elder brothers and sisters of expanded consciousness who compassionately point out the best route to travel upon the spiritual path. Each lesson in this book gives exact instruction on building the *New Shamballa*, that is, the Golden Grid of Light that holds and contains the Golden Cities. We access this sublime grid of light through our spiritual practice along with physical travel to one or a predicated series of Ascension enhancing geophysical points—a spiritual pilgrimage. In order to help students to ably understand this teaching, I added a special section of full-color illustrations of Golden City Hierarchs and explanations of each of the fifty-one Golden Cities. This book also features in-depth Appendices that explain the Golden Cities with detailed illustrations regarding their soul-expanding Adjutant Points that leverage and calibrate consciousness from Third to Fourth, and then onward to Fifth Dimension experience and expression. This instruction also includes how to identify their multidimensional locations, presence, and attributes.

Chapters also include valuable teaching we received on our spiritual journey to the Golden City of Malton, located in Illinois and Indiana. From the momentum of *The Garden* instruction, my student Rosalie volunteered to help record and transcribe sessions. We initiated our collaboration with a five-day October excursion to the Southern Door of Malton, in the Illinois wetlands, near the rivers of the Shawnee National Forest. This trip was breathtakingly magical, and we were accompanied by numerous Devas, playful Gnomes, benefic Nagas, and the Royal Fairies of the Elemental Kingdom overseen by the Master Kuthumi, Lady Nada, and many other new Masters and beings of Light who reveal themselves in these teachings, along with their eagerness for the Ascension not only of humans, but for the many hidden Kingdoms of Creation.

Ascension has many different forms to mirror the bountiful Rays of Light and Sound, but perhaps the most provocative technique shared in these pages is the cultivation and use of *Group Mind*. Group Mind is the invaluable precursor to experience and understand the Oneship, a form of consciousness often used by two or more Ascended Masters. Throughout time immemorial, the Group Mind has been known in many Mystery Schools as one of the quickest methods to swiftly and seamlessly infuse a cornucopia of spiritual knowledge along with enabling students to acquire vital personal experience. In computer language this is akin to the ultimate software and system upgrade. The Masters refer to this spiritual experience by several names including the Oneship, Collective Consciousness, "Two or More," the Golden Orb, Unana, and the Guiding Light. The use of this technique is foundational to obtaining Mastery and the technique and nuances of this important knowledge are outlined with detailed exercises.

In keeping with his ever vigilant theme of personal liberty and freedom, Saint Germain continues his contemporary teaching and soul-freeing initiations of the Right-hand Path. This spiritual path is filled with the inspiration of the Aspirant, the discipline and love of the Chela, the service and faith of the Initiate, the wisdom and charity of the Arhat, the skillful, benefic power of the Adept, the guiding instruction of the Master, and the perfected, adoring presence of an Ascended Being. Through every step in our ever-evolving spiritual journey, we are taught to engage with self-determination through our choice and developed free will. In simplest terms, we are to be free, and free from tyrannies of all sorts. This includes the obvious economic tyranny that forces manmade government into corruption and insane politics, but onward to our soul's freedom from the tyranny of our own self-created shadow.

The New Shamballa is not only a grid of spiritual pilgrimage and Golden City Light; it is a state of consciousness. As we move from human to HU-man in our spiritual evolution, let us now state this level of consciousness and life as ours. May we claim eternal victory in the light of Ascension, and step-down the God-perfected light of love, wisdom, and power upon our precious Earth, our beloved Babajeran.

With love, at every level,

Lori Toye

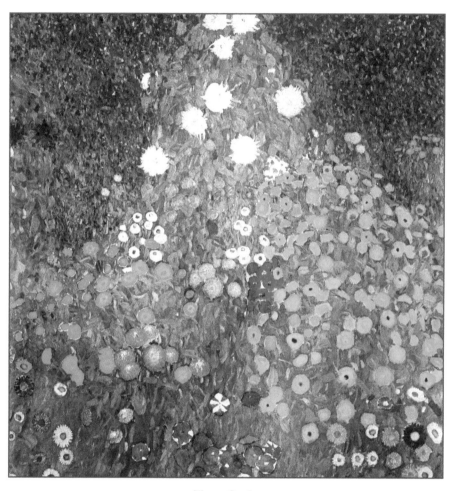

Flower Garden
Painting by Gustav Klimt, 1905-1907.

Chapter One

In the Garden

Saint Germain, Sananda
with students of the I AM America Teachings

Greetings in that Mighty Christ that I AM! I AM Saint Germain and I stream forth on that Violet Ray of Mercy, Transmutation, and Forgiveness. As usual Dear hearts, I request permission to come forward.

All respond: *Please come forward, Saint Germain.*

VIOLET FLAME AND THE GOD SOURCE

It is with great joy that I come this day . . . in joy and celebration for I am aware of the work that you have achieved in service to the Hierarchy, the Great White Brotherhood of Breath, Sound and Light. Yes, it was I who sent you through the Southern Door of Shalahah, and I overshadowed every single step along the way.

To my right is Beloved Brother Sananda, he is present to give advice and discourse should you need it; however before we begin, I would like to give a brief discourse on that Mighty Violet Ray of Mercy, Transmutation and Forgiveness.

As you well know, the Violet Flame was brought from the Lords of Atlantis who transconducted this energy into the atmosphere of the Earth; prior to that the great Lords of Venus brought forth this Mighty Flame in physical form and engineered it into the DNA and genetic structures during the Atlantean epoch. The Violet Flame transmutes the emotional body of mankind, and in the time of Atlantis, consciousness rose and then fell to a (never before) low point in the Astral level. This low point in the Astral Plane created great wars among the cultures and the society became divided. You may already know and understand this. Then the Violet Flame was engineered into the Eight-sided Cell of Perfection. This engineering insured that the Heart Chakra and the Mighty Will's connection to the God Source could never be depleted. Dear ones, Dear heart, it is in this God Source where we find that most refreshing drink, is it not?

Group response: *Yes.*

It is this most refreshing drink that reinvigorates you and gives you the energy to always pursue the (spiritual) path and the work at hand.

THE DYNAMIC GROUP MIND

Your journeys through the Southern Door were requested by me, but overshadowed by Beloved Brother Sananda so you could begin to understand the great work of the Brotherhood—not only the abundant work of compassion and healing, but also so that you could open your hearts to understand your group as Group Mind. For you see Dear ones, it is Unana that is leading you, guiding, and directing you. It is not just the ONE or the Oneship—though these are very important and critical for spiritual evolution—the power lies in the Group Mind and Unana. This is not to say that the Mighty I AM Presence is not the most important aspect, for it will be the integration with your Mighty I AM Presence that leads you into the pathway of Ascension. However, it is so important to understand every dynamic of the Group Mind, for the Group Mind contains within its own *record and memory* that you can use to direct your Co-creative consciousness to manifest your creations.

Len: Is *this information to be included in the I AM America work?*

If you so choose . . . as I have always stated before, whatever I give in discourse, I give freely to humanity for its use.

DIET ASSISTS THE VIOLET FLAME

Now, on that Mighty Violet Ray, it is important to understand that as it evolved into the Atlantean heart, this also evolved the Eight-sided Cell and the Unfed Flame of Perfection. This is why we have given much discourse upon the diet in prior teachings, but it is also important to use this Violet Flame on a daily basis and keep your focused consciousness upon the Violet Flame hour-by-hour . . . its transmuting effect is very important.

FEEL THE GROUP MIND

Worry not over those who do not agree with the way you see things. Worry not over the (differing) political allegiance. First, work to *feel* the Group Mind for greater Oneship, for Unana, and higher consciousness.

I shall take my leave from this plane, and I wish for each of you to *feel* the overshadowing of Beloved Lord Sananda as he walks among you.

LORD SANANDA AND THE CHRIST CONSCIOUSNESS

Sananda is coming forward to walk among us . . . he has placed his hand atop a student's head.

Do I have permission?

Student response: *Yes.*

Sananda is moving to another student, and he has placed his hand on her back, directing energies.

Do I have permission?

Student response: *Yes.*

Saint Germain comes forward.

Greeting chelas, students and initiates . . . this was brought purposefully, not only for the overshadowing, but for the initiation into the Christ Consciousness. Remember this, and carry this knowledge always.

Now Saint Germain is walking among us, and the Violet Flame is moving in, through and around each one of us. There is great heat and the Violet Flame is expanding.

Now, I will provide a few answers to any questions you may have.

Student question: *What was going on yesterday with Lori at Steptoe Butte?*

SAINT GERMAIN'S INTERVENTION

I sent one of my Violet Flame Angels to your circle and I was signaling to Lori, many others in the circle felt that as well . . . you and I have known each other before, have we not?

Perhaps you do not remember Dear one, but I will overshadow you so that you will begin to feel my presence and my energy. I have come this day through your purity of heart and your desire, have you not been asking for this relationship?

Student response: *Yes.*

Then as you have requested, I am here and I shall always be with you Dear one, to gently guide you and instruct you.

In that Mighty Christ, I AM the Victory of the Ascension.

In this one statement is that Mighty Victory and energy of Ascension that can set you free!

I know Dear ones that you traveled to the apex of the Shalahah Vortex. Did you not feel the purity of the energies there?

Student response: *Yes.*

BUILDING THE ASCENSION BODY

For this brought you closer to the work of this Great White Brotherhood and know that as you continue in your path, in this great path of light, there will be many, many more initiations that will come. This was the first of many that you will receive in the Stars of the Golden City Vortices, for it takes this purity of energy to build the Ascension Body.

Many of you have begun to feel the energetics of your Eighth Energy Body, and now we are getting ready, not only to initiate that Eighth Energy Body, but to also inspire the integration with the Ninth, Tenth, and Eleventh Energy Bodies. These energetics are absolutely essential to build the force and the field for the Ascension. Now, it is important to understand that the Ascension can be obtained in one lifetime, but it is also a process, is it not Dear ones, dear hearts?

All respond: *Yes.*

THE IMMORTAL CONSCIOUSNESS

It is a process that is carried within the heart, it is also carried within the energy bodies. One must develop with surety and sanctity the Eighth, Ninth, and Tenth Energy Bodies in order to secure the memory of the process as you traverse from one lifetime to the next. For as you well know you drop the lower three energy bodies with the dissolution of the physical body. Now, I state:

"Down with death,
Immortal Consciousness arise!"

It is very important to train the consciousness to respond to immortality, for this is the immortality that is carried from one lifetime to the next.

The use of the Violet Flame clears and builds the spiritual infrastructure that is needed to carry over from the Fourth and Fifth Dimension. Do you understand?

All respond: *Yes.*

Saint Germain directly addresses the guest-student.

THE NEW SHAMBALLA

Dear one, you know that your work has been in Klehma, and this will bring a great purity to your soul. I specifically asked for the Southern Door to be assigned to you so that you could carry forward the necessary cleansing and healing for the work at hand. As you are in this Vortex you will feel the energy of Master Serapis Bay, once a great Archangel who brought his energies to help in the construction of the etheric city of Shamballa. Klehma will become as a New Shamballa, and not only will the new capital of the United States be present, you must now hold the focus (first) in the Fourth and Fifth Dimensions. Hold the clarity within this Vortex for the building of the New Shamballa and this will occur through the energy of the Southern Door

As you have suspected, some of the doorways and Adjutant Points number (identify) as masculine, feminine, masculine, feminine, each of them have their unique energies and they will change throughout the ten-thousand year Golden Age. Some will morph from masculine to feminine, some will morph from feminine to masculine; however, each point contains both masculine and feminine qualities. Presently at the (Klehma) Southern Door, it is a dominant masculine force, however, we would ask for you to spend time in the Southwest sector of this Doorway and there you will continue upon your path to ready these energies of building the New Shamballa. Questions?

Student question: *I am currently working in the Southwest Doorway, not the pure Southern Door . . . should I do more work in the Southern Door?*

We are aware of your efforts and applaud this; however, there will be a greater force and impetus given to you as you move into the Southwest Adjutant Point of the Southern Door. [Editor's Note: This is the Klehma Gateway Harmony Point.] What you have known as the Child Point will also give you great energy for your efforts. Do you understand?

Student question: The Child Point of the Southern Door?

[Editor's Note: A Child Point is also known as a Golden City Heavenly Ashram, see Appendix D: *The Difference Between Spiritual Retreats and the Golden Cities.*]

That is correct, and there you will fully feel the energies of my beloved brother Serapis Bey, Archangel of the White Ray of Shamballa. Questions?

Student question: *How do I raise my vibration to the level necessary to interact with Serapis Bey?*

LOVE AND DEVOTION

Keep your focus upon that Mighty Violet Ray of Mercy, Compassion, and Forgiveness. Call upon my assistance, as you have felt this blazing flame in, through, and around you. You will feel it again Dear one, dear chela of my heart, you will feel this yet again . . . like a soft glimmer and you will begin to build your relationship with beloved Serapis Bey. Questions?

Student question: *Is increased discipline a part of building this relationship with Serapis Bey?*

It is the increased love and devotion through which all of our activity streams. It is only in our love and devotion for humanity and (through) the Brotherhood and Sisterhood of Light that we exist. Now, if there are no other questions, I shall take my leave and again come forward at your request.

I AM a Being of Violet Fire,
Be the Purity of God's Desire!
Hitaka!

Chapter Two

Every Push, Every Pull

Saint Germain, Kuthumi

Greetings in that Mighty Christ, I AM Saint Germain, and I stream forth on that Mighty Ray of Mercy, Compassion and ultimate Forgiveness. As usual Dear heart, Dear ones, I request permission to come forward.

Response: *Dear loved one, please come forward. You are most welcome.*

Dear ones, Dear hearts, Dear chelas of mine, there is much work still to be accomplished upon this Earth Plane and Planet. I come forward with great import and light, I understand you would like to continue this work, is this so?

Response: *Yes.*

VIOLET FLAME FOR OBSTACLES AND PROBLEMS

I come forth to serve on that Mighty Violet Ray of Mercy, Compassion, and ultimate Forgiveness, but what is this Mighty Violet Ray? It is the Law of Transmutation in action, is it not? It is the law that comes forward to give completion not only to the process of liberation, but it also helps in the transcendence of any type of problem that you may have. As I have always recommended Dear ones, it is important to always use the Violet Flame for any type of problem you may be experiencing:

Mighty Violet Flame come forth and pave the way
To remove any obstacle that may be occurring!

This is what I would recommend for you at this time. You can always insert a specific problem that you are encountering, and then that Violet Ray of liberation will come forward and remove any obstacle that you are experiencing in your pathway. It is important also to understand that when you come into the tutelage of an Ascended Master, you can call upon that Master. Their energy field will be present for you to solve any difficult situation that you may be experiencing.

A TIME OF POLARITY

I know that it is difficult at times, especially at this time, in this great Time of Change. This time is not only a Time of Testing, but also the great Time of Change that we have spoken of before in so many past discourses. The current Time of Change is a time when you will see many extreme weather events and Earth Changes. For there will be great polarity that will exist not only in your political and social systems, but will also exist in all of your relationships. I am certain that all of you have experienced this to some degree, have you not?

Response: *Yes.*

A LEVELING EFFECT

This polarity brings forth of course a type of cleansing that is necessary for the New Times that humanity will be entering. For you see, now a certain amount of karma must be transmuted . . . or discarded, this might be another way to understand this. This leveling effect that happens before we enter into this great Time of Grace or the Golden Age is absolutely essential Dear ones, Dear hearts. This leveling of karma, or should I say a balancing effect with the karma, must occur in order for those who have the eyes to see, and the ears to hear can understand the Great Time that is upon all of you. Now, as you have noticed, I have just said *all of you* . . . every single man, woman, and child will experience not only this great Time of Change, but will also experience this great Golden Age.

However, we have always said it is that Point of Perception that helps one to understand this.

ADVERSITY AND NEGATIVITY CREATE OPPORTUNITY

There are also many changes that are happening within your solar system, changes that are affecting the Earth in many adverse but also in positive ways. For you see, it is sometimes the adverse conditions that strengthens the will so one can achieve a much more positive result. There are those who will say, "There is so much negativity!" Yet, this is that great opportunity is it not, through which karma can be balanced and then a positive result can be achieved? El Morya has always said that in the great tempering of the will, the strongest of steel goes through that fiery furnace of light. And now Dear ones, unless if you have any questions, I would like to continue more discourse upon the changes of the Earth Plane and Planet.

Question: *Are there any instructions for our journey to Malton?*

There are several adjustments that can be achieved. However for this to occur, before the end of this discourse, I will summon Master Kuthumi to come forward and give that explanation. Will this suffice?

Response: *Yes.*

A GREAT RADIATION

The changes that are now happening on the Earth Plane and Planet are happening throughout the galaxy itself. For you see, there is energy radiating from the Great Central Sun and causing an explosion of energies to happen on many other planets. We are also seeing these energies undulate and buffer themselves upon the Earth. Some of these energies enter within the North Pole and the South Pole. These energies travel to the light core of the Earth itself and then radiate out. This also brings a great radiation within the Golden Cities themselves and the other retreats that the Masters know and serve.

LUNAR AND SOLAR ECLIPSES

The Golden Cities temper these energies and buffer the forces, especially the energies from the Great Central Sun and energies through various lunar and solar eclipses. As you know the United States went through a complete solar eclipse within the last year and there will be another within seven years. This eclipse will completely activate the United States and this will mark the beginning of the great Time of Change. How severe the changes occur of course relies on the Collective Consciousness. For as we have prophesied so many times to you Dear ones, Dear hearts that "prophecy is not prediction," instead it is a spiritual teaching that is imparted to you so that you can make a difference in your heart and primarily in your mind.

THE MENTAL BODY IS A COMPONENT OF GROUP MIND

It is the training of this great Mental Body that we are most concerned with at this time. For the Mental Body is the first component that is always associated with the Group Mind and of course at this time, the Group Mind is of great importance, it is not Dear ones? For the Group Mind is a secular form of Collective Consciousness—the best way to understand it at this time. However, it does draw its force from the universal and unifying effect of the

ONE. It is in essence like a Oneship, that you are all aligning your Divine Will towards.

THE IMPORTANCE OF GROUP MIND

The Group Mind is brought forward in many cases to activate a Golden City Adjutant Point. Entrance into the Star of a Golden City can activate energies to bring them forward for concerted efforts. The Group Mind is always of greatest importance, and it is important to understand the primary function of the Group Mind and how it can move one forward or backwards. For you see, after your last experiences in the Shalahah Vortex were you not always affected by that Group Mind? Could you not feel every push and pull it made upon you? And thus it affected your emotions, and onward from your emotions into your activities. This is why the development of your Group Mind is of vast importance. For it is the way that we, (chela and Master Teacher), can become the true Step-down Transformers of the times to come.

ONE STEP AT A TIME

Through conscious intent, one can enter within the vibration of the Group Mind. Through conscious intent, one can leave the auspicious nature of the Group Mind and enter into its (individual) soul experience. Now, there are many other layers of development that we could discuss, but in your journey—right now—on your spiritual path, it is the development of this Group Mind that we are most concerned with. This paves the pathway to Unana. This paves the pathway for the Christ Consciousness. Do you see Dear ones is it baby steps, incremental steps, one at a time that you shall take. Then, you are able to enter into that Mighty ONE that rules the achievement of conscious effort upon the Earth Plane and Planet. Then you are able to understand the unity of Ascension, and are able to begin to build the Ninth, Tenth and even the Eleventh Energy Body.

"TWO OR MORE"

Remember, the Eighth Energy Body functions ideally off the Group Mind. It is very difficult to achieve without the presence of "two or more." For you see the Ascensions that were achieved in the past were always brought about through group effort, and while one may think it is a solitary path it is not. It is a path that is achieved through entering into the Group Mind. Now, one may meditate and through their levels of meditation enter and achieve through the Group Mind. As you practice and achieve your own Group Mind, there will be that Group Mind that you can enter into with your Master Teacher. This is achieved in such a manner, especially in the development of any school or any ashram. Questions?

THE SEVEN FORMATIVE RAYS OF GROUP MIND

Response: *Yes, it was a very interesting experience, but I didn't find it uplifting. It was entirely too much push and pull.*

This was because you (your group) had not been trained in how to calm the Mental Body and then enter into the Group Mind as ONE. Now, it is suggested that before you enter into any form of ceremony or activation points in Golden Cities that you gather not only in groups of three, four, and five, but seven is always the suggested amount. Each participant holds the energy of one Ray Force and attunes their vibration to the Seven Rays of Light and Sound. Each holds the essence and energy of that (one) Ray. Once you attune yourself to the energy of that Ray, the Group Mind can enter. The Group Mind holds the focus for the Aquamarine and Gold Ray. Do you understand?

The Aquamarine and Gold Ray has a calming effect on the Mental Body. I suggest you call forth each of the Rays and each of the Archangels and Elohim associated with that office (Ray Force). As you call forth each Ray into your circle, signal for each (Ray) to come forward. Each of you serves as a formative Step-down Transformer of that Ray Force. Do you understand?

Response: *That will take a little practice.*

USE OF THE SOOTHING AQUAMARINE RAY

It always takes practice does it not Dear ones, Dear hearts? But as you well know, practice not only makes permanent, practice turns the adaptation into adeptship. From there the Aquamarine and Gold Ray can then form not only the nucleus for the Group Mind, but it has a melding effect—that is why is it associated with the Group Mind and with Unity Consciousness. It soothes the mental bodies of everyone who is present. Call forth:

Beloved Archangel Crystiel,
In the name of that Mighty Christ that I AM,
Lord Crystiel come forward!
May the Aquamarine and the Gold Ray sooth my Mental Body,
And pave the pathway to Unity, Oneship,
And the ONE Unana, I AM.

You see Dear ones this is of vast importance. Now I shall tell you more about the Shalahah Vortex and your journey there.

TAME YOUR EMOTIONAL ENERGY

It was important for you to gain insight into the nature of all of the students involved in this journey. For you see Dear ones there may be those who are willing, but not yet ready. There are always those who want to accomplish more, to become not only the chela, but also the initiate. But they have barely just experienced the energies of the aspirant!

The aspirant, you see, is very much intoxicated with even the idea of spiritual study. They longingly search for the beloved. The beloved they seek is within themselves, and in the great sanction of the Flame of the Heart. But you see Dear ones it is the discipline that then must come forward. For the spiritual discipline then allows one to not only identify and tame the emotional body, but to also have the experiences at the astral level where the *eyes and ears* are developed. To know the difference between these subtle energies is of vast importance, especially when traveling to Adjutant areas.

STEWARDS OF THE ADJUTANT POINTS

It is also important to be in tune with the steward of each Adjutant Point. As you know there is a Master Teacher who is present at every single one of these divine retreats of the Golden Cities. Each of these divine retreats holds a specific energy and carries forward not only the Ray Force of that specific Golden City, but there also may be a combination of Ray Forces that will be present.

MASTERS OF SHALAHAH'S SOUTHERN DOOR

Let us travel through the Southern door of Shalahah where you will learn even more about the beloved points that you have visited. The first point that you entered was an Adjutant Point of the Blue Ray, and did you not feel Archangel Michael present and your alignment of your will to the Divine?

Answer: *Yes and no.*

Then you must spend more time in meditation to reach this Ashram—it contains within it the energies of the fiery Will of God. The second point that you were not able to travel to carries energies of enlightenment, and the Yellow Ray of Archangel Jophiel. There were also energies of different Master Teachers who were also present to give counsel at Jophiel's Ashram. Present were Ascended Master Lady Nala—she has worked for many, many lifetimes with Lady Master Nada. Nala will come forward in future information that will be dispensed to those traveling to this Vortex area. Her Divine Counterpart, who is the Elohim of Strength known as TronXR. TronXR is an Elohim who aligns and helps many to achieve their Ascension through the manifestation of the Blue Ray as the Electronic Blueprint around their physical bodies. There are even more Divine and Cosmic Beings who serve at the Outer Child Point and the Inner Child Points of these doorways. This information is specific for Shalahah and for now, I have given you enough information. Now for information of Malton, we shall refer to Beloved Brother Kuthumi.[1]

Beloved chelas, I AM Kuthumi. Do I have permission to speak?

Response: *Yes you do, please come forward.*

RED, WHITE, AND BLUE

Let me explain what I am seeing. Kuthumi has a bluebird on his right shoulder and a red cardinal rests on his left shoulder.

As you see my Beloveds, I have brought two symbols for you: the bluebird which represents the first Abundance Point, the red bird, the cardinal represents the second feminine point that you shall visit in Malton. However as we well know the center point which is known as the Outer Child is represented as the white dove.

He is holding a white dove in his hands, and he releases the dove and the dove flies up into the air.

"IT IS NOT QUANTITY, BUT QUALITY"

As it flies, does it not fly with a sense of messenger and peace? You see, these points are very important: Harmony, Abundance and the peace that comes forward through both. For you see Dear ones we, as the Four Pillars, have our service to bring forward at this time. I bring forward my service not only for the Elemental and Deva Kingdom, but I will also give you great assistance to bring your school into its manifestation to the physical plane. The bluebird, red cardinal, and white dove will always be your symbols for the school. For this will show how two should work together and form one of

---

1. See Appendix A: *Shalahah Southern Door and Adjutant Point Hierarchs*, page 241.

great peace and inner activity, you see each of these birds have their different disposition, their different color, even their different Ray Force as a species, yet they all fly in the air, do they not? They are all members of the animal kingdom, yet they carry a consciousness that is swift and certain.[2] In the forming of your school, it is important that each of your students is certain in their footing, and that they are ready to move forward into new teaching. As I have said before it is not the *quantity* but the *quality*. Questions?

THE GREAT TABLE

Question: I have often wondered in my personal interaction with you why it is usually just one-on-one, and now with the creation of a school it is many people?

Yes, and those with their agendas of course, and also their collective karma. But it is important to understand the great service that you give. Some students will come only for a simple drink. And as Sananda has said, some will pull themselves, "Up to that great table and feast." And there will be those who take it all in, and digest it fully, and become yet another teacher. And some will come and pass this information forward, then achieve the glory of their own Ascension! For is this not the goal Dear ones . . . the achievement of Ascension? In glory and light, I AM.

Saint Germain now comes forward

ASCENSION IS YOUR BIRTHRIGHT

Dear ones it was important too, that you spent time in Ascension Valley and were able to absorb its vital energies not only at the gateways, but also at the mine location. For you see the water contains and carries that vital glacium that can move your light bodies onward, not only until the Eighth Light Body experience, but onward into Ninth Light Body experience.[3] It is always important that there is some physical representation when you are building these (Light Bodies), and that is why glacium has been given. As you well know, each of these locations is very important, very select, and achieves a different result. Indeed, I have said before, "There are never, ever any mistakes!" And there was not one mistake with any student who was present at that moment! Do not doubt, Dear ones, for doubt is only a form of

2. See Appendix B: *Golden City of Malton and Symbology*, page 245.

3. See Appendix C: *Ascension Valley and the Presence of Glacium*, page 249.

fear. Know that Ascension is your birthright and your divinity is within the Eight-sided Cell of Perfection. With each flicker of the Unfed Flame you are growing, learning, and evolving. Trust in this, Dear ones. Questions?

Question, Guest-student: *Did we achieve what we were to gain from our journey to Shalahah?*

SHEDDING KARMA

There was, as you well understand with the visit to each Adjutant Point, a shedding of karma and an opening of Divine Purpose. As you well know, to let go of karma is not an easy thing. As you entered that point, what happened? You all incurred karma, and as you held your will through that process, the Mighty Teacher came forward you were able to persevere, did you not?

Answer, both: Yes

Then onward you traveled to the Star, and there was Lord Sananda overshadowing you with the beloved energies of the Christ. And so it is.

Answer, both: So it is.

Questions?

Question, Guest-student: *Are any of the current students ready for any type of graduation? Is there anything special we must do to prepare the students?*

ENTERING THE SANCTUARIES

They must continue their study of the Golden Cities, be secure in their knowledge of the Adjutant Points, and be able to accurately identify the Ray Forces associated with each doorway and each Adjutant Point. This must not be a knowledge that is given to them orally, but received at a level of inner guidance. They too must gain entrance into the sanctum of each of the Sanctuaries as they exist in the doorways. This is important, because there is much more instruction that can be achieved. I do not mean to be vague, but this is of great importance. Perhaps as you spend more time in the sanctum of each doorway you will begin to understand that of which I speak. For instance, in your own Gobean Vortex in the Southern door at the Service Point, did you not feel the energies of the Elohim Claire? There was that beautiful White Ray of Purity, streaming in, though, and around that Vortex point. Right now, Claire is working in stewardship, training a new Master Teacher, a Step-down Transformer who will come forward (later) at this point. Do you understand?

Response: *It is indeed the experience and until you actually go, you can only have the experience there.*

"I HOLD THE LIGHT FOR YOUR ASCENSION"

It is always the experience Dear ones, Dear hearts, is it not? And until you have had these varied experiences through at least Five Different Golden Cities, you are not properly prepared yet to teach. Remember this (teaching) is only for those who have the "eyes to see and the ears to hear," do you understand?

Answer: *Yes, but I would also include myself as not yet properly prepared to teach.*

Ascension is always a do it yourself project, is it not Dear ones, Dear hearts?

Answer: *Yes.*

I hold the light for your Ascension:

Mighty Violet Flame,
Come forward into my energy fields,
And may the White Ray of Purity initiate my consciousness
Into the eternal gift of Ascension.
So be it.

Questions?

EXPERIENCE THE ENERGY

Question: *Does that mean we need to take physical journeys to the Five Golden Cities?*

It is important to feel the difference between the energies. Travel only to the Golden Cities where there has been a level of activation. Do you understand?

Answer: *That would include all the ones in the United States?*

They are all ready to serve, but it is important to travel first to a Northern Door, then to an Eastern Door, onward to a Southern Door, and conclude in a Western Door. It is best to experience different Golden City Vortices, so you can sense the difference in the energies. Of course there may be only travel to just one Golden City, for instance in your beloved Gobean, but this is not enough experience.

Question, Guest-student: *Should that be done at a group level?*

LIGHT AND PURIFICATION

It can be done at a group level; however it can also be done individually. I realize it is a great sacrifice for the chelas to achieve this. However, this is the initiation as we have suggested before. The Golden Cities are brought forward to not only instigate the building of the great Light Bodies, but also to purify the Mental Body so it can be used at a much higher level. Do you understand? Questions?

Question, Guest-student: *Does this current group of students still have work together as a Group Mind, or will some choose a different path?*

Everything comes forward through choice does it not? Everything is always a choosing. If they choose, so then it will be. Unless there are other questions, I shall take my leave. I will be happy to return to give advice.

Question: *How often would you like to meet?*

I am always available to help and assist, as you well know. I am always present, for you see Dear ones, I AM within your heart.

In that Mighty Christ that I AM,
May the light now shine among humanity,
For the Ascension and the Group Mind.

I AM, Saint Germain.

A depiction of the Cintamani being carried by the Lun Ta (Windhorse)
Painting by Nicholas Roerich, 1936. The Cintamani is known in
western culture as the *Philosopher's Stone.*

Chapter Three

Acceleration

Saint Germain and Kuthumi

I AM Saint Germain and I stream forth on that Mighty Violet Ray of Mercy, transmutation and ultimate Forgiveness. As usual Dear hearts, I request permission to come forward.

Response: *Please come forward Saint Germain, you are most welcome.*

THE GOLDEN CITY RETREATS OF SHAMBALLA

As I have said before, there is still much work before us, much work, of course, to be dispensed through I AM America. There is much work that can be achieved among the chelas and those who are the stalwart of heart. Also, there is much work to be done in the Golden City Vortices, for you see Dear ones, we must properly prepare the Golden Cities not only as a place of refugee in the great times to come, but also as a place of sanction and spiritual growth and evolution. These are indeed the great retreats of this time, and while there are many other retreats that are held in the great union of the Great White Brotherhood and Sisterhood of Breath, Sound, and Light, there are also the retreats that exist for the Seven Rays of Light and Sound.[4] These are the retreats that are open for the chelas at this time. Shamballa was formed many years ago so one could properly prepare their light bodies in order to gain entrance into the Brotherhood.

GOLDEN CITIES CALIBRATE GALACTIC LIGHT

The Golden Cities can be entered by anyone at anytime; however, as one develops the "eyes to see and the ears to hear," then they can properly enter the Golden City. Each of the points has their own timing and intent, and as I stated before in our last discourse, each of the points has its own great pillar of light that is a sponsor who is in charge of the retreat above each of the Adjutant Points and the Outer and Inner Child Points. Each of them contains a consortium of energy that is used to help humanity at this time, for each of the Golden Cities holds not only the great inner sanctum of the

---

4. See Appendix D: *The Difference Between Spiritual Retreats and the Golden Cities*, page 251.

Ray Force as it streams from the Great Central Sun from the core of the Earth on upward to the Golden City where it is dispensed in its centripetal force, but it is also used at this time to calibrate and to help the energies flow from other Ray Forces as they stream forth from the Great Central Sun and from other planets. For you see, Dear ones, Dear hearts, there are many other planets that have evolved in their spiritual evolution and they too carry great light. This light is also assisting many others at this time, and is especially helping humanity to evolve and to grow in this great Time of Change. It is important to understand this, for the Golden Cities calibrate every form of light that is used for the spiritual evolution of humanity.

THE NEW HUMANITY

In this Time of Great Change we will see many changes in humanity. Yes, life spans will extend, but it is also important to understand that the respect for spiritual knowledge will strengthen. This is why I AM America will become as a clearinghouse for the new humanity. The new humanity is the evolution of humanity spiritually and evolutionary. Yes, this is the path of Ascension, but there will also be many, many spiritual expansions that will be observed on the path to Ascension. I would like to spend some time outlining how this works so you can begin to understand this, not only is there an expansion of the human aura, there is also the growth and development of energy bodies. I have explained these before as the development of the Eighth, Ninth, Tenth, and Eleventh energy bodies. Of course this is of great importance, and the chela who is on the path and traveling towards Ascension will understand the development of these and how each of them assist this process.

There is also a sense of rapport that is telepathy—understanding the difference between subtle and gross energies. This, of course, is very important to understand the difference of how one's energy will respond to another differing energy, and to understand the difference between negative and positive energies. This is the polarities and the great Hermetic Laws. There is also a sense when dreaming at night, the ability to remember dreams and to dream in full color, but to also have experiences in other planes of consciousness. This is very important. All of these experiences develop alongside the development of the Eighth, Ninth, Tenth, and Eleventh Energy Bodies.

INTENTION AND THE GROUP MIND

As I have described, it is that Eighth Energy Body that is responsible for the formation of the Group Mind. Now, the Group Mind holds together through unity, Unana, and the Oneship. It is focusing upon a singular goal at hand. For instance, if a group is traveling to a Golden City you are focusing upon the Group Mind in that travel. The next step is to clarify your intention of what you are to achieve within that trip. As you have already explained that you wish to travel to Malton, it is very important to state your intention of why you are going on this journey. I suggest that this intention is written down and preformed as a write and burn. This will affirm your intention within your energy fields and then this is released through the spiritual law.

FORGIVENESS AND COMPASSION

These levels of spiritual evolution are important, but perhaps the greatest of all of these is the use of that Mighty Sacred Fire, the Violet Flame. The use of the Violet Flame unencumbers the karmic residue that creates obstacles in your spiritual growth and evolution. This, of course, is of great import at this time. To understand the Law of Forgiveness and Compassion is perhaps one of the highest levels that a chela can achieve. For it is only in this level of forgiveness and compassion that one begins to develop the detachment that is necessary for the next level of the spiritual journey.

SERVICE OF THE INITIATE

As you move from the chela who has taken on the devoted discipline, you will be ready to encounter the arena of the initiate. As the initiate you give your great service to your Master Teacher. This great service comes forward to serve humanity, and is also a service to the Great White Brotherhood and Sisterhood of Light.

THE BODHISATTVA, THE PROPHET, AND THE ARHAT

Of course from there, there will be many different levels of understanding. Some of these have been development through the Bodhisattva, but also through the Prophet. These two pathways lead one into a greater development and understanding of working with the Group Mind. How does the Bodhisattva carry forward its great focus of compassion? Through the Group Mind. How does the Prophet garner the energy and the support to understand it is not prediction, but indeed prophecy? Through the

Group Mind. All of these function through that greater understanding of unification. Then one is prepared to enter into the pathway of the Arhat. The Arhat is perhaps the greatest of all teachers, for the Arhat has already passed through both the initiation and the devoted discipline of the Chela. For one to enter as teacher, this is one who has the vital experience.

PURPOSE OF THE GURU

Perhaps it is a bit confusing at times to understand the difference between mentor, a teacher, and a Guru. Each of these has differing levels of devotion, differing levels of connection to students, and also differing levels of spiritual application. The Guru transmits not only the information and instruction, but is also present on a steady day-by-day basis to transmit vital energies that are used not only to learn but to perfect the discipline to achieve liberation. The Guru has the ability to transmute karma and to raise the student into the levels and knowledge of the transmutation of karma. The Guru can actually help to free the student from the bondage of reincarnation. This is the true role and purpose of the Guru and this has been misused in this time of Kali Yuga.

MASTERY OF THE TEACHER

The teacher has Mastery over the knowledge that they share and transmit. This, too, is a very different understanding, and has been misused in this time of Kali Yuga. The teacher has complete Mastery over the information that is shared and can exhibit and demonstrate through vital experience the knowledge imparted.

THE MENTOR IS A WAYSHOWER

The mentor is a way shower. The mentor can prove through the vital will and choice the way that something is not only experienced, but is placed in vital daily practice. These are the subtle differences between Guru, teacher, and mentor, and I am certain this knowledge will be of great assistance to you. Do you have questions?

BUILD THIS KNOWLEDGE

Question: *Do you want us to build a school building?*

The school itself is built within your hearts. This is the most important building that anyone shall take upon themselves. However, if you wish to, it may be of vital importance. All is a choice Dear ones, Dear hearts, but more important is to build this knowledge, as a way shower, showing the way that has worked for you, and share your methods and methodologies.

As a teacher, what do you share? Your vital experience that has proven itself in the past, present, and will prove itself again in the future. Do you understand?

Response: *Yes.*

So all is a choice, Dear ones, Dear hearts, always, all is a choice. It is important to not take on too much at this time, but to just put one foot in front of the other.

Response and question: *I agree, the thought of building a school building is probably a lot of unnecessary karma at this point, just activity. However, I do understand what you are saying, about just 'in the heart.' Do we still call the school, the School of the Four Pillars?*

That was a dispensation for that time period; this shall be a gathering of the I AM America Teachings.

LEVELS OF MASTERY

Question: *So the title of the school is?*

I AM America Spiritual Teachings.

Response and question: *Thank you. Next question I have is the Golden City comparisons from Adjutant Points and doorways . . . so if we are going to the Northern Doorway say of Gobean, and we go to the Western Adjutant Point, do we need to go to the Western Adjutant Point of Wahanee to do a comparison of similar points and similar doorways?*

Now that you understand my criteria, when we say the word "teacher" we understand the great levels of Mastery for the teacher is an Arhat and has not only fulfilled their missions of service, but they have also exhibited their levels of Mastery. Do you understand?

Response: *Yes.*

For the Teacher has traveled to each and every one of the five Vortices, understanding each of the four doorways and the energies of their stars.

Now the mentor is very different and perhaps this is what you should pursue in your training of those who are available to mentor, but not to teach. Mentoring is based upon knowledge of practical experience with spiritual practice, practical experience of understanding, entrance into an Adjutant Point, practical experience of meditation and ceremonial order within the Star and the Vortices. These are each levels that are attained and sometimes they are attained in one lifetime, sometimes they are attained in hundreds of lifetimes.

TWENTY-YEAR CYCLES

Question: *Each of the doorways is a Ray color, the Gobean Vortex is the Blue Ray, the North Door is a color, but each of the Adjutant Points is a specific Ray color itself with a guardian or a Master overseeing each of these points?*

They function in a twenty-year period, each twenty years a new Master Teacher will appear at the Adjutant Points, each of them sponsoring a different Ray Force for the energies that are at hand for that time period. Do you understand?

Question: *So my questioning you, for example if we start at Gobean, in the North Door, is a specific color which I do not know and I ask you for each of the Adjutant Points colors and the name of the Master teacher. I don't know if you wish to share that?*

They will always be changing, as you have well known, these twenty-year cycles are based upon the elements. It is important to understand the Cycle of the Elements and then you will begin to understand the change of the Ray Forces.[5] Now, there is a primary Ray Force for each Golden City; however, all Seven Rays of Light and Sound are always present within each of the Golden City Vortices. This is how someone can obtain their Mastery within just one Golden City; but, remember the Arhat has perfected the art of meditation and Astral projection, so Golden City doorways and Adjutant Points can be visited through the Astral Plane. Do you understand?

Response: *Yes, I understand that. Sometimes there is a great sense of adventure and joy to physically go to each of these locations.*

---

5. See Appendix E: *The Twenty-year Cycles of the Elements,* page 269.

THE NEW JERUSALEM

Yes . . . for then we see the law as it is mirrored, "as above, so below." And there is also a great shedding of karma that happens through travelling to the Adjutant Points. It is as if traveling from one Temple of Consciousness to the next, is it not? And there you perform each of the sacred ceremonies as they relate to each of those Adjutant Points.

What I am pointing out to you Dear ones, Dear hearts is that there will be many changes that will occur throughout the Golden Cities. These changes will be very profound for the Seven Rays of Light and Sound as they come forward in their timing and in their intention.

Now, in twenty years each of the Adjutant Points will shift and change with new stewards, new Angels, new Masters, and of course new Elohim. This is important to understand, for this is indeed the building of the New Jerusalem. It is a Jerusalem of freedom; it is the Shamballa of the Golden Age. Questions?

Question: *I would like to ask that the way is made clear for Lori and I and those we choose to join us, to visit every Adjutant Point in these United States, that the way is made clear time-wise, health-wise, energy-wise, financially so we may have this experience.*

Focus not only on that Mighty Violet Ray, but also focus on your decrees of abundance, opulence, and supply. There are many lightworkers who feel that money is a sin; however, remember that money itself is only a tool for the achievement of freedom.

Answer: *Yes, just because it is mismanaged by evildoers, doesn't mean that blessed things can't come and be achieved with it.*

ACHIEVE THE ASCENSION

It is true that the Golden Cities are an intervention for this time of choosing, this time of Armageddon, if you wish to call it that. It is a time of development of the will and choosing eternal life over death; that is, Ascension over the endless cycles of lifetime over lifetime. Ascension you see Dear ones, after you enter into the path, you can achieve your liberation within only one lifetime. However if you choose to take yet another embodiment you will have the opportunity to enter into the path of Ascension yet again. Often it takes no less than seven lifetimes to achieve the Ascension in this manner; however, through the use of the Sacred Fire and the spiritual techniques I have given you, you can achieve your Ascension within one lifetime.

MIGRATORY PATHWAYS

Dear ones it is important that you always enter into meditation, into the ashrams of those retreats of light that reside within the Golden Cities. These are locations that accelerate the light bodies and help you to accelerate your own Ascension opportunity. It is important to commune and spend time in each of the doorways, in each of the Adjutant Points, and also then into the Stars. As you well know, there is a migration pathway that is used for different results and I'm happy to share those pathways with you as needed.

For Ascension I recommend always starting in the Southern Doorways, for there you are able to bring out the healing qualities first, and then focus upon your knowledge, your hard work and uniting as the Family of Man. Then enter into the Star, where you then can achieve a purity of intent and foci of light. Questions?

INTENTION AND FOCUS

Question: *Yes, so I'm going to state my personal intention for going to Malton . . . it is specifically for the attainment and fruition, for there are many things that Lori and I have worked out to attain and have not yet to come to pass, and it is time that these things are put to rest and we move on.*

It is true Dear one, to re-establish the intention of what you wish to focus upon and the great service that you give as an Initiate. You see Dear ones, a focus must still be placed upon the publication of all the Golden City material, for it is very important for those who have the eyes to see, and the ears to hear to know where these great centers exist, but also how to access and utilize them. I am happy to give more information regarding this.

If you wish to establish an I AM America School, this too is important, but remember that the teacher is not yet the focus—the mentor is your focus, and this, itself, is enough to be accomplished in one lifetime. Do you understand?

Response: *I do understand.*

However if there are those who would like to study and become the Arhat of that teaching, of course I am available to give discourse.

THE MASTERS AND RAY FORCES OF GOBEAN'S ADJUTANT POINTS

Question: So, in the North Door of Gobean, the Northwestern point, what Ray color is that?

It is the Ruby Ray.

Question: *And who is the teacher?*

Uriel has been training a great Mahatma, who is known as Mahatma Ishmar.[6]

Question: *And in the North Door of Gobean, the Northeastern point, which Ray is this?*

It is the Violet Ray, and there is the great Lady DeNaire.

Question: *Then the Outer Child Point of this North Door?*

An Elohim of the wind element, known as the Elohim Veenon.

Question: *Which Ray color is this?*

Since it is a combination of both, it functions as a Violet and Gold Ray.

Question: *And the Inner Child Point?*

Now this child point resonates only with the Gold Ray—the teacher is Cassiopeia, the great Elohim of the Yellow Ray. However, this is a higher vibration of the Yellow Ray and brings forth an Ashram of the Gold Ray. All of these, of course, will change at the end of the twenty-year cycle which by the end of the year 2023 and beginning in 2024. Then, new assignments are made.

Response: *However between now and then, if we can call upon each of these guardians as we go to these points throughout the five Golden Cities of these United States and we create our personal alignment and intentions as we go to these points,*

---

6. See Appendix F: *The Hierarchs and Ray Forces of Gobean's Adjutant Points* page 271.

whether it is metaphysical or physical, then our knowledge and relationship with them grows.

It is true Dear ones, but remember the flux is between five to ten miles, where you can feel those great Spiritual Retreats that are built not only in the Fifth Dimension or Fifth Density as you would call it, but also in the Astral levels, Fourth Density and Fourth Dimension.

Question: *If I go to the Eastern Door of Gobean, to the Northern point, which Ray is this? The Eastern Door of the Northern point of Gobean.*

This is the Green Ray, and there you will find an overshadowing of the beloved Elohim Vista, who is currently training one of his stalwart chelas, the name is not yet to be released.

Question: *If I go to the Eastern Door, the Southern point, the Eastern Door of Gobean, which Ray is this?*

This is the White Ray of purity, which is served by the Angel Cresta.

Question: *The Outer Child Point of the Eastern Door?*

Again, it is a combination. This is a very interesting point and serves the Aquamarine and the Gold Ray.

Question: *Who is the guardian?*

The Elohim Pacifica is overseeing this, and the name of the steward shall not be released.

Response and Question: *I understand. And the Inner Child Point, which Ray is this?*

This is a Gold Ray, overseen by Cassiopeia; however, the Elohim of Focus will be serving here.

Question: *Do we have a name for that Elohim of Focus?*

Arien is the Elohim.

Question: *And the Southern Door of Gobean, to the Eastern point of the Southern Door of Gobean, which Ray Force is this?*

This is a very fascinating doorway for this carries the energies of Ancient Egypt, for you see the Gobean Southern Doorway covers areas that were once Atlantean. From these civilizations there was a migration, not only of consciousness, but also social and cultural groups who then helped to establish Egypt and the teachings of Akhenaton.

Question: *And the Ray color?*

As I have mentioned before, we have that great White Ray of service that is extending out to the other two points, so these are all a focus of the White Ray of purity.

Question: And the guardian is?

The guardian names are kept somewhat in secret; however, one is known as Akhenaton on the masculine, and Nefertiti on the feminine.

Question: *So when I go to the Southern Door of Gobean, the most Western point, that is also the White Ray?*

They are all carrying the White Ray for the purity of their strength.

Question: *And that is Nefertiti?*

Yes. However, she has attained a higher name, which will not be released.

Question: *And the Outer Child Point which is also the White Ray?*

Correct, and this has not been released.

Question: *And the Inner Child Point is also the White Ray?*

That, of course, contains energies of the Aquamarine and the Gold Ray.

Question: *And the Elohim Claire is there?*

Claire is present in the Inner Child, I am speaking of the Outer Child.

Question: *We don't have a name for the Outer Child?*

These will be released at a later dates, for you see they are overseen by these great stewards and they are training those Masters who will then come forward and form those offices. Do you understand?

Response: Yes.

Question: So if I then travel to the Western Door of Gobean, and I go to the Northern point of Gobean to the outer, I guess it would be North and West, which Ray color is this?

This contains elements of the Yellow and Pink Ray in its service. You see, sometimes two Ray Forces come forward to serve a point. If you were to travel to this point you would have complete understanding of this.

Question: Who is the guardian?

Eliah is the guardian.

Question: *If I go to the Western Door of Gobean to the Southern point, which Ray color is this?*

Yellow and Blue Ray, and there is the Divine Complement of Eliah— Aloah.

Question: *The Outer Child Point, which Ray color is this?*

This again is an Aquamarine and Gold Ray, this retreat is served by the Elohim of Inner Vision, known as Sein.

Question: *And if I go to the Inner Child Point of the Western Door of Gobean?*

It, too, is a focus of the Blue and the White Crystal Ray, again overseen by the Elohim of Strength, Hercules of Stienta and Gruecha . . . this name (of the incoming Hierarch) not to be released.

Response and Question: *I see, so we won't include that name in the book?*

YOUR SACRED TRAINING

Names will be added at a future date, as you see, everything is moving and changing, now it is important to understand as you reach your Ascension within an Ashram of a Golden City, you too will come into your sacred training and you will oversee one of these Divine Points. Do you understand?

Answer: *Yes.*

It is also an evolution of consciousness; you see Dear ones, Dear hearts, "As above, so below." Each of these Golden Cities are part of the building of the New Shamballa. This has been released in prior discourse, and each of them serving with the energy and intent of these great retreats of light and consciousness.

Question: Is there enough energy to go onto the next Golden City?

I am here to answer your questions and then I shall take my leave.

Question: Since we are intending to travel, I am going to need some assistance and focus so all the financial needs are taken care of so we can go.

As I have said before, focus upon that Mighty Violet Flame and it will help to ameliorate the obstacles that are in your pathway. Also, focus upon your decrees for abundance, opulence, and supply. And now if you are ready and willing, Beloved Kuthumi is here to give discourse.

MASTER KUTHUMI, HIERARCH OF THE GOLDEN CITY OF MALTON

Saint Germain is backing away, Master Kuthumi is coming forward.

Dear hearts of this Mighty Gold Ray! I request permission to come forward. I AM Kuthumi.[7]

Response: *Kuthumi please come forward, you are most welcome.*

I realize now your great planning and intent to travel to the great Vortex of Malton, and I am here to overshadow you and give you instruction upon these points. For you see Dear ones, Malton has been used to help transmute the Animal Kingdom, but also many of the kingdoms of the Fourth Dimension and the hidden kingdoms that lie within. When you are there you will feel their magic, their energy, and their contribution at this time. There

---

7. See Appendix G: *Master Kuthumi*, page 277.

are many other kingdoms of creation that humanity has not even begun to understand. As you well know, there are many kingdoms and subspecies that exist within the Inner Earth or what is known as the striated hollow Earth. However, we do deal with the kingdoms that do exist upon the Earth Plane, and as they go through there great changes and their own spiritual evolution. For they too have a scheme of evolution that works not only to help them spiritually evolve and to grow at this Time of Great Change, but to also reach their own Ascension Process. Even the animals, plants, and the minerals are working on an Ascension Process. All of them are evolving and growing, changing. Yes, changing very much!

LADY NADA, HIERARCH OF THE GOLDEN CITY OF DENASHA

As you also know, I align my energies with Lady Master Nada of the great Vortex that lies above Scotland.[8] You too will feel the push and the pull of the energies as they pulse between one another. [Editor's Note: The Golden City of Denasha and the Golden City of Malton.] Each of the Golden Cities has their own great timing and intent. Some align with others, and yet some do not at all and exist primarily through their singular Ray Force and of course the sub-Ray Forces. I realize you will be traveling to the Southern Door of Malton, how can I assist?

Question: *Yesterday you spoke of the bluebird and the abundance point, my understanding is that the abundance point is the Southern Door, most Eastern point. Is that where we are to start?*

Yes, this is the place to start for this is the focus of your trip, is it not? It is indeed. To bring this into manifestation the bluebird is a representation of Saturn as the Blue Ray in its highest form, the hard work, and the earnestness of the path that it takes to achieve anything and bring it into manifestation.

Question: *And the next point to go to would be in the Southern Door, the Western point which is the Red Cardinal?*

This represents the healing of the nations; the color red represents Mars as the Divine Warrior. For once you have achieved the great work through Saturn, then it must be brought forth again and shared with others. Do you understand?

---

8. See Appendix H: *Lady Master Nada*, page 279.

Response and question: *Yes. And then the Outer Child Point is the White Dove?*

This states that the intention for our teachings is to give you great, sublime peace.

Question: *If I go to the Northern Door of Malton and I go to the most Western point, what color Ray is that particular point?*

At this time, I am not allowed to share this information, however at a later date more shall be given and this information shall be known.

Response: *Then in going to Malton, to these three points in the Southern Door, I hope I can walk arm in arm with you.*

As you know Dear Brother of mine, this area is a great refuge for the invisible kingdoms, and it is my great desire that I share this with you when you are there. OM Eandra, I AM as ONE.[9]

Master Kuthumi is backing away. Saint Germain is coming forward:

And now Dear ones; if there are any other questions I shall open the floor.

Question, Guest-student: *Could you elaborate on going to all five Golden Cities?*

THE INITIATIONS OF THE FIVE UNITED STATES GOLDEN CITIES

The Five Golden Cities are five very specific initiations that take the soul through a liberation process of Ascension. First, is Gobean and the initiations held through Beloved Brother El Morya. Second, is Malton and the initiations taken through the great philosopher Kuthumi. Remember in Gobean, this is for the development of the will, and Malton is for the development of the mind, both play a great role for the development of the Group Mind. Wahanee is the great Vortex that holds the Sacred Fire of forgiveness and is present so you can easily place the Violet Flame into your own personal daily practice. But Wahanee is also present so that the great Sacred Fire is held for all of humanity on the Earth at this time. Lord Sananda serves the next great initiation in Shalahah, and it here that we find healing at every level. This is where the great healers will seek their initiations and move forward in their own Ascension Process. In Klehma is Serapis Bey

---

9. See Appendix B: *Symbology of the I AM America Teachings through Malton's Southern Door, page 245.*

and he holds all the initiations of the White Ray, for indeed he is the Great Trier. Does this help?

Answer: *Yes it does. I hope that before we travel to these points for each of these locations, that we have guidance on the Ray Force and the specific guardian for each of these locations so when we are there physically or in meditation that we may commune with them.*

As you can see, it will take a great flexibility of consciousness to access each of these points, their Ray Forces, and their stewards. Do you understand?

Response and question: *Yes.*

But that is just part of the path, and now unless there are other questions, I shall take my leave from your density.

THE GROUP MIND AND LIKE VIBRATION

Question: *I have only one. In creating the Group Mind is it advisable that we join with others or just create the Group Mind under the I AM America spiritual teachings?*

Remember the Group Mind is also created through the hermetic principle of like vibration. It is difficult to create Group Mind when you have dissimilar vibration. Place your focus upon creating a higher vibration that all may resonate with.

Answer: I see, and we can use the Violet Flame to transmute, to create that higher vibration.

In that Mighty Violet Flame is that most refreshing drink of which you shall never tire.

Response: *We will go to Archangel Crystiel for that Group Mind creation.*

So Be It, Dear ones.

Response: *I am complete, thank you.*

With love and adoration for the liberation of humanity, I AM Saint Germain.

Chapter Four

Leveraging Consciousness

Saint Germain, Kuthumi, and Lady Nada

Greetings Beloveds, In that Mighty Christ I AM, Saint Germain, and I request permission to come forward.

Response: *Dear Saint Germain, please come forward, you are most welcome.*

THE ACTS OF HUMAN INTERVENTION

Greetings and salutations Dear ones, Dear hearts and we welcome you to this beloved Golden City of Malton. We also applaud your effort and the great sacrifice that each of you has made to be present this day. Dear ones, there is still much work to be accomplished on the Earth Plane and Planet, much work to assist and help humanity, yes. But also much work to assist the beloved Golden Cities.

As you well know, the Golden Cities could exist without any human intervention whatsoever; however, with each act of human intervention comes forward a shedding of karma for humanity in the Collective Consciousness. For the Golden Cities are those locations where the Collective Consciousness can indeed be leveraged. In this Time of great Change, this can bring about many, many other scenarios. Yes, in consciousness, but also ameliorating many of the Earth Changes, and the more horrific Earth Changes that are still held within possibility.

TRAVEL TO ADJUTANT POINTS

For you see Dear ones, the Collective Consciousness is held though the collective thought of very man, women, and child who is in embodiment on the Earth Plane. Though prayer and intervention many of these Prophecies can be ameliorated. However, one of the greatest things that can happen to help ameliorate the Prophecies of Change, especially those of Earth Change and that can affect the lives of so many at this time, is your work within a Golden City. This is accomplished through traveling to specific Adjutant Points with certain timing and of course intent. Above all, the intent is the most powerful.

GOLDEN CITIES' INFLUENCE

Each of the Golden Cities holds within their scope the ability to help a certain culture and even certain countries. And in a different context, they also hold and embrace certain geographies and political nations. It is important to understand how each Golden City works and how you (and they) can bring about a change of heart that indeed can change the world.

Gobean, as you well know, has always been aligned to Africa—Egypt specifically.

Gobean assists the African nations to come together in greater harmony and to hold within that greater consciousness—Unana, the Oneship, and the ONE. Of course, now you are in Malton, and this Golden City holds all of Northern Europe in a greater harmony and affects its Collective Consciousness.

Wahanee is also aligned to Africa, but primarily it is a Mighty Transmuting Vortex. For it holds the energy of the Sacred Fire for all of humanity to learn forgiveness and how to apply that Sacred Fire. Now, when you consider how few know about this Mighty Flame in action, you can see the great work that Wahanee holds for all of humanity. Shalahah, of course, holds parts of Asia but primarily India in its Collective Consciousness. All spiritual work that is done there (in Shalahah) can have an affect upon its (India's) coastlines. Klehma holds the energy for the United States, and it does have some influence upon Canada and Mexico. But this is the primary Vortex that will be used to ameliorate extreme weather, extreme Earthquakes, and other Earth Changes that are prophesied. We decided that it was important to dispense this information at this time, so you could begin to understand yet other important uses of the Vortices.

SACRED ACTIVITY

Now, I well understand your intent for coming forward for the work of I AM America in this Golden City of Fruition and Attainment. And we realize how important this is at this time. For the work is held in the hearts of humanity, it is a work that you must put into its own sacred activity. As I have said before, you become our hands, our eyes, our ears, and our feet. You are the ones that walk the path, and share the material with others in the same way that we have shared the material with you. I realize you have many questions and now I open the floor for questions.

Response: *I am just looking for any direction or guidance for this very day, and for the next days where we take on the ceremonies for each of these Adjutant Points.*

Dear ones, to my Right is Beloved Brother Kuthumi, and to my Left is Lady Nada. Behind me stands Beloved El Morya. Beloved Kuthumi would like to speak.

Saint Germain is taking a few steps back and Kuthumi is coming forward.

"WE ARE MOVING SWIFTLY"

Greetings Dear hearts in the Golden Harmony of all that is, I AM Kuthumi and I request your permission to come forward.

Response: *Dear Kuthumi, please come forward, you are most welcome.*

The point that you travel to today will not only help you as you seek additional finances, it also assists the Collective Consciousness of humanity to achieve a greater harmony with their economies. So hold the people of Northern Europe today in this Mighty endeavor. For long they have been held prisoners by those of a dark mind and a dark heart, but I shall not spend too much time upon this for I realize that time is of the essence. You are moving swiftly not only in this Great Time of Change, but you are also moving swiftly with your endeavor of teaching. I hold the I AM America Teachings within my heart, and I will help and assist in whatever way that I can. The teachings, of course, must be brought through with great simplicity in that Divine Heart of Love, for the teachings are inevitably the expressions of the Heart of God. This is also the Heart of the ONE. The ONE that exists in all of creation, that exists in your hearts and the hearts of all humanity, and the creation that exists in all of nature.

MANY KINGDOMS OF CREATION

Today as you travel to this Adjutant Point and perform your ceremony, remember those Kingdoms of Creation: the gnomes, the fairies, the undines, the salamanders, and the sylphs. They can give you great assistance in this endeavor. As you see, the Elemental Kingdom also plays a role in the great abundance that you require for the school and the teachings that you bring forward. As you well know, they hold a space for the creation of the funds that you need. Call upon all four of their kingdoms, and do not forget the Beloved Plant Kingdom and the Beloved Mineral Kingdom. For they too help, do they not? They hold a space within the Collective Consciousness that also helps and assists in the creation. Animals are transmutative of your own emotions. So call forth that Kingdom as well so you may obtain a Mastery over your feeling world.

RESPONSIBLE CO-CREATION

As you well know, with great abundance comes an even greater responsibility. It is my hope that you are now prepared and ready Dear chelas. This is an awesome task in front of you, and one that cannot be taken lightly. I do not give this warning in sternness, I give this warning from my great Heart of Love and compassion, for there will be many decisions and many choices that must be made. Questions?

Question: *I ask for your aid and assistance, that at this point that we are able to ask and put forth the energy for the Elemental Kingdom to help us with all of our processes. And to the Plant Kingdom and the Mineral Kingdom and all members of the Spiritual Hierarchy that support the work of I AM America. But, I also ask for one other thing. Can we free the people of the world from all the types of slavery that exists? Can we free the animals of the world from all the types of slavery that exists? Can we set this into our intention for the upliftment of all?*

Yes, of course you can. Are you not the Co-creator of the will, of the light, and inevitably of the Heart of Love?

A HU-MAN STAR

He is walking forward to you Len, and he's holding his palm outward. And in the center of his palm is a five-pointed star. He is projecting the radiance of this energy into your Third Eye.

This Star represents the kingdoms of which I speak. Of course, the final of these is that of the HU-man Creation. Use this symbol today in your ceremony and it will give you the assistance that you require.

HEART OF ACTION

He is walking over to you (our guest-student) and he is projecting the star into your Heart Chakra. The energy is moving into your heart.

Dear One, this energy will move you not only into the Heart of Love, but into the Heart of Action. This, too, is a symbol that I ask for you to use today. It will give you the intention and the creation that you seek.

He is backing away. Saint Germain is coming forward.

Dear ones, and now I shall share my great symbol with you.

THE WESTERN MIND UNFOLDS

He offers Len a white rose.

This white rose is the Rose of the Brotherhood and Sisterhood of the Great White Dove. It is our symbol that we use in all of our ceremonies and rituals, for you see it represents the unfolding of the Western Mind into the understanding of esoteric and occult knowledge.

He's backing away. Lady Nada is coming forward.

Greetings my beloveds I request permission to come forward.

THE CHANGE WITHIN

Response: *Please Lady Nada come forward, you are most welcome.*

I AM Lady Nada and I hold the symbols of truth, justice, and balance for humanity. As you well know, I hold my focus over that great Vortex of Glastonbury, located above Scotland. I have long held in my mind's eye truth and justice for humanity. At this Time of Great Change I work with beloved Brother Kuthumi to help compensate the energies of balance as they move between the Golden City of Malton and the Golden City of Denasha. You see Dear ones; there are many other changes that are prophesied to happen: great changes of ice sheeting, great changes of volcanic eruption and the rifting of the tectonic plates. However the most important is the change within you. This change moves each and every one of you into the truth of your BE-ing through the uniting of the Mighty I AM Presence that is your own God Perfection. Call forth your God Protection in any ceremony, and hold in your mind's eye that great truth and justice in which all life shares. Life exists for life, and this principle begets balance.

Lady Nada is moving towards you (the Guest-student). She's handing you a yellow rose.

Would you accept this Dear one?

Answer: *I accept with gratitude.*

To help and assist the school of the I AM America Teachings, to help those who come forward, to nurture them, to help develop their spiritual wisdom and insight? This my Dear one, is your symbol.

THERE, I AM

Lady Nada is backing away. Saint Germain is coming forward.

Greetings chelas and initiates. I recognize the great service that you are bringing forward with this, and I too shall overshadow you every step of the way. Know that I follow you everywhere you go:

> In the Truth of the Unfed Flame of Love, Wisdom, and Power,
> There, I AM.
> In the Truth of the Sacred Fire,
> There, I AM.
> In the Beauty of the Eight-sided Cell of Perfection,
> There, I AM.
> Unite with your Mighty I AM Presence, and the gift of Ascension.

Now, I shall open the floor for your questions.

Question: *Is there any specific intention that you want us to put forward in today's ceremony and service?*

UNITED AS ONE

Hold today the Northern Lands of Europe, also help and assist the whole Northeast of the United States. For you well know, not only the weather and the political turmoil that the nation (the United States) is in, we know you are aware of the great conflicts that are held in its political system. Through the Child Point that you attend to, it is our hope that you can help to bring balance. This also will affect Malton, but also Denasha—which has a great influence on those who hold control on the monies of the world. Now without saying too much, you know what I speak of, do you not?

Response and question: *Yes, I do. Now, I am going to ask, is it within my small ability to call forth the removal of their control?*

Call forth your own eternal freedom first, Dear one. For in your freedom, then you can extend your service even at a much higher level, do you understand?

Response: *Yes I do.*

For this, we do:

United as ONE,
In the Great White Brotherhood and Sisterhood
Of breath, sound, and light.

DARKNESS IS A TEACHER

The Dove, of course, is our symbol of peace and the symbol of our lodge, of our stewardship—not only of the planet; but, also our stewardship of the continuing spiritual development and evolution of humanity. Realize that darkness, too, is a great teacher. Darkness, too, allows one to see so clearly with great clarity the difference. And as you well know, as Lord Sananda has always said, "The difference is always the experience." So in the experience comes the varying experiences from which create those great textures of life, the great feelings, the great thoughts. Questions?

Question, Guest-student: *Is there anything we can do to strengthen our Group Mind?*

GROUP MIND: ONE MENTAL BODY

In this moment you are strengthening such. And each ceremony and ritual that you perform together as one strengthens such. You can also call upon Brother Kuthumi, for he has united the great Kingdoms of Nature into one Group Mind, and he holds the key to this. Call upon him in your prayer and your meditation. Of course, I have found the use of the Sacred Fire is perhaps one of the best ways to clear the pathway for the use of the Group Mind. Meditation is also good, along with contemplation. Essential time spent in silence also can clear the mental space. For what is the Group Mind? It is the uniting into ONE Mental Body that function at a higher level and aligns its will to the Divine Plan. Does this make sense?

Answer: *Yes.*

Questions?

Response: *My sense is we should tarry not, and get going.*

I agree, and in that Mighty Name of Christ, may abundance rain down upon you and I AM America. May all the funds, all the money that you need be there and available for you to take Divine Action!

Response: *So be it.*

Hitaka! I AM your Brother eternal, Saint Germain.

Chapter Five

A Great Love

Saint Germain, Sananda, and Kuthumi

Greetings in the Brotherhood of Light, I AM Saint Germain. Today Dear ones, Dear hearts, to my right is beloved Lord Sananda, and to my left is beloved Lord Kuthumi. And before we begin, we request permission to come forward.

Response: *Please come forward, you are most welcome.*

THE GROUP MIND IS ONE

We all come forward this day as representatives of the Great White Brotherhood of Breath, Sound, and Light. And our Collective Consciousness also forms, what you would call at your level of development, a Group Mind. However, at our level of development, we know this simply as the ONE and also the Oneship. We agree to merge our consciousness as ONE, and then as ONE, we come forward into your density for teaching. As I have always said, there is still much work to be accomplished upon the Earth Plane and Planet. The Golden Cities of light are activating one at a time in their intent and their timing so that the Collective Consciousness of mankind can be lifted to yet another level.

ATTUNE TO THE MIGHTY CHRIST

However it is most important to understand, that the Golden Cities at this time, yes, have been given as a divine intervention. Also, they have been given to each one of you individually so those who have aligned their will to this Divine Plan and the work of I AM America, can use them to develop the *"eyes to see and the ears to hear."* I realized yesterday, that as you walked among Kuthumi's beloved forest, that you attuned yourself to the elementals of life and the kingdoms of creation that many are not yet aware of. This helped you to attune your consciousness to yet a even a finer level, a level that is held not only in the reaches of the ONE, the Oneship, but is also held in that Mighty Christ.

A SUBTLE DIFFERENCE

Dear ones, many of the terms we use are analogous, but yet are separated by a very subtle difference. This is very important, and why you need to develop the "eyes to see and the ears to hear." Sometimes it is a subtle difference in the layer of energy. It might be that the aura takes on a soft tinge of pink or soft tinge of gold, and it is this subtle difference that you will also need to develop.

LINEAGE OF THE VIOLET FLAME

But first things first, and we must begin to put one step in front of the other toward the great work at hand. This is the application and use of the Mighty Violet Flame, known in our inner retreats as the Sacred Fire. The Sacred Fire, you see, cleanses not only the outer layer of the human aura, but also clears the way for the inner light of the Eight-sided Cell of Perfection. Use of the Violet Flame is very important and you need to apply it on a daily basis. If you feel you need more, take this discipline unto yourself three times a day. If you do not have the time to decree, hold your focus upon that Mighty Violet Flame and say aloud,

I AM the Violet Flame, manifest within me and without me, now!
Almighty I AM, Almighty I AM, Almighty I AM!

In that moment you have invoked the essence of the Mighty Transmuting Fire, whose lineage comes not only from Atlantis, but also from a civilization prior to that and held (the Violet Flame) in the Temples of Venus. The Violet Flame is an energy and a law that was sponsored by the Lords of Venus at the creation of Shamballa. It was brought to help humanity bring forward a level of spiritual cleanliness in times of great change and be able to use to help ameliorate difficulties not only within the Collective Unconsciousness, but also help difficulties within societal levels, cultural levels. We realize of course that in the time you are now experiencing, this Great Time of Change, that many, many things are being brought to the light . . . things that you could never even imagine to be truths. As you discover each and every one of these, it seems at times a bit sensational, does it not?

VIOLET FLAME GROUPS OF SEVEN

Use this Mighty Violet Flame to help calm and sooth your emotional bodies. If you feel incensed over injustice, if you feel incensed over this great war of good vs. evil, call upon that Mighty Violet Flame in Action, call upon it for the Collective Consciousness, call upon it for all social, cultural, and political situations. It is also advised to work in groups of seven with the Sacred Fire and appoint a time to use the Violet Flame for specific aspects and cultural anomalies that will be brought to the Light.

In these groups of seven, we also ask for you to choose a appointed time that you each shall speak aloud a minimum of seven times a chosen Violet Flame Decree for the situation you are addressing.[10] This will bring about a momentum of energy that can quicken and hurry the amelioration of these types of karmas. It can also create a soothing grace that is much needed among humanity at this time. While using this chosen decree, whichever one you choose to mediate upon, it is also important that you realize that you are a Step-down Transformer of energies, and as you call forth that Mighty Sacred Fire, you are also carrying the energy of the Violet Flame, in, through and around you throughout your daily activities. I also suggest if you choose one day of the week to give to (practice) this discipline, and indeed, this is like a sacrifice to help your present day situations, that you choose Saturdays. For that is the day of that Mighty Violet Flame, and practice on this day will increase its efficiency, ten-thousandfold. Also call upon the Kuan Yin lineage of the Violet Flame, and each of the teachers of that Mighty Violet Flame of Compassion, Mercy and Forgiveness will come forward.[11] It sounds so simple, does it not Dear ones, Dear hearts? Yet the effect will be profound and accomplish a great deal for humanity.

It is in this loving grace of the Violet Flame that I now step back from this podium and Beloved Sananda will now come forward.

CHRIST CONSCIOUSNESS

Sananda looks very much like the Savior, the Christ that we see in biblical times; yet, he has on a Seamless Garment, a white robe, and he too has a Dove resting on his left shoulder. He is engaging what we call the Sananda Mudra from the palm of his hand, and gold light is streaming from it to the three of us.

My Beloveds, I AM Sananda, and I request permission to come forward.[12]

Response: *Please come forward, you are most welcome.*

It is with great delight that I come forward. For I realize the great sacrifice that each of you gave to attend to the Christ Consciousness of Shalahah. I

---

10. See Appendix I: *The Three Standards*, page 281.

11. See Appendix J: *The Lineage of Gurus*, page 283.

12. See Appendix K: Lord Sananda, page 285.

know it was a difficult journey for many of you, for as each of you traveled though each Adjutant Point, there was indeed a transmutation of karma. Many of you were shedding the burdens of not one, two, or three, but even of five different lifetimes simultaneously. This, of course, caused great fatigue and energetic dissociation, as well as many other anomalies which you are now more aware of.

This was absolutely necessary for me to begin an overshadowing of you, to initiate you into the Christ Consciousness. The Christ Consciousness does indeed function through the Group Mind, which you are now beginning to understand in detail. The Christ Consciousness comes forward not only to give you healing and peace, but also to meld your consciousness together as ONE for a greater service and your own spiritual evolution. Beloved Brother Saint Germain has reminded you this is also a necessary step for Ascension. Not only does it build the Eighth Energy Body, it also builds the beginning of the Ninth Energy Body. It like a foundation on a house and from that foundation, brick by brick, the house then comes together. But what is the mortar, what is the clay that holds each of these bricks together? It is that Mighty Christ Consciousness that creates the interface though which you can interact. This consciousness is built not only on service, but also, inevitably, on love. For as I have said so many times, "Love one another." Love creates a higher frequency and we are not talking about accepting another or lowering your frequencies for another, but instead acceptance through the ideal of love.

SERVICE, LOVE, AND FORGIVENESS

This tenet of the Christ Consciousness is built upon service and love. These two aspects are very important to cultivate. The last tenet of Christ Consciousness is Saint Germain's forgiveness. This is why we have given so many discourses on the topic of forgiveness. Forgive one another, for all of you have human frailty. Forgive one another, for all of you will attain yet another understanding of an ideal of consciousness. Forgive one another, for in this Mighty Christ lies the gift of eternal light and the freedom of Ascension.

Sananda reaches for the dove perched on his shoulder, holds it for a moment, and then releases it.

May Peace reign supreme into all of your Energy Bodies, Dear ones. I AM Sananda, and I love and bless you dearly.

Saint Germain is now coming forward.

Dear ones. Now we realize you have much work to attend to in the Golden City of Malton, and today to help and assist you, and to give you guidance is Beloved Kuthumi.

Today Kuthumi has on a brown robe, with a red sash around his waist. He wears a small brown hat with a gold band about it.

Dear Brothers and Sisters of the Gold Ray, I AM Kuthumi, and I request permission to speak.

Response: *Please come forward and speak, you are most welcome.*

"TO EVERY BLADE OF GRASS"

My Dear Brother Sananda speaks of the great love that guides not only the Group Mind, but the consciousness of the Christ. It was this love that I used to attain my own Ascension. It was a love that I gave freely—a love to all creation, to every blade of grass, to every song the birds sang, to the kingdoms of creation. The Gnomes, the Fairies, the Deva Kingdom, even the Salamanders of Fire—I appreciated every detail about them. A love I gave to the crawling creatures of the Earth, to those who are looked down upon and discarded. A love I gave to the lowest and even the highest of humanity. This love, if generated within, extends to all around you. Not only as a Step-down Transformer, but as a Sun (son) of radiation, this, you see, is the nexus of Golden Harmony. Golden Harmony draws from the center of love, and that love radiates as the Sun does, as our eternal father shines upon us. Every beam of light that comes to you is the essence of this unconditional, never-ending love.

GOLDEN LIGHT

Love is not only what ties us together as ONE, but love invigorates our journey and gives us joy, laughter and ceaseless, unending peace. For it is love, that does indeed bring us to this experience, love that drives this experience, and it shall be love that you remember always, in your journey of Golden Light. The Golden Light, you see Dear ones, is the light of Ascension. It is that great fatherly light of freedom.

DARKNESS AND CHOICE

Now, when I speak of the father, I speak of the masculine energy that is complemented by the darkness, that being the feminine energies. Darkness you see, gives contrast to light. Darkness is needed in almost all situations in order to have clarity to choose. And in this great choosing, one then is able to cultivate and develop their will. Through the developed will one can understand the difference between bondage and freedom. Bless those who test you, for they are indeed your Brothers. Bless those who test you, for they are indeed your Sisters. As beloved Saint Germain has reminded you, there are never any mistakes, are there not Dear ones?

Response: *True.*

"FOCUS ON THE LOVE"

Everyone who comes along your path is brought through that great Law of Attraction and through this great law, spiritual evolution unfolds in a magical journey of light and the Golden Sun. Today, as you travel to this Adjutant Point, focus on the love that is within, the love that surrounds you, and the love that you radiate. For in this love comes that first principle, which is the principle of harmony—masculine and feminine in their most perfect blending of energy. In this perfect energy is the balance, and from this balance all exists as it should. All expresses as it can. All is, as it is. And I shall stay here now for a brief moment for your questions.

Response: *Do you have specific guidance for today's intention to be fulfilled?*

Today as you enter into the Adjutant Point, feel the love of which you are. This is the love that lights that Mighty Monad in the crevice of the heart in the Eight-sided Cell of Perfection. Love comes forward to show the light removing darkness. Focus upon love as you enter the apex of the energies of this point. Feel the love and how you place your Mighty Will in action through love. For love is what brings you on this journey, is it not?

Response: *Yes.*

Give deep gratitude and appreciation for the love of this journey and there within you will find the Golden Peace. You see Dear ones, each Adjutant Point not only philosophically ties you to this Great White Lodge, but helps you to incrementally build each layer at a time the Seamless Garment of Ascension. I am certain you understand exactly of what I speak. Questions?

Response and question: Yes. So it takes seven present, holding a focus for one to ascend?

I shall step back and allow Saint Germain to give your answer.

Greetings Dear ones, yes, seven is ideal; however, to break the hold of the Earth Planetary Field, five is always a better number. For you see (the number) five controls a certain sacred numerology or sacred geometry for better understanding. The seven breaks the hold of convention and gives access to the higher, Spiritual Mental Planes and the concept of purity can be achieved. Do you understand?

Response: *Yes.*

Now Dear ones, unless there are other questions, I shall take my leave.

Response: *I have no further questions.*

I thank you, and I love you all from the BE-ing of my source. In the Trinity of that Mighty Christ, I AM Saint Germain. Hitaka!

Jacob's Ladder
Painting by William Blake, 1799-1806.

Chapter Six

Human to HU-man

Saint Germain, Kuthumi, and Lady Nada
as ONE Group Mind

Greetings and salutations, I AM Saint Germain, and I stream forth on that Mighty Violet Ray of Mercy, Transmutation, and Forgiveness. As usual Dear hearts, I request permission to come forward.

Response: *Please come forward, you are most welcome.*

CHRIST CONSCIOUSNESS AND THE ASCENSION PROCESS

Today I come forward with great joy in my heart. For on my right is Beloved Lady Nada, and on my left is the Hierarch of Malton, Beloved Master Kuthumi. Together we perform a consortium of energies that is a Group Mind or a Collective Consciousness. However this Group Mind contains within it a component of Christ Consciousness that helps humanity to transcend to a new level of spiritual evolution. For you see Dear ones, it is the Christ Consciousness that you must access before you can attain your Ascension. The Christ Consciousness is as Brother Kuthumi said yesterday that energy of "ultimate love." It is also the energy of ultimate Forgiveness.

The Christ Consciousness, as Lord Sananda has taught you so well, overshadows you and helps you to perfect (connection to) the Mighty I AM Presence. As you well know, the Ascension Process itself is governed and guided by the Christ Consciousness, for when you receive your inner guidance in your most early stages of development of the Eight-sided Cell of Perfection alongside that Eighth Energy Body, what are you calling upon? But that Mighty Christ within. It is that Mighty Christ that allows you then to traverse multiple layers and dimensions of energies. It also allows you to move in your perceptions and how you are able to see things with a much more truthful perspective.

FIRST, DEVELOP THE ONENESS

The Christ itself has been brought forward to help you attain the Ascension, but it is also very important that you use the Christ Consciousness to promote Brotherhood and Sisterhood. This you see is also very important, Dear ones, Dear hearts for moving into the ONE, one step at a time. Now, let me explain. The ONE, from the human to the HU-MAN and obtaining a sense of Brotherly and Sisterly camaraderie, is a step at a time. First, you develop the Oneness. This Oneness, Dear hearts, is felt not only in the Group Mind that the three of you have achieved, but it is also felt when you walk in harmony in nature. For yesterday in your walk at the Harmony Adjutant Point, did you not feel the sublime Oneness?

Answer: *Yes.*

THE ONESHIP

It is this Oneness that paves the pathway to take the next step, that next step is the Oneship, and allows you to meld your consciousness to another. Very often this happens in the sacred agreement of marriage, for two shall become as ONE. As you do your research in past I AM America Teachings, you shall see I have said, "That two shall become as ONE or where two are, there I AM." This is the process of the Oneship. It is also another way of understanding the Group Mind. Go back; remember the teachings of beloved Mother Mary, beloved Kuan Yin and how they merged their consciousness to become as ONE. That indeed was the Oneship that they preformed.

UNANA, THE ONE, AND FIFTH DIMENSION

As you add yet another level of consciousness to the Oneship, you step up into Fourth Dimensional consciousness, but also into Fifth Dimensional consciousness. The Fifth Dimensional consciousness is where we enter into Unana, this is known as the ONE. In the ONE come many levels of healing, spontaneous healing, as well as your understanding of the immortal, light giving body. These are the bodies of light that are developed at the Ninth, Tenth and even Eleventh layers. These are essential for understanding the pathway to Ascension.[13] Do you have questions?

THE EIGHTH ENERGY BODY

Question: *What are the steps to developing the Eighth Energy Body?*

The Eighth Energy Body, as you well know, is held through a collective Chakra System. Even now as the three of you are seated for this transmission, there is a Chakra System that is being formed and is comprised of the three

---

13. See Appendix L: *The Light Bodies of Ascension*, page 287.

of you. Now, look out at least three feet in front of you, from your heart center and your Solar Plexus, do you see a globe of light?

Response: *Yes.*

Each of you are creating this beginning chakra, this is one of the anomalies of the Eighth Layer of the Energy Field. Do you understand?

Answer: *Yes.*

Of course there are other chakra fields (systems) that develop through the Eighth Energy Body—it also uses a collective energy of the Crown Chakra. Now, in your mind's eye, travel to the Third Eye and the Crown Chakra, then look out again another three feet. What do you see?

Answer: *A star.*

This is the beginning of yet another vital chakra that forms the nexus for the development of the Ninth Energy Body. As you well know, that Ninth Energy Body is where much conflict can occur, but that is why we have counseled you to depend upon the Group Mind. For this can give a much balancing effect to the Ninth Energy Body. Do you understand?

Question: *So the step-by-step process to create the Ninth Energetic Body is it a natural course of evolution through the Eighth Energy Body?*

SPIRITUAL DEVELOPMENT THROUGH ONENESS WITH NATURE

It is indeed, however there are many who have obtained this without the vital influence of the Group Mind. They have obtained it as Brother Kuthumi has exhibited through a Oneness with nature. This is why so many travel to the retreats to spend time in solitude, and in meditation, so they can use the energies of beloved Mother Earth Babajeran to develop the Eighth Energy Body.

In this time period, the Golden Age of Kali Yuga, the Eighth Energy Body can be built through the HU-mans who are developing the "eyes to see and the ears to hear," and I would like to add, this is a much swifter course—using the HU-man (Group Mind) for spiritual evolution.

Response and question: *I see. So going to the Ninth Energy Body, ultimately we will need the HU-man at the point of Ascension?*

It is one course of development, as always there are choices. Remember when you discovered that there is a difference between Ascension and Rapture?

Answer: *Yes.*

SPIRITUAL LIBERATION AND THE ASCENSION

Now, there is a difference between Spiritual Liberation and Ascension, do you understand?

Question: *Can you be more specific in that difference?*

Spiritual Liberation is a form of freeing the consciousness to new levels and heights of ecstasy though using and understanding the energy fields of the Earth, Babajeran. Ascension is a pathway that has been brought through development and cultivation of the Christ Consciousness, and applying this through the use of the Group Mind.

Question: So you are saying that the Group Mind is the main pathway to the Christ Consciousness?

Indeed it is. For within the Christ Consciousness, does it not too use the Group Mind?

Answer: *Yes, I would say you are correct there.*

So it is based upon the synergy that is brought from the Group Mind itself. Questions?

Response: *So in going to the Ninth Energy Body, and establishing a Group Mind agreement or harmony . . .*

THE NINTH ENERGY BODY

The Ninth Energy Body can be very difficult sometimes (harmonizing), with the Group Mind. For there the wills must come into complete and absolute harmony, do you understand?

Response: *I see, that could be a challenge . . .*

And it is important to understand the difference between the individual and individualization. This too, is brought about by that which cannot be divided, that which is the Ray Force which you love, serve, and place your utmost devotion.

Question: *So the individualization is the contribution of each person to the Group Mind?*

This is so, and in the Ninth Energy Body—that is where fear is finally dropped. If you go back and research the previous lessons you will understand. Questions?

THE TENTH ENERGY BODY

Question: *So then to go to the Tenth Energy Body, what is that procedure?*

This is the process where one is freed to yet another level and Mastery is obtained.

Response and question: *Yes, but what is the process?*

For now I have given you enough, go into past lessons and there you shall find your answers.

Response: *Then I will do so.*

Because time is of the essence.

Question: *Is there anything specific for today's journey?*

I shall now turn the floor over to Lady Nada.

LADY NADA AND THE GOLDEN AGE

Lady Nada is coming up to the podium, and I would like to describe her. She has beautiful, long, flowing hair, and very green almost green-blue exotic looking eyes, and she has roses in her hair—they are pink roses. She is wearing a beautiful yellow gown.

Greetings my beloveds, I AM Lady Nada, and I request permission to come forward into your energy fields.

Response: *Please come forward, you are most welcome. Thank you for coming.*

As you know Dear ones, Dear hearts, Beloveds of mine I AM Lady Nada, I serve as Hierarch of Denasha, but also I have served on many councils for the Earth itself. At one time, I served on the Karmic Council that oversaw the karmic burden of humanity. It was decided through timing and intent that a great Golden Age would be dispensed to the Earth Plane and Planet, so those who were willing and were developing themselves spiritually would have an opportunity for Ascension—this is the period of time you are now experiencing. While it will be timed out as a ten-thousand year period, there may even be a longer period that will be applied to it—this is contingent upon humanity's use of the Golden Cities and their attainment of Ascension.

Just so you can familiarize yourself with my mission for the Earth Plane and Planet, I represent Divine Justice, harmony, grace and peace for humanity. And I, too, have served in the Earth Plane and Planet, reaching my own Ascension in the days of Atlantis. Yes, I incarnated in those early epochs of Rama, of Lemuria, and during the great wars of Atlantis. It was there, through the greater councils that I sought my liberation and found it through the energies of Quetzalcoatl, which at that time was also known as the great Group Mind—you know as Christ Consciousness. We found through compassion, great love and mercy for the human condition rests our eternal freedom. I ascended in that time before the great sinking of Poseidis, and I too, served on many councils in physical form working for peace, harmony for all people, races, and especially for the Chimeras. For as you know, there were many who sought to alter the DNA of the human at that time. And as you are aware of, there have been many more alterations of this DNA. I can give more detailed information.

A PORTAL TO INNER EARTH

For today I am here to speak about the Child Point, which you will travel to and perform your great ceremony. But it was important for me to give you some background about this. For it is important to know and understand, and to protect yourself with that Mighty Gold Ray of the Golden Age as you bring together two vital points of energy. Dear ones there lies a great portal where you are traveling to, and this is a portal to the Inner Earth. It was not just those of evil who escaped into the Inner Earth, but many of who were made of the Chimera. Do you understand that their DNA had been altered, and that they too can rise in vibration? But it is very difficult for them to achieve there Ascension, especially through Group Mind. But some day, somehow, in another epoch, they too will obtain their level of liberation. Do you have question?

Question: *My only question, because time is of the essence, is there something specific you need us to attend to on this particular child point?*

It is important to keep your eyes and ears open and attentive. There will be much you will discover in this trip, things that will expand your consciousness beyond your experience and beyond your belief. Call forth my energy and my essence as I will overshadow this particular activation of this Adjutant Point. Now, unless there are other questions, I shall turn this floor over to my Beloved Brother Kuthumi.

Response: *There are no other questions.*

Nada is backing away, Kuthumi is coming forward.

Greetings Brothers, Sisters of the Gold Ray, I AM Kuthumi, do I have permission?

Response: *Please come forward, you are most welcome. Thank you for coming.*

TWO VITAL LEI-LINES: HARMONY AND ABUNDANCE

Yesterday, I was with you in my beloved forest of Elemental and Deva Kingdoms, Plant Kingdoms, and Mineral Kingdoms that I take such delight in, and today you too shall feel this delight and joy for the merging of these two vital lei-lines between Abundance and Harmony. Harmony and Abundance can never be separated; they are one concept and the same. When you call forth your need for finances, for money, what are you calling forward? Your need for great harmony. Where does this harmony come from? From the love within your heart; feel this love, live this love, and BE this love.

Today as you come to this great point of the child, the inner marriage of yin and yang, left and right, masculine and feminine, recognize again love as the great equalizer that creates balance within. Here, call forth your great decree for finance, your great decree for harmony, your great decree for love, and it shall be manifest—this I assure you Dear ones. Do you have questions?

Response: *I completely understand that, I have no further questions.*

In that Mighty Gold Ray of Brotherhood, Peace, and Understanding, I AM Kuthumi.

He is backing away and Saint Germain is coming forward.

In that Mighty Christ, let us proceed.

I AM the flame of Unana,
ONE, in Brotherhood,
ONE, in heart,
ONE, forever and immortal.

Response: So be it.

Hitaka!

Chapter Seven

The Golden Orb

Saint Germain, Kuthumi, and El Morya

Greetings Beloveds. In that Mighty Christ, I AM Saint Germain and I request permission to come forward.

Response: *Please come forward, you are most welcome.*

A LIFETIME OF EXPERIENCE

As usual Dear ones, Dear hearts, there is still much work to complete, for the work upon the Earth Plane and Planet is still before all of us. As you have eyes to see and ears to hear know that I AM an Ascended Master who works for the upliftment of humanity and that I am here to give you service.[14] It is the upliftment of humanity that concerns the Great White Brotherhood and Sisterhoods of Light. For you see Dear ones, Dear hearts, our message is brought forward to uplift your hearts, and too uplift your energy fields. But of all things, this service is to uplift your mind and lead you into these teachings of breath, sound, and light.

These teachings of course are not gained just in the reading of one book, but they are gained through a lifetime of experience. And through this experience is always the difference, is it not Dear ones, Dear hearts, Dear chelas of mine?

Response: *Yes.*

This experience you see, not only gives you the capacity to then place these teachings into action, but it also gives you great joy. For you see Dear ones, is it not the joy itself that is the nexus of love?

Response: *Yes.*

---

14. See Appendix M: *Saint Germain, the Holy Brother*, page 291.

LOVE, AT EVERY LEVEL

Love, as beloved Kuthumi has taught you, is indeed where all of these teachings lead themselves toward.

It is the experience of love at every level,
Is part of the Mastery you seek.
It is not just the feeling of love,
It is the sensing of love.
It is not only the sensing of love,
It is the knowledge of love,
It is the faith of love,
And the thoughtfulness of love—
As love has many expressions.
For love in service,
Breathes the breath of life for all.

When you understand,
"It is indeed love that will catapult you
Into a new life and beyond."
The life that you seek,
Is life eternal in the light.
This is the Process of Ascension,
And love is the basis of this teaching.

For love is the beginning,
And it is the end,
—the Alpha and the Omega.
Love is where your life flame started,
And where it is from.
Love is the life flame,
That will take you into the reaches of freedom,
Into Spiritual Liberation,
And into Ascension.

THE ASCENSION SPIRAL

There is also much work that must be completed with that Mighty Violet Flame, to call this Mighty Violet Flame in action say firmly:

I AM the Violet Flame in action in me now.
I AM the Violet Flame, to life and Ascension I bow!

Dear ones, when you call this Mighty Violet Flame in its eternal action for Ascension, you are scrubbing away the karmic residue of lifetime after lifetime that has held you back. For you see, as you gain the knowledge of successive lifetimes you see how the wheel continues to turn and turn and turn. But what you really seek is not the turning of the wheel, but the spiral. The spiral is brought forward, not only through that Mighty Violet Flame but also through its application and breath. It starts in the lower chakras, moving into the Solar Plexus onward through the Heart Chakra, onward up into the throat, into the pineal, and onward into the Crown Chakra. From the Crown Chakra this then takes this Mighty orb into that Eighth Energetic and forms again the Group Mind. Now, to apply this into Group Mind, visualize now (the Orb) between the three of you as you sit here as a great and Mighty force, circling itself as a spiral, lifting you into the glory and the liberation of the Ascension.

GOLDEN ORB TECHNIQUE

I prefer to call forth that Mighty Violet Flame in action first. Command the HU (or HUE) in its vibration and force, and then visualize that Gold Ray. As it starts (appears) between the three of you, the center of the triangle and it moves itself, its own energetic, embracing all of you in a tornadic type of whirlwind. Yes, indeed it is a whirlwind, but it is a controlled whirlwind— you control it through your breath. Now, I would like the two of you to practice this and let me walk you through it:

1. Between the two of you, visualize a Golden Orb of light.
2. From this Golden Orb, command the HU into its action and activity, (vocalize the HU together).
3. As this moves forward in its action and activity, do you sense the pulsing of that Mighty Golden Orb between you . . . and notice a golden tinge on its outer periphery?
4. It is important to apply the breath within the HU itself, for the HU is like the Mighty Breath of God. The Violet Flame is in action as it moves throughout your Chakra System and is released through the Throat Chakra.
5. Now, this Mighty Orb forms the foundation of the tornadic activity.
6. Close your eyes, and visualize with me, through this Mighty Orb of Light.
7. A circular motion comes forward between the two of you; it begins with a lower rate-of-spin.

8. As you are ready, increase the rate-of-spin. Do you feel this motion now?
9. This motion is controlled through your breath; now, try a breath in unison.

I'm going to describe what he is showing me. He is showing me this Golden Orb, and from the base of the orb radiates a tornado. It is swirling and it is moving energy between the two of you, your Third Eyes and Throat Chakras are also connecting to it. The Throat Chakra, Third Eye, and Crown Chakra is the Orb's higher chakra activity. Also, you can increase the rate-of-spin through your breath; you can control it through your Third Eye. Len, you are doing this!

Dear ones, Dear hearts, as you can see, this tornadic activity is one way to instantly join in Group Mind. Now it is important as you are experiencing this for you to share a single focused thought. For this first single focused thought, I ask for you to place your focus on the White Dove of Peace. Signal to me when you both have this held in your mind's eye.

They both signal.

So be it. Now form one expanded thought with the Dove of Peace. Keep this silent unto yourself, and place it into your memory. Now, I would like for you to gradually disconnect by slowing the rate-of-spin down of the tornadic experience.

I will describe what I am seeing. You want to slow this Golden Light tornado, slow its motion, and eventually dissipate its energy back into the Golden Orb.

Now, open your eyes. Reach your hands forward and touch the Golden Orb. Then, withdraw your hands from this Golden Orb . . . one at a time. What was the one thought you shared as you held Group Mind?

Response: *The dissolution of the control of evil across the world.*

Response, Guest-student: *The next step for the I AM America School.*

TECHNIQUE: MOVING INTO HARMONY

So you came close to the next step. This was the union that you shared in your Group Mind. Let us perform this experiment one more time, and see if you can bring your thought into a harmonious, momentous ONE.

Let us begin again:

1. With the tornadic golden light, visualize the energy streaming from your Throat Chakra, your Third Eye chakra and also your Crown Chakra.
2. Place your thought now on the White Dove of Peace, this provides a plan of unison.
3. Now, expand the rate of speed of the tornadic golden light.
4. Dissipate it; you can also dissipate the rhythm through breath.
5. Open your eyes and each of you place your hands on the Golden Orb.
6. Share your thoughts.

Response, Guest-student: *My thought was how to bring greater peace on Earth.*

Response: *I could see Kuthumi holding the dove.*

This is excellent, for both of you have focused on a single purpose, even though each of them is individualized. This is perhaps one of the best exercises to move into Group Mind, quickly and fluidly. It not only uses the work of the Violet Flame, it also uses that Mighty Gold Ray in action.

THE GOLD RAY

As you know Dear ones, the Gold Ray is the next step after the use of the Violet Flame, it is a harder spiritual practice but as you can see, it completely unifies and leads one into the Group Mind. It arcs itself from that Great Central Sun, but instead of triangulating through the Fire Triplicity, it enters only the solar Sun and from there arcs its energy into your Energy Field. And in this case, the golden torsion field that you created of light.

Mighty Golden Ray,
Stream into and around my light-fields,
Leading me into the unison of the Group Mind.
So Be It!

You have been requesting more information of how to work and use Group Mind, and this should be your next step. Practice it at will, and you will receive great result. Now Dear ones, since I have given this teaching to you, are there questions?

Response and question: *The tornado also looked to me like it would ground to the core of the Earth too. It is best that it always uses the Golden Orb as its source of energy, do you understand?*

It can be used with other ameliorations later on; but first, perfect its use through the Golden Orb.

Response, Guest-student: *I felt my heart rate increase when we were spinning the Golden Orb.*

This is because of the activity of the Eight-sided Cell of Perfection, for it uses the energy of the Eight-sided Cell of Perfection to refract the energy and to calibrate the rate-of-spin. Questions?

BELIEF SYSTEMS

Question: *The transmutation of the Ascension Process—when we are talking about the spirit, basically, what we are doing is freeing spirit from incarnating again, true?*

This is correct, and as I have explained in past discourse, there is of course the Rapture that is brought about by the momentum of the belief system. You understand this, do you not?

Response: *Yes, the belief system is very creative.*

"TWO OR MORE"

It is indeed. Brother Kuthumi has explained his great vision of nature, which can also bring about unison of energy and open a portal or pathway, for Spiritual Liberation. This is one of the techniques that is employed more in Eastern Thought, or though the work of the Bodhisattva and the Buddha. It is indeed a Path of Awakening, but it is a singular path and can take many, many lifetimes.

Though the effort of the Group Mind, one can accelerate their spiritual development; for you are pulling upon a group energy that is created of *two or more*. Now that you have had this experience, do you understand my statement?

Response: *I have a better understanding that I did before. It is no different than when you are standing in front of a great audience and you are performing on that stage. You are indeed working with a larger Collective Consciousness—a Group Mind, and it uses the same premise; however, it is a direct utilization of the energy though the light-fields and the Chakra System.*

Response and question, Guest-student: *So as we focus our thought upon the dove, the power of the Group Mind will give the (energy of) two or three of us working together. Will it help our thoughts to become harmonized, even though we say it differently?*

Yes, indeed. And as you obtain more practice with this, there will be greater harmonization and as I have brought forward, along with my Beloved Brother Sananda and Beloved Brother El Morya, and the many other Masters of light. In the Jurisdictions it is Harmony first that creates Abundance, does it not?

Response, Guest-student: *Yes.*

So in your request for the abundance, let us now focus on the great harmony. Questions?

ADJUTANT POINTS AND THE GROUP MIND

Response and question: *So back to the spirit being freed from the incarnation process . . . what the spirit has done is incarnated multiple times and had experience, but the experiences have not been balanced. . . it has not been energy-for-energy. So since they are not balanced, that's the remainder to be transmuted?*

These experiences remain then like a ball and chain, chaining the human condition again and again to the grosser energies of Earth; but what you achieve though this is creating a higher energetic that is used to lift you into the Ascension. This indeed can also be increased exponentially though visits and performance at Adjutant Points. Each Adjutant Point can increase the efficiency of the Group Mind ten-thousandfold. So you see Dear ones, this is why we encourage the visits to Adjutant Points, for these are sensitive areas in the Golden Cities that have also been overshadowed by the Great Ones. They, too, use their energy to lift you into the glory of the Ascension. As I explained to you, in the different levels of mentoring, teaching, and the Guru—the Guru, though the Adjutant Point emits the vital energies. But again, the Cup must be readied to receive. The tornadic Vortex that you create functions like an open chakra. What is the open chakra? It is the open Cup though which sublime, eternal light can pour though. Do you understand?

Response and question: *Yes, it is like when the chakras terminate though the eight layers, they terminate into a ball.*

Now Dear ones, are there other questions before I proceed?

Answer: *No, we will have to practice this to become more proficient about it.*

At Saint Germain's right is Beloved Kuthumi, and to his left is El Morya. Kuthumi is coming forward to speak.

THE GOLDEN FOREST

Grace and eternal peace to you, I AM Kuthumi, do I have permission to come forth?

Response: *Please come forward, you are most welcome.*

Peace in the eternal Gold Ray, my Dear hearts. It is with such gladness that I come forward this day. Joy for your visit to Malton, and for the work you performed while there. I realize while you seek this Golden perfection, that there will still be many twists and turns along the path. But I overshadowed every moment with you and walked with you in the Golden Forest. Within this forest there is a retreat that you do not yet see, but as you develop the "eyes to see and the ears to hear" you will begin to see its beautiful golden, jeweled and gem encrusted walls. There is a beautiful gateway through which you can also gain entrance. That is why it is important to visit Golden City Vortices and these spectacular points so you can begin to discern and gain entry into the sublime retreats.

This first retreat that you attended to, which was in the progression to the Abundance Point, is indeed an Abundant Point of the Green Ray. It is served by the being Visheeah, who has also been overseeing many of the Elemental Kingdom and their activity there. Visheeah is a being of water, and that is why when you visited this great retreat over this Adjutant Point, he sent the rain for you. Visheeah, you see Dear ones, not only sends water, but also can be called upon in your prayer to bring water in times of drought. This is the work of the Nature Kingdom and as they move forward in their own evolutionary process, they too reach levels of enlightenment and purity of thought. You also had many experiences of the Elemental Kingdom, did you not while you were there?

Response: *Yes.*

There was also another being who jokingly left his belt for you, this was the being Thronana, for Thronana is of the Earth Kingdom (gnome) and represents a village of Earth Beings who exist primarily in the Fourth Dimension. He did this jokingly, and he is happy that you saw it, examined it, and left it.

They are amused and chuckling.

Now let us move over to the Harmony Point and this is where the Goddess Sinerna resides. Could you feel the beauty of the feminine and the Pink Ray as it streamed though this harmonious point? Sinerna oversees a Kingdom of Fairies and Elementals, and they were all present with you as you opened this gateway.[15]

He is backing away, beloved El Morya is coming forward.

Greetings chelas, stalwart ones, in that Mighty Blue Ray, I AM El Morya. I request permission to come forward into your energy fields.

EL MORYA'S INITIATIONS OF THE BLUE FLAME

Response: *Please El Morya come forward, you are always welcome.*

It is the third point of which I shall now concern myself. For this third point, I too overshadowed and one of my stalwart chelas is now in training, and will come forward to serve in their Ascended state. This will not happen for several more years, but for now I do oversee this area with that Mighty Blue Ray. Perhaps you felt the strength of my force when you were there?

Response: *Yes, there was a lot of force there.*

This, you see Dear ones, is an ancient site, not only of Atlantis, but also of the times of Lemuria. It is also, as Lady Nada pointed out to you, an entrance into the Inner Earth, but there is also a great pyramid that exists that I oversee where many initiations of the Blue Flame come forward. I often say, "To do, to dare, and to be silent." This is a point where one gains great inner strength, and where one can meditate to achieve union with their Mental Body. Their thoughts, their feelings, and their actions lead them into great fruition and attainment. Essentially what am I saying? This is a point of Mastery. Do you have any questions?

---

15. See Appendix N: *The Hierarchs and Adjutant Points of Malton's Southern Door,* page 295.

Response: *There seemed to be a lot of activity at that point, in the Earth plane.*

There is a lot of activity of the Deva and Elemental Kingdom present there, as well as an entrance to the Inner Earth.

Response: *We had a discussion while we were there, that we thought the snakes (cottonmouth) of that area were designed for protection.*

THE CHIMERAS OF LEMURIA

You refer to the Chimeras which were created in the time of Lemuria. Lady Nada also referred to this. At the time when the two continents began their fight with one another, the battle was carried out not only in the higher reaches of Third Dimension, but also in Fourth Dimension. Many Chimeras were created—this form of snake was created at that time. Not only does it have the ability to fight viciously in Third Dimension, but it can also enter into the Fourth Dimension. That is why you "pick up," as you would say and have an eerie feeling when you are near these types of areas, do you not?

Response: *Yes.*

They are entering into the Fourth Dimension, so it is very important when you are meditating in this area that you always call upon Archangel Michael's Blue Flame of Protection. Are you familiar?

Mighty Blue Flame,
I call you forth in full force activity!
Empower me with the Blue Flaming Sword of Protection.
Surround my physical body,
Surround my Fourth Dimensional body,
Surround my Fifth Dimensional body,
All my light-fields,
My Chakra System.
Mighty Blue Flame in action,
I call you forth now!

Before I depart, are there questions?

THE EVOLUTION OF LORD NAGA

Question, Guest-student: *I felt dragon energy there as well.*

What you feel is the Fourth Dimensional breath of that Mighty Serpent. For you see it too has its own level of evolution. Though scientifically created at one time, they have created a Group Mind. Lord Naga, their spiritual leader, is of the Blue Ray and does indeed exist. You may have had some contact, but he is still within the training field. Do you understand?

Answer: *Yes.*

Perhaps I have told you too much!

El Morya is chuckling to himself.

Question: *I do have a question . . . will the Nagas and the snakes accept harmony and unconditional love?*

There are many that already do live within this great harmony of the Beloved Mother Babajeran and the great changes that she is now undergoing. They too await this great change and the time when they too shall be freed from there Chimera existence. In that Mighty Blue Flame, I AM as ONE heart, El Morya.

Saint Germain is coming forward.

And now Dear ones, it is important that we address that Mighty Point of Service. To my right is Beloved Lady Nada..

Greetings Dear ones, it is I, Lady Nada. With joy and happiness, I stream forth into the Earth plane upon the Mighty Yellow and Gold Ray in service to humanity. Do I have permission to come forward?

Response: *Please come forward, you are most welcome.*

LADY AMARYLLIS

In her right hand she is holding another Being of Light–an Elemental Being, who appears to be about twelve to fourteen inches tall. Let me describe her to you. She has long brunette hair, green eyes, and she is wearing a white dress that resembles a white lily.

This Beloved Being of Light has been under my stewardship for many hundreds of years. I would like to introduce Lady Amaryllis.

Lady Amaryllis is coming forward.

Greetings Dear ones, do I have permission to speak?

Response: *Yes, Lady Amaryllis, you have permission to speak and come forward at any time.*

I represent that beloved Plant Kingdom at the Point of Service. For there you felt that golden, radiant white light. This is a Service Point of the White Ray, and leads one onward into all the kingdoms of creation. This beautiful Kingdom of Plants are here to assist the Ascension of humanity. It is important to understand that the Plant Kingdom, in its wisdom and ultimate medicine, is also available to assist the Ascension of humanity. We work in harmony with humanity at all times, but we also work in harmony with the Animal Kingdom, the Mineral Kingdom, the Insect Kingdom, and many other kingdoms of creation that exist. Understand that there are many, many more kingdoms. However, this particular Point of Service exists for the Plant Kingdom and the focus here is for the cultivation of new plants to help and assist the vibration of the Earth. For you see you went through many agricultural areas, did you not?

Response: *Yes.*

And could you feel the energy, almost in a twenty to sometimes thirty-mile radius from that point? This, you see Dear ones, Dear hearts, will become a great focus for the development for many new crops that will come forward in the New Times. Underneath that lake you visited is a large deposit of White Gold. This explains the sublime energy that you feel in this soil. This (deposit) is several thousand feet below, but it is also important to understand that it too, in its timing and intent, will come forward as it arcs energies into the soils of the Earth. There are also many other entrances (to Inner Earth) and aquatic beings that reside within this area. I am in tune with their forces and I serve always the great Light of the Divine. Questions?

THE PLANT KINGDOM AND ASCENSION

Question: *Is there a specific native plant that will be helpful in the Ascension Process?*

From this area there are two that you can research, one is a white-flowering plant that resembles a lily; however, it is not of the lily family. If you do your research, you will find it. And the sunflower is always of great assistance, for it carries a combination of the Yellow and Gold rays. There will be many new cereal crops that will be developed in this area in the New Times. However, it is important to attend to the Service Point, for you see, the more spiritual activity that is brought among the humans and those of the Plant Kingdom will help to control a much more conducive climate. Do you understand?

Answer: *Yes.*

This has to do with the glacial activity and the Polar Vortex that was experienced in this area several years ago. Perhaps s student will come forward and offer their complete service in this area. I ask for them to call upon me, Lady Amaryllis, and I shall step-down my energies of service. Do you have any further questions?

THE MAGIC OF ALCHEMY

Response, Guest-student: The magic of this area is stunning to me. I can still see it in my mind's eye.

The magic and alchemy of the White Ray will always be present there for you Dear one, Dear heart. This magic of alchemy is the ascent of light, is it not . . . and in the joy of service?

Response: *I know we have to go back.*

TEMPLES OF THE SUN

She is stepping back, Lady Nada is coming forward.

I AM Lady Nada, and now will share a bit of knowledge regarding this specific point, for it too contained at one time in the time of Atlantis, a great Temple of the Sun. You felt the remnant of this great temple, and if you carry out more of your research you will see that this has been suspected for some time by archeologists. This (temple) was one of the great transmitters of vital light during the Time of Peace. There was a time of war among civilizations and continents, and then the great Time of Peace came about through the building of many Temples of the Sun. Questions?

THE GREAT TEMPLE WITHIN

Question: *Is there any way we can help with doing something at that location or any other location to magnify that light to bring about a great peace again to this planet?*

The building of the great temple is within the HU-Man. This is achieved through uniting the heart and mind as ONE. When Beloved Saint Germain came forward and said to, "Build the school within your heart," this is exactly what must be done first. First, this great temple is built within humanity. I hope you understand and are not frustrated by my answer.

Response: *No, I'm not frustrated. This requires a lot more self-discipline.*

Within all of your hearts is the light sublime to achieve this goal, and if there are no further questions, I will return the floor to Beloved Saint Germain.

Response: *Thank you.*

Saint Germain comes forward.

Dear ones, I realize I have given you much to think about and ponder. Now, are there further questions before I take my leave?

Question, Guest-student: *I have a question from a Dear friend. She is currently suffering from both fatigue and emotional depression and she wants to know is it her time to leave yet? Is it time for her Ascension? And if not, what does she need to do to further serve you?*

VIOLET FLAME FOR DEPRESSION

Of course all is a choice and this Dear chela has served me well, yet there are ten more years of service that she can bring to the Earth Plane and Planet. Of course, it is the open heart that always serves, is it not? And for this Dear one, it is important to spend time in meditation upon my Beloved Sacred Fire, the Violet Flame. Visualize the Sacred Fire burning away the stress, the worry, and the depression. Call forth:

Mighty Violet Flame,
Come forward into my energy fields.
Dissolve and transform my depression.
Dissolve and transform my disease processes.
Lift me into Joy!
Lift me into the Light of All Life!
Violet Flame transform,
Violet Flame blaze in, through, and around me.
So Be It!

This alone has the force and the energy to change all conditions, now my message to this beloved, dear one of mine, my daughter and heart of my heart, I ask of you. Please stay just a little longer, can you not?

Now unless there are further questions, I shall take my leave.

"I AM THE EMBER, I AM THE FLAME"

Response: *Only one. A good priestly thing to do is to call upon the Violet Flame in all circumstances and situations.*

Indeed.

Question: *And the best way to start?*

Use of the Violet Flame can start at any level: beginners, aspirants, chelas, initiates and even the Arhat, call upon that Mighty Sacred Fire to achieve the end result.

In that Mighty Violet Flame,
I AM the ember,
I AM the flame,
I AM the transmutation
Of the Mighty Violet Flame in activity!

So be it, I AM Saint Germain.

Response: *Hitaka.*

The Annunciation
Painting by Henry Ossawa Tanner, 1898.

Chapter Eight

The Guiding Light

Saint Germain, El Morya, and Kuthumi

Greetings beloveds. It is I, Saint Germain, and I stream forth on that Mighty Violet Ray of mercy, transmutation and forgiveness. As usual Dear ones, I request permission to come forward.

Response: *Please come forward, you are most welcome.*

THREE MASTERS

There are three Masters present. Beloved Saint Germain, and to his left is El Morya and to his right is beloved Kuthumi. El Morya is stepping forward.

In that Mighty Will of God, I AM El Morya, and I request permission to come forward.

Response: *Please come forward, you are most welcome.*

In that steely Blue Ray of the Lord of Lords, I AM El Morya.[16] Today I come forward along with my Brothers Saint Germain and Kuthumi to give you further discourse upon the work of the Group Mind. For you see Dear ones, Dear hearts, the Group Mind functions through your individual will, but it also contains its own will. This is the discourse today: understanding and knowing the Group Will of the Group Mind.

The group will is engendered within the Divine Cause, and the Divine Cause is engendered within the great Divine Plan. It is important to understand that as you align your will to the Divine Will, then the Ascended Masters—this hierarchy of Light—can come forward and utilize that for the greater working of united Brotherhood and Sisterhood. When you call upon that Mighty Divine Will are you not then asking for the Blue Ray of Protection and the God Will of protection to stream in, through, and around you?

---

16. See Appendix O: *Master El Morya*, page 299.

DIVINE PROTECTION

Answer: *Yes.*

This you see is vital and important, for yesterday Beloved Brother Saint Germain taught you the basis of how the Group Mind is structured, its infrastructure, and its many points of cause. However, it is also important to understand that alongside this exercise, you must also call upon Divine Protection before entering into the process of using Group Mind. Call forward that Mighty I AM God Protection,

I AM the God Protection of all of life.
I AM the God Protection imbued with the Blue Ray Force.
I AM the God Protection that is engendered
through the Mighty God, I AM.

"A SACRED PACT"

When you call this forth in its power, throughout the scheme and infrastructure of that Mighty Group Mind, you are placing your Group Mind into the hand of the Holy of Holies. This is not only a devoted act; it is, of course, a sacred pact. As you call upon the Group Mind and then add a third, a fourth, a fifth, maybe even a sixth or seventh (person) you are merging your Chakra Systems and energy fields together as ONE. This creates an even greater force that can be used and directed with sublime focus.

GOD PERFECTION

This is of course the way we work with you. For the Mighty Blue Ray and its focus and God Concentration delivers that grand Co-creation. It is the Co-creation of God that we are looking to engender, is it not? And it is also the Co-creation that leads one step-by-step along this path of perfection. The path of perfection leads to the path of Ascension. We seek the God Perfection that leads one onward into Ascension. God Perfection does not hold its standard by that which is human or HU-man. It holds itself engendered by that Grand Creator's eye, brought forward for time immemorial. And it serves that Mighty Plan or will in action, through the host of the Mighty Angels and Archangels, through the activity of the Mighty Elohim, and onward from the beginning—Alpha, to the end— Omega. It is as it shall always be, and is held within infinity.

The idea of perfection has always been held as an ideal; however, God Perfection itself, serves that Mighty Plan. Perhaps the best way to understand the Path of Perfection is to understand the Path of Service. Self-realization through the Mighty Will used by a higher will. I have given many discourses on this, but I ask for you to pray each day to your Mighty I AM Presence and to that Mighty Stewardship for the God within,

> Align my will to the Divine Will, to the Holy of Holies,
> May I serve the plan of the Great White Brotherhood,
> The Alpha and the Omega, the beginning and the end.

THE RIGHT-HAND PATH

You see Dear ones this too is done through the right use of your will. It is important to understand that there are those upon the Earth Plane and Planet at these times, who are directing (energy) through a Left-hand path. We have always taught the Right Use of Will though the Right-hand Path.[17] This you know has been brought though a provenance of teachings, the Right Use of Will was taught in the early days of Mu, and traveled onward into the times of Lemuria, through the mystery schools of Atlantis, then it was brought forward at the beginning of the twentieth-century and held in all the Theosophical texts. And now Dear ones, it is important for you to understand that the Right Use of Will is engendered in the teachings of I AM America.

We hope to imbue this Right Use of Will, not only among you, as devoted chelas and initiates, but we also hope to imbue this Mighty Will within those students of I AM America. When one turns their will over to the Mighty Divine Plan, not only is the God Perfection held in the mind's eye it is in its outworking, in its holy perfection, but this Mighty outworking is the unfolding of the Divine Plan. The Right-hand Path never imposes upon the will of another, yet it aligns its will to the Divine Plan. Now its use within the Group Mind is of haste, and it is important for you to call upon the use of the Divine Will, within that Mighty Orb of gold light. It is done with an in-breath and an out-breath, now let me explain.

I ask for the two of you to visualize that Golden Orb, signal to me when you are complete.

---

17. See Appendix P: *The Right-hand Path*, page 301.

THE LIGHT OF GOD PROTECTION

They both visualize the Golden Orb and signal that they are complete.

Remember yesterday when Saint Germain said, "See around it that beautiful hue of Violet Light." I ask you to take that Violet Light, and in its mind's eye, see its perfection, its separate qualities that bring out the Pink Ray and the Blue Ray. The Pink Ray covers the inner peripheral of the Golden Orb, and throughout the outer periphery is the Blue Ray. The Pink Ray is God's Love that is the most perfect of God's Love. The Blue Ray is God's Protection. Together, call upon Beloved Archangel Michael:

> Archangel Michael enforce the Blue Flame of Protection
> In, through, and around this Golden Orb!

Now, as I repeat this decree, do you see how the layer of blue fluctuates and then creates a hardening or steely blue effect of protection around this Golden Orb?

Answer: *This is very much like when you gave us the candle meditation.*

Indeed, and that is perhaps one of the best precursors to use to understand how you are controlling at all times, the undulations of this golden sphere of your Group Mind.[18] Now call it forth together:

> I AM the God Perfection,
> Manifest in me now.

And observe the blue light. Questions?

Response: *It gets a lot bigger, the blue light.*

Indeed, and have you also noticed there is a rotational spin within the orb?

Answer: *It also has a pulse . . .*

Indeed, for it is a living, breathing consciousness. Perhaps this is the most important thing that you must begin to understand.

---

18. See Appendix Q: *The Candle Meditation*, page 305.

Question: *Is this something that we can set up as an energy pattern and then just step into it?*

It can be, however that is an advanced technique and I shall leave that for dispensation by Beloved brother Saint Germain.

Response: *Thank you.*

Response, Guest-student: *I just saw a brief flare of blue when we called in Archangel Michael.*

Michael, you see Dear ones, also provides that activity of God's Protection. For you see, the Blue Ray itself, holds the perfection of God Protection; however Archangel Michael is the activity of that Mighty Will of God Protection. Do you understand?

Answer: *Yes.*

And now Beloved Kuthumi will come forward.

El Morya is backing away, Kuthumi is coming forward.

Greetings my Dear hearts, I AM Brother Kuthumi, do I have permission to come forward into your energy fields?

Answer: *Please come forward, you are most welcome.*

LOVE, THE UNDERLYING ENERGY

I come this day through the Heart of Peace, but I also come through that Mighty Heart of Perfect Love. El Morya has instructed you on that layer of God Protection, I shall instruct you on the pulsing layer of pink that you are observing in this orb. I ask for you to both close your eyes and look through your Third Eye, or your mind's eye at the pulsation of this Mighty Orb in activity.

Identify first that layer of pink light. Now identify the feeling, it is a feeling of warmth, is it not? What you feel shrouding your entire body, is the perfection of God's love. God's love that is neither male nor female. God's love is the eternal creation. When you call forth this Mighty Perfect Love:

I AM the perfection of God's love in action,
In me Now.
I AM the perfection of love,
Now.
I AM the perfection of God's love radiating around me,
Now.

You see Dear ones, Dear hearts, this thoughtful prayer is given to activate that layer of pink love, for you see, love itself is indeed the beginning and the end. It is the Alpha and the Omega that Beloved El Morya has spoken of, it is held in eternal protection and in eternal perfection. Love, you see, is the underlying current of energy, of any Co-creative activity, so indeed love itself should stream to this Golden Orb!

Now I ask for activation, not only of your mind's eye, but an activation of your Heart and Throat Chakras. From these, direct another beam of pink light towards this Pink Ray.

Now begin this process. I ask for your comments and your questions.

Question, Guest-student: *It pulses as a living consciousness. Do we breath in time with the pulse?*

As Saint Germain instructed yesterday, it is important to feel that pulse, for it is a living thing. It is a child of your higher consciousness.

THE HOLY CONCEPTION: PROTECTION AND LOVE

Response: *There is a portion of it in its pulse that almost looks like an eye.*

This you see is the Eye of Perfection—it holds within it the conceptual child of perfection. This is that holy conception that was taught in many of the Gnostic and Judaic-Christian teachings. This holy conception is not that of male or female, it is of the Co-creative activity through the combining of Mighty God Protection and that Mighty God Perfect Love in activity.

Now, unless there are other questions, I shall step back.

Question, Guest-student: *How often should we practice this?*

Until you feel complete with this teaching . . . until you can feel that at any moment you can call upon the essence of this Golden Orb.

Response: *There's a lot more going on with this, than what you are explaining to us, because we haven't experienced enough with it.*

Of course Dear chelas, but today, is this not your first experience?

Response: *Yes.*

THE SEED OF CO-CREATION

So today is indeed a holy day. Today is the seed of your Co-creative consciousness germinating to yet a new level of Conscious Co-creation. Do you understand?

Response: *So, technically we can Co-create this no matter how far apart the three of us may be?*

Precisely, for now you have had the experience. It is very similar to one who is walking in snow and what do they do leave? A footprint. Are you accessing the snow or the footprint? But both Dear ones, Dear hearts. In your mind's eye as you recall each flake of snow as it fell upon the ground, in its perfection, in its God Protection and in God's eternal love . . . feel its completeness. Questions?

Response, Guest-student: *In my mind's eye, as I am looking at the gold orb, I do see it similar to a womb . . . like bringing new life forward.*

Indeed it is, and this is perceptive, for it holds the potential of each Co-creative activity and you, of course, are commanding this through your Collective Consciousness. Questions?

Response: *I see. The very creation of this makes it an alignment of harmony and the continued sustainment of this, allows calling forth a Co-creative action that is either of a spiritual nature or a physical nature.*

This of course is of the higher choosing. Now, I shall step back and allow Beloved Brother Saint Germain to explain in further detail. I thank you and love you from the eternal heart of perfect love.

Saint Germain is coming forward.

FORCES OF THE VIOLET RAY

Dear chelas, do you see that layer of pink and that layer of blue? We consciously separated these apart so you could see in your own God Protection and God Perfection of Love eternal the forces at work when you call upon that Mighty Violet Ray in action. This, of course, is the higher activity of the Violet Flame. I ask for you to return to this Golden Orb, and observe these two layers of light melding as ONE. This is the process of the Violet Flame in its conscious activity.

Response, Guest-student: *So it intensifies the golden light when I am looking at it, and it magnifies it.*

Indeed, and it was important for you to understand conceptually the forces that are at work in this Holy Trinity.

"WHERE TWO ARE GATHERED"

Question: *So does it take three to make this?*

It only takes two, for where two are gathered, there I AM. This is the law eternal, written in the Alpha and Omega, the beginning and the end, this is the path of the Co-creator. [Editor's Note: When learning the creation of Group Mind, it is best to first work with a group of three.]

WHITE FLAME OF PURITY

Now in your mind's eye, separate away from one another, call upon the Mighty White Flame of Purity.

Mighty White Flame of Purity,
In the name of I AM That I AM,
Come forward and purify all who are present.

Now, observe that fact that you are no longer linked at your chakras or energy fields. With your mind's eye, observe again the Golden Orb of Light.

Response, Guest-student: *It looks much smaller to me, and the pulse is not as intense.*

Yet it still exists, does it not?

Answer, Guest-student: *Yes.*

This is the process of engendering, feeding, and understanding the presence of the Group Mind.

THE CO-CREATIVE GROUP MIND

Question: *So, we are creating a subjective energy body, but consciously?*

Precisely. Now you must always hold yourself in the highest of God Protection, God Perfection and God's Love in this form of Co-creative Group Mind. For you see, the Group Mind itself holds within it, a Seamless Garment of light that is engendered through Co-creative activity. Yesterday when I taught you about the tornadic funnel of light, what does this do but bring expansion to the presence of the Group Mind. Now hold it eternally in the White Flame of Protection, and it will always continue in its function and activity until the two of you unite and call upon its force. Do you understand?

Question: *So what you are saying is that it's still sustained because it has been created?*

It has been created. Now those upon the Left-handed Path know and understand this practice. They create a Group Mind programmed upon the degradation of the Co-creative activity. They create a Group Mind that is programmed though fear, distrust, and suspicion.

This (Right-hand Path) is a Group Mind that is programmed through God Protection, though the Mighty Will and the Divine Plan of God, eternal protection, lack of degradation and the most holy premise of all—love. For *Love Eternal* is the law written among your hearts, it is the law that has programmed the Eight-sided Cell of Perfection and if you review the Evolutionary Pyramids and Evolutionary Pathways, you will see that love is the beginning, and that love is that final breath of Co-creation.

Question: *So technically we could expand this orb to cover the whole planet?*

Whatever you choose Dear ones, Dear hearts, remember it is truly the conscious focus of your Co-creative activity.

Response: *We could expand it to cover a galaxy.*

Dear ones, in your Mastery you shall know and in your Mastery you shall be free.

Response: *I love you, and thank you so much for teaching us. I have much gratitude.*

The gratitude and love is mine, Dear ones, for I too live to serve humanity. Are there further questions?

Question: *Is this something to practice on a daily basis?*

You may choose to practice on a daily basis, however presently at your level of development and evolution, monthly would suffice.

Question, Guest-student: *So, when we get together we should practice this, look at it, and feel it?*

Of course I will not tell you how often to access, how often to use, for in your own experience will come your own God Protection and God Perfection.

Question: *I understand, we have to have the experience.*

This is true Dear ones. Now I sense there are other questions, please proceed.

GOD'S PROTECTION, PERFECTION, AND LOVE

Response and question, Guest-student: *So have we created a subjective energy body?*

This is a body created of life's pure substance, engendered through God Protection and God Perfection, and of course, the Mightiest of all principles—love. Subjective energy is (intentionally) created through the Left-handed path, do you understand?

Response: *Yes, meaning unconscious as opposed to intentionally coming forward though the Law of Love and God Protection.*

PURITY OF THE GOLDEN ORB

This Golden Orb, is indeed your golden Co-creation, held within, not only your mind's eye, but in your Mighty Heart of Love. It has not been created with even one unconscious thought, it holds indeed its own consciousness—a purity through the conception that you have held for its creation. Do you understand?

Answer: Yes.

Question, Guest-student: *So it's alive and present, now that we have created it, all the time?*

Indeed it is, and it does contain at one level, its own sense of higher consciousness. Now, it is important as you proceed with this Mighty Golden Orb to engender its life force. When you separate from it, use that Mighty White Flame of Purity. Why is this? For the White Flame of Purity seals it again, without the leaching of the energy into the Earth Plane and Planet. For this Golden Orb of light exists and yes, can perform miracles at the third density as you would call it, but it functions primarily at Fourth and Fifth Dimensional levels. It is created to hold, your perfection, protection and Holy Love Eternal as you enter into the Ninth Energetic.

The Ninth Energetic is where you will face the great trial, and it is sometimes known as the Ascension Body. But the Ninth Energetic as it comes into its manifestation is where Beloved El Morya says, "One does the choosing." Now, I shall hold all of that information for further discourse, but for today, are there further questions?

Question: *So what you are saying is that with the Ascension Process, you have to create a gateway at some point?*

Precisely, and you must engender that gateway with these three principles: protection, perfection, and love eternal.

Question: *So it's not really necessary to expand it?*

It will seek its own level of expansion when the time is needed. It seeks its own expansion when you add more to its collective force, do you understand?

Question, Guest-student: *So right now we are separated from it, and it is present. But when we are joined and merging, it automatically seems to expand and pulse brighter?*

At this level, it is often referred to as the Guiding Light. Now this Guiding Light is with you eternally.

Question: *So the three of us have this shared guiding light?*

Indeed, and you can call upon this Guiding Light for solving problems, and for entering into a higher level—Group Mind—of conscious effort.

Response: *All right, and so be it.*

So be it! Upon my return, I will instruct you on the Ninth Energetic. Are there other questions you may have this day?

Question: *So what you are saying is that we have started the process, the three of us of the Eighth Energetic?*

Indeed, for this is the intention. I know that you are looking for ways to engender this school for I AM America, but are we not upon this pathway now?

Response: *Yes.*

Then let us proceed in that great Guiding Light of God Protection, God Perfection and eternal God love. I AM yours eternally, Saint Germain.

Response: *Hitaka.*

Chapter Nine

Temples of Ascension

Saint Germain, El Morya, and Kuthumi

Greetings Beloveds, in that Mighty Christ and Blessed Shamballa, I AM Saint Germain. I stream forth on that Mighty Violet Ray of Mercy, Transmutation and Forgiveness. As usual Dear hearts, I request permission to come forward.

Response: *Please come forward, you are most welcome.*

SHAMBALLA IS A STATE OF CONSCIOUSNESS

Greetings my beloveds and blessed Shamballa to each and every one of you, For you see Dear ones, on this first day of Shamballa we are very excited to share not only the messages as we have brought forward through the many years, but also excited to open Shamballa to you! This is a time when Shamballa is open to those who want to develop the "eyes to see and the ears to hear" to come forward and gain not only entrance into Shamballa itself, but also move into Shamballa as a state of consciousness.[19]

For you see Dear ones, Shamballa, as a state of consciousness is the path to learn about the traditions of the Great White Brotherhood and Sisterhood. Consciousness paves the pathway to eternal freedom, for you see Dear ones, Shamballa is a retreat where we carry not only all the archetypes of consciousness, but also where we teach many different forms of Ascension. This is the liberation that humanity is seeking at this time.

There is also much work upon the Earth Plane and Planet, and we as the Great White Brotherhood and Sisterhood of Breath, Sound and Light gather at this time to not only determine what should happen to humanity for the next coming year.[20] But we also share our ideas and focus for humanity and the Earth Plane and Planet.

There are many changes that are happening on the Earth Plane and Planet, are there not? And these great changes, as they come forward, we then send our eternal love and radiance to the Earth. Yes, there are many changes that

---

19. See Appendix R: *Shamballa and Sanat Kumara*, page 307.
20. See Discography, page 383.

are happening that one would deem as negative, but also there are many changes that are happening that are also very positive and this we shall place our focus upon.

THE SCHOOLS OF ASCENSION

Shamballa was a place not only where one could gain entrance into the Mighty mysteries, but where one could also gain development of consciousness through the varying Schools of Ascension. Each School of Ascension focuses on one of the Seven Rays of Light and Sound. Dear ones, I have divulged to you in past discourses, that there are indeed different forms of Ascension, and the ways that this has always been taught in Shamballa, is that there are Seven Pathways, one for each Path of Light and Sound. I will break this down for you.[21]

RAPTURE AND THE BLUE RAY

Let us first start with that Mighty Blue Ray, for you see the Blue Ray contains within it not only a focus of Mighty El Morya, but also contains a energy that aligns itself to Egypt and the ancient mysteries. This is a form of Ascension that is brought though a form of complete devotion and sometimes we refer to this form of Ascension as a type of Rapture—devotion alone that creates this level of freedom. So some may attain this form of freedom specifically through their belief systems and we have known this in the church of Christianity. Christianity applies this aspect of the Blue Ray.

THE PINK RAY AND SPIRITUAL LIBERATION

Now, let us move on to the Pink Ray of Love and this form of Ascension comes through devotion as an aspect of the Blue Ray, but also through the great love that is given through Mother Earth. We have spoken of this before as a form of Spiritual Liberation, where one begins to meld their energy fields with that of the Earth Mother. This, too, achieves a type of spiritual liberation or Ascension. When we speak of Ascension Dear ones, Dear hearts, we are speaking of that eternal freedom from the need to reincarnate again into a physical body. This also means you are no longer tied karmically to the Earth Plane and Planet; however, there may be incarnation aspects that will occur in Astral and Causal Planes. These, too, require their own law of understanding, for as we have said so many times before, "As above, so below." This law is eternal truth.

---

21. See Appendix S: *The Eight Pathways of Ascension*, page 321.

ASCENSION THROUGH THE ENLIGHTENED MENTAL BODY

That next pathway of Ascension is based upon the Yellow Ray of Enlightenment, and this is a form of Ascension which humanity is focusing on at this time. But this requires a complete and absolute purification of the Mental Body. How does this come forth? Through your actions; it is only through spiritual practice that one can ingrain within the Mental Body that great Ray of Illumination. This form of Ascension can give you freedom eternal from the Earth Plane and Planet.

ASCENSION THROUGH THE NEUTRAL POINT

The Fourth Ray is the White Ray of Beauty, and this form of Ascension comes through the seeking of balance. In many of the teachings we speak of the Neutral Point—that point of balance. One achieves this through their devotion, their love of Earth, but also through the Mental Body. Eternal balance creates the neutral point. Achieving the Neutral Point no longer requires incarnation and after that lifetime the individual is granted the Ascension. Do you see Dear ones how all of the Rays work together in harmony and cooperation?

ASTRAL HEALING AND ASCENSION

Ascension through the Green Ray is based upon healing. This is a healing process, not only of the mind, but of the Astral level. This is achieved through a great harmony that occurs in the Astral Plane, and this then affects not only Causal levels, but has its influence upon the physical body. Through this healing eternal and calling forth the great beauty of healing, Ascension, or shall we call it a form of liberation of the physical body, occurs. Sometimes this is known as the dropping of the body and many of the yogis of times past have encountered and used this form of Spiritual Liberation where their consciousness moves swiftly out of the physical plane and onward into the Astral Plane of existence.

WORSHIP, GROUP MIND, AND ASCENSION

The Sixth Ray (Ruby-Gold Ray) is a form of Ascension that is brought though balance and great worship. This is a form of Ascension that was brought forward in other epochs and time periods known in Atlantis and also in Lemuria, through the culmination of the great Group Mind. You have been taught some of the aspects of this Mighty Group Mind today.

You are learning the Group Mind for its application with the Mental Body. Your Ascensions will be brought through that Mighty Yellow Ray and the Gold Ray of Purity. The Group Mind that comes forward in this time uplifts consciousness and many will drop their body and bring dissolution to the physical form. This has also been referred to in the Book of Revelations where two are standing in the field and then one leaves. The one left becomes the Mighty Witness. So you see Dear ones, there are six forms of Ascension.

DISSOLUTION OF THE PHYSICAL AND THE ASTRAL THROUGH THE SACRED FIRE

The seventh form of Ascension is a form that can come forward in the time you are experiencing and this is through the use of the Sacred Fire. It causes the complete dissolution not only of the physical body, but also of the Astral Body, and moves the consciousness directly to the Causal Planes. This happens through the use of that Mighty Violet Flame in Action. The seventh form of Ascension creates dissolution of the karmas as they move from the physical plane into the Astral levels, and onward into the Causal— this is a purer form of Ascension. Yet, this is a form that can be achieved in the time period you are experiencing.

Very often, when you enter into this path of the Sacred Fire, it is for one thing and one thing only, for the dissolution of the karmic holds upon the physical body, so you can move into your final liberation. Many of you have had these experiences I am certain, where you have dreams of certain experiences that are very karmic, yet you have not experienced them in the physical plane. What happens is the driving of karmic actions to the Astral level through the use of the Sacred Fire. Karmas are acted upon and driven yet to another level of experience and understanding. For you see, sometime karmas must be acted upon and in this case, this is the pathway for that Mighty Violet Flame.

I know I have summarized much detail of this, so now I open the floor for your questions.

Question, Guest-student: *I have a question about the Group Mind that the three of us created last time we were with you Saint Germain. We are having students come in a few weeks, do we add them to our Group Mind, or is that two separate Group Minds?*

SYMPATHETIC RESONANCE OF THE GROUP MIND

These are separate Group Minds that are created, in your case, for the purpose of learning. Now, that does not say that this does not have an importance, for indeed it does. You can add new people to the Group Mind through seeking their permission; however, there may not be the rapport you see. I was able to help you create your Group Mind through Sympathetic Resonance, do you understand?

ASCENSION THROUGH THE GOLD RAY OF VICTORY

All must be in great harmony together, even in this moment as I give discourse, there is harmony between us, is there not? So the Group Mind is an aspect of Ascension through that Mighty Gold Ray of Victory. The Yellow Ray is there to help purify and assist the Mental Body, and I have also given you the direction of the Group Mind to assist your Co-creation activities. Questions?

ENERGY-FOR-ENERGY

Question, Guest-student: *The three of us were looking at creating more abundance on the Earth plane, is that a good use of Group Mind as long as the intentions are pure?*

Yes, indeed it is, for as you well know, everything upon the Earth plane, functions upon energy-for-energy and at the Astral level and Causal level. It is, "As above, so below," is it not?

Response: *Yes.*

EXPERIENCE OF THE ONESHIP

So everything has its equal measure met as energy. Dear ones, even as you decree for great abundance, you too must create the great answer of energy-for-energy.

Question, Guest-student: *As we work with the students, how do we work with the Group Mind?*

I would suggest that they create their Group Mind. The three of you create your Group Mind and then later on, if the experience merits so, we shall merge them together as ONE. For you see Dear ones, we are giving you the experience of the Oneship. Do you remember how I have taught you that there is Oneness, Oneship, and then the ONE? Each of these is a level of consciousness that you pursue. Questions?

SPONSORSHIP OF THE FOUR PILLARS

Question, Guest-student: *What is the next step for the school and the students? Lori would like to channel for them to help them with the Overshadowing. Is that a good acceleration of their growth? Are they ready for that?*

We shall be available, for you see Dear ones, we as the Four Pillars have always been available to give this sponsorship to those who wish to develop through the I AM America Teachings. Questions on the discourse?

Response: *It is dually noted in my experience with you, that you have achieved your Ascension on the Violet Ray and Flame. El Morya has achieved his Ascension on the Blue Ray and Flame. Sometimes I have asked each of you questions and you will give me a similar answer, but with the perspective of each Ray. It is interesting how the Rays interact, but it is also interesting how the Rays are individualized. Could you address the individualization of the Rays?*

THE SHAMBALLA TEMPLES OF THE SEVEN RAYS

Each individualization process of the Rays has been brought forth through its focus. That focus is held in the intention of Shamballa, for you see, there is a temple at Shamballa devoted to each of the Rays of Light and Sound. There is the great temple of the Blue Ray, of the Pink Ray, of the Yellow Ray, of the White Ray, of the Green Ray, of the Ruby Ray and also of that Mighty Violet Ray. And I received my Ascension yes, at the Temple of the Mighty Violet Ray at Shamballa. This is where the final initiatory rites are administered and then one gains their freedom, according to the devotion of that Ray Force. Then that soul comes forward and serves upon that Ray Force for a given time period as the soul develops in its own process and evolution. Sometimes the soul can also give service upon another Ray, for you see sometimes an individual, and when I state this, one who's become Individualized through the Ray Force, then comes forward, also upon another Ray Force. Beloved Lord Sananda has served several different Ray Forces along with beloved Mother Mary. I have kept my Ray Force quite singular of course, always focused upon that Mighty Violet Ray of Mercy, Transmutation, Alchemy and ultimate Forgiveness, for this fit my consciousness the best.

ONE-ON-ONE WITH THE MASTER

Each of you in understanding and choosing your individualization process will then begin to know and understand what Ray Force fits your consciousness the best, you see it is a process choosing and the Master

Teacher helps to refine. This is why there is the vital overshadowing that does happen at a certain point of the development of a chela—especially the soul moves from chela into the initiate. As the one-on-one process begins with the Master Teacher, their the soul's consciousness begins to understand the individualization process and, as you well know, this individualization process is accompanied by very specific Ray Force.

THE TEMPLE OF THE GOLD RAY

You, Dear ones, Dear hearts, are all children of that Mighty Gold Ray, and so its existence upon the Earth Plane and Planet now comes forward in a higher frequency—to be realized in the higher reaches of the Golden Age of Kali Yuga. This requires individualization upon the Yellow Ray. It is important to know and to understand that there is a Gold Ray, and there is a Temple of the Gold Ray in Shamballa. At any time during this celebration of Shamballa, this is open to the three of you.

Response: *Thank you. The Ray Forces seem to affect many people in the population in different ways. And the Ray Forces seem to, in effect, have their own group focus and individual focus. But that individual focus, does it take effect only when you become consciously aware of the Ray Force?*

This is true, for you see it is important to gain entrance into the temple of the Ray Force you are attuned with. For there you will meet other souls of kindred spirit, and those who are working upon the same pathway that you are working. Now, let us go back to when we formed that Group Mind. I chose the three of you to come together in that group experience because you all will individualize your consciousness upon that Mighty Yellow Ray. Again, this is an outreach in this time of Kali Yuga of the Gold Ray. Later on, as you achieve your Ascension, you shall serve in that Temple of the Gold Ray located in Shamballa.

Response: *I see. We still have choice, even though we are children of the Golden Sun?*

"WITHIN EACH PATHWAY LIES YOUR FREEDOM"

Of course Dear ones, Dear hearts. For all in this world of Co-creation is based upon that Mighty Fulcrum of Choice, is it not? So things can rapidly change through different choices, for this is indeed the basis of Co-creation. It is a great gift to know and to understand the Ray Force of which you serve. For some search lifetime after lifetime wanting to know and understand their great purpose. Celebrate with me as you raise your Cup to Shamballa for each of these Mighty Seven Rays of breath, sound, and light! Within each of these different pathways lies your eternal freedom, your Ascension into the realms of light, your freedom from the shackles of reincarnation lifetime after lifetime. Dear ones, focus upon that Mighty Yellow Ray, an aspect of the Gold Ray within you, for this is indeed your freedom. Now you can also focus upon the Mighty Violet Ray of Mercy, Transmutation and Forgiveness and it will accelerate your pathway into the halls of Ascension, for Dear ones, the Sacred Fire can also help you achieve this liberation. You are to achieve the individualization of your consciousness. Now do you understand?

Answer: *Yes I do. So this evening when I sleep, I think the three of us should go to the Temple of the Gold Ray, since it is open to us.*

These eight temples are open to humanity, now it is important to understand that an aspect of the Gold Ray is also the Aquamarine Ray, and it too shall have a Temple coming forward for humanity in the future. Do you understand?

Answer: *Yes.*

However, for now the Rays function in their purest form under the auspices of their light and sound frequencies.

Question, Guest-student: So for our Group Mind to be successful, or cohesive, you need to have not only an agreement, but also a similarity of the Ray that the members function upon?

THE GREEN RAY AND I AM AMERICA

Ideally, yes. Sometimes this can be identified within the Jyotish chart, however sometimes it cannot. For you see one comes forward balancing out the Rays of Sound and Light, and it is sometimes very difficult to understand. That is why the overshadowing of a Master Teacher is of vast importance. Now, I shall let you know about those who that are coming to receive instruction through the I AM America Teachings. They will vibrate to the Green Ray, for all of them are healers in their own right, and this is why they have come forward to form their Group Mind. They, too, shall achieve their Ascension upon that Green Ray and it is the Temple of the Green Ray that shall be open to them.[22]

---

22. Note: Throughout the years we have noticed that many students attracted to or studying the I AM America Spiritual Teachings often resonate with two Ray Forces: the Green Ray and/or the Yellow (Gold) Ray.

Response, Guest-student: *I see.*

They are healers of sound and light and many of them have had numerous lifetimes where they have pursued this in different qualifications; however, that is their form of Ascension in this lifetime.

Response, Guest-student: *I see. That is very helpful for our work with them; I thank you for this guidance.*

Question: *So I'm assuming that Shamballa has a theme for this year?*

THE MASTERS OF THE SEVEN RAYS

At this point I will not announce it, however there are several other Beloved Teachers that I would like to introduce who are here today, each of them comes forward in this form of teaching, representing the Seven Rays of Light and Sound. Beloved El Morya of the Blue Ray, Beloved Mother Mary of the Pink Ray, Beloved Lady Nada of the Yellow Ray, Beloved Serapis Bey of the White Ray, Beloved Hilarion of the Green Ray, Beloved Kuthumi and Lord Sananda of the Ruby-Gold Ray, and Beloved Portia, my Divine Complement of the Seventh Ray (Violet Ray).

Now, let me explain. They all are stepping forward as he introduces each of them, each of them holds a candle representing their Ray Force.

Now, together we shall form our Group Mind, our Oneship.

A great Vortex of light is enveloping all of them and they are protected by it.

As you see Dear ones, this Group Mind is not only that through which we Co-create, but also though which we seek our Divine God Protection.

LIGHTING THE SHAMBALLA CANDLE

Now, all of them are moving forward to a singular candle. Saint Germain will speak for the Oneship.

Today we light this in honor of Shamballa—that has served humanity though time immemorial to raise consciousness into Oneness, into the Oneship, and onward into the ONE.

OM Sheahah, I AM as ONE.
OM Eandra, I bless this Earth.
OM Shanti, God Protection.

They light the candle as ONE, and back away.

As you see Dear ones, this Mighty Light of God, never, never faileth, and is open now for all of you to travel to, not only in your meditations, not only in your dreams but also in your light bodies tonight. I invite all of you to come and visit Shamballa, and tour this beautiful lighting of the ONE Candle. I also invite each of you to visit the beautiful Temples of the Seven Rays.

Response: *Thank you, we will take you up on this invitation.*

Now they all create a mudra, with their right hand over their hearts and from the center of their left palms, they are streaming energy to us. There is a trilling in the air of Angels.

May you be blessed in this Mighty Oneship,
The Unana, which we love and serve.

And unless there are further questions I must return to the activities of Shamballa.

Response: *No further questions at this time. Thank you.*

In the Love of that Mighty Dove of Unity, Oneship, Brotherhood and Sisterhood, I AM Saint Germain.

Chapter Ten

From Shadows to Light

Saint Germain and Hercules

Greetings Beloveds in that Mighty Violet Ray, I AM Saint Germain and I request permission to come forward.

Response: *Please come forward, you are most welcome.*

"ALL ARE LINKED AS ONE"

Greetings and Blessed Shamballa, I AM Saint Germain. Dear ones, Dear hearts there is much work in front of all of us, is there not? Much work that must be accomplished upon this Earth Plane and Planet, but also there is much that is occurring right now at Shamballa. For you see Dear ones, this is the week of the Earth itself. Yes, earth, as it exists as an element in your third dimensional world, but also much work that will occur for the upcoming year and the Spiritual Hierarchy.[23,24]

For you see Dear ones, Dear hearts during this period, many of the prophecies, those events that are prophesied to occur upon the Earth Plane and Planet are entertained by us this entire week. It is important to understand, that as each of these Earth Changes does occur, big changes do happen with humanity as well. For you see, all are linked as ONE, and as each change occurs on the Earth Plane and Planet there is also a great spiritual change concurrently with humanity.

SACRIFICE AND BLISS

Now this is not to say that there is not suffering with these events for indeed there is. And you well know in its darker version there is energy-for-energy, and all must rise out from lower states of consciousness and evolve into higher states of consciousness. None of this happens through an easy evolutionary journey, it is a journey that has work attached to it. This is your own energy that is given at this (physical) level. Sometimes this is known as sacrifice—for sacrifice is indeed needed in order to experience the bliss.

---

23. See Discography, page 383.
24. See Appendix T: *The Spiritual Hierarchy*, page 323.

"ERUPT WITH LIGHT AND CAST AWAY SHADOWS"

The changes that will happen will be many, for you see Dear ones, there is much that is occurring on the inner planes, and much is moving out of the shadow and into light. This is the theme that we will see, as mankind is ready to face their shadow. Politically, the (world) governments are all working to face their own shadow and what they have created. It is the same with each of you as individuals. You, too, have your own shadow that you have created and it is important to bring the shadow into conscious light and activity. Because of this, there will be many Volcanic Explosions are prophesied to happen. Each of them, of course, with timing and intent; but also each of them designed to erupt with light and cast away shadows. Shadows of evil—yes, but also shadows of self-doubt that you may hold. The shadows you hold when you refuse your own inner light!

This inner light is ready to come forward and to explode and bring you to new levels of enlightenment in your journey of Ascension. You see Dear ones, we at our hierarchal level then work to lessen such changes, but it is also important to know that interconnected with each Volcanic Explosion are also movements of tectonic plates. These of course have had a hold placed upon them by the dark side of your government, yes—that shadow part of your government. Your governments can create and also orchestrate earthquakes that occur at certain strategic times; however, we of the light know and understand this and send our light frequencies.

KARMIC IMPLICATIONS

You must understand that Beloved Babajeran in her own energetic movement can release energies at certain strategic times, and volcanic explosions seem to be the best way that she can release this energy with the least occurrence of death and chaos upon the Earth Plane and Planet. You well know everything that happens has karmic implications, does it not? Everything is energy-for-energy, cause and effect, this you know as the Law of Attraction, but we see it somewhat as the Law of Compensation. As one gives, so another receives. This is as it is in the Earth Plane and Planet, Dear ones, Dear hearts.

EMERGENCE INTO LIGHT

So we would ask that you be prepared to give, to give as your group, as you gather to learn and to apply the I AM America Teachings, to hold as you will, as a Step-down Transformer of Light. Place your focus upon the shadow emerging into the light, and this first place will be the emergence of volcanic explosions and softening their effect. If you are prepared, I would like to give you the locations of some of these anticipated explosions of light that will be coming forward. But first, of course, do you have Questions?

Response: *Yes.*

Response: *I am assuming that on the plane there are others than just our small group, who will take up the work that you have put forward, but who are also advanced to a level, who can help to mitigate these disasters, that your energy works through them.*

Indeed it is so, yet many of these groups, such as yours carries forward their intention and also their group consciousness in silence, for you see, within the great silence is the greatest of protection.

Response: *I understand, I offer my service to be available for whatever energies you deem necessary to put forward into the planet.*

THE MOVEMENT OF ENERGY

Dear ones, Dear hearts, now unless there further questions I shall proceed with some of the locations and the movement of the energy behind this— movement into explosive light. First, we will deal with the Americas and there will be movement in South America.

- Look to the country of Chile and along the western coastline, for this is most vulnerable for volcanic explosion. This will be the first movement of the energy; for it moves from I AM America and forward into the Greening Map.
- There will again be some movement that will be released in the Cascadia fault lines, and also in the San Andreas. But we have calibrated the San Andreas to move as in a breathwork type of motion, that is, we dispense the energy and then release in smaller movements. This, too, is an area that has been targeted by the shadow government.
- It is important to hold your foci of light around both the South American coastline and also the Western coastline of the United States.
- Central America, which is the umbilicus of energy of I AM America, will also experience vulnerability.
- As this energy moves forward, it moves to the Greening Map and there the Philippines will also have great vulnerability this year, then throughout Indonesia with great vulnerability for release of energy through tectonic movement.

There are many other changes (prophecies) that will be dispensed during Shamballa. I will share if you are willing to receive that information, as it is forthcoming.

Response: *Yes we are willing.*

Now, it is important to also understand as this energy moves that it creates vulnerability at your North Pole, and again there will be movements throughout the state of Alaska, especially within the Aleutian Chain of Islands.

As this energy moves though the Greening Map, it moves to the Map of Exchanges and there again there will be great vulnerabilities throughout both Iran and Iraq. This whole area has great vulnerability. Throughout the Middle East and Afghanistan, there is also great sensitivity of Earthquake release.

Let us move onward into that Map of Exchanges, and there is a great vulnerability within the country of Turkey; however, you know we have also sponsored that great Golden City of Ganakra. Its presence, held though the eternal wisdom of the Elohim Vista, will help to dispense and dilute some of this energy frequency. Each of the Golden Cities also play a great role in ameliorating these drastic changes, do you understand?

Response: *Yes.*

THE STEP-DOWN TRANSFORMER

I would also like to give you further instruction on how to hold your energy as a Step-down Transformer. Are there questions?

Response: *Please proceed.*

It is important to ground yourself to the Golden Light. See yourself as a conduit of the Golden Light frequencies. You may recall that you have always used the technique of circulating energy from the core of the Earth to the core of the Sun. This is most important to use as a Step-down Transformer as your energetic responsibility as an Earth Healer. Now, as you are circulating the energy, stand up straight—tall, feel the energy enter through the bottom of your feet, and though your Grounding Chakra, it is a simultaneous pull. This, of course, comes though the breath. Breathe out that first breath of light, focus it into the heart, now the breath circulates up through the Crown Chakra, and from there the Crown Chakra extends to the center of the Sun.

When I speak of the Sun, I do not speak of the false Sun, I speak of the one true light, do you understand? [Editor's Note: The false Sun is in reference to the alleged satellite Sun(s), launched by the shadow government.]

Response: *Yes.*

"FOCUS YOUR LIGHT"

This (breath) then circulates through the Sun itself and meets the energy in equal measure in the heart. From the heart, this energy radiates out though the Heart Chakra. You will feel its pulsing and pulling and as it creates its own orb within. Then this energy releases to the area where you are standing. This is used to step-down transform and to change any area that you may be bringing forth healing. Now, as you are performing your work for these different volcanic and tectonic explosions, it is important that you place your hand over your heart. Work with a map of the area, and focus on the area of the Map through the Sananda Mudra. Remember—the energy flows from the heart and to the center of the palm of the hand. Center a beam of focused light into that (map) area that I have identified. Pay attention to current events, and I warn you that it is important to not watch or listen to your media, for they do not report accurately. Identify and follow alternative sources of media at this time, so you can get a true understanding of what is happening throughout your planet. Do you understand?

Response: *Yes.*

I will bring forward information directly to you at this time. To some degree you can pay attention to the scientific community, but it too has been infiltrated by the shadow. Now to be preemptive, I would say to focus your light upon these areas and I will give them in their level of importance:

1. The west coast of South America, hold this throughout the year.
2. The Philippines must also be watched this year, for they are vulnerable.
3. Your third watch shall be that of the West coast of the United States and when I say the West coast, focus your energies to Los Angeles. However, it is the entire West Coast that is under vulnerability this year.
4. Alaska and the Aleutian Island Chain.
5. Afghanistan and throughout the Middle East.

When I identify these areas, they are general of course. This energy moves as it does in energy meridians, and this is how Babajeran is constructed. Now, there are some points that are interconnected to other points and where this healing can be much more effective. I have always taught you Dear ones, that it is in the Stars of the Golden Cities and if you have the time and the inclination to go to a Star of a Golden City you can be much more effective in your healing efforts. This can be the Star of any activated Golden City. As you may know, not all the Golden Cities are in there complete activation, but since they are being held in conscious focus and intention until they reach their full maturation, all Golden Cities are functioning at sixty to seventy percent. Now, Dear ones, do you have any questions on this technique?

Question: *Is this something to be shared with the incoming students, since they are of the Fifth Green Ray and healers?*

Yes, of course it is, and this is to be shared within the teachings of I AM America and anyone else who is readied and has their ears and their eyes open. Do you understand?

Response: *Yes.*

THE BELOVED ELOHIM, HERCULES

And now Dear ones, I would like to introduce someone who has come forward today to share with their message. To my right, I would like to introduce the Beloved Elohim Hercules.

I would like to describe him. He is entirely blue, and his light bodies are electric blue. He is muscular in some ways, but he is very strong in his auric energy! While he displays himself as a masculine being, I also sense feminine energies radiating from him. His eyes are a piercing blue—similar to El Morya.

Greetings chelas and students, I AM the Elohim Hercules, is your permission granted?

Response: *Yes, please come forward, you are most welcome.*

Yesterday I observed you, I watched you like the Silent Watcher as you entered to that Point of Cooperation, and I would like to share with you more teachings upon Cooperation. Cooperation comes though the meeting of two minds and from this comes strength eternal. Is it strength that you seek when you travel to each of these points of this Vortex? I serve under the auspices of the Hierarch of Gobean—El Morya, but I too was his teacher in another time and epoch. I would like to share some of the provenance of my teachings.

Much of what is left is really myth of my teaching. My teaching comes, not only out of the strength of Group Mind, but as two willing to come together in complete harmony and cooperation. One who is versed in this knowledge and in the strength of this teaching is indeed strong, for they recognize the eternal wellspring within, which is spiritual strength. However, when two come together, as Dear Sananda has said become as ONE—this is truth. Two come together not only in the Christ Consciousness, but the two have brought their wills together as ONE. They weave themselves together almost as a twining braid of rope, this you see is their Chakra System, working together as ONE energetic to form an intention and to carry forward a grand Co-creation. This interplay is strength. It is not only the strength of will; it is also the strength of focus. Now, as you come within this Adjutant Point, did you not feel the flux of that Mighty vital lei-line as it arcs its energy from the Star of Gobean?

TIME TRAVEL

There are also techniques that you can do to access this vital energy, similar to what Saint Germain has taught you in step-down energy information. This is also the knowledge of the lei-lines and how they function. This is a teaching that I shared in many other Mystery Schools in other epochs of time. You will find this is the basis of understanding not only of Ascension, but also time travel. Understanding how to access this energy is also the understanding how to travel through time. As you access and enter two lei-lines in physical proximity, you will always feel a bending of time that is a flux of the energy about you. First, it will squeeze (contract) and then it releases . . . then it squeezes yet again and then it releases—much as a muscle does in the human body. As it reaches to grasp, all is a contraction and then there is a release of the energy. This is the first thing to understand, it is the same as breath in the body. As you take energy in there is a contraction with a breath, as you release the energy there is a flow into the ONE.

BREATH AND THE FLOW OF TIME

As you enter into certain frequencies of lei-lines and especially the condensation that occurs at lei-lines at specific Adjutant Points, you have the ability to not only change future events but to transform events of your life. This is what I taught, how to surf time, and to pit (oppose) negative elements that have happened in your own lifetime and to work within them to transcend them to different outcomes. I realize I have given you quite a bit to understand, but I have given you enough to begin to practice.

As you enter into these points, you can begin to control them in the same way that I have described. You can use the muscles within your body, but best to use the breath. This is a form of breath that works within the time, and you will feel the flow of time. First, you feel the rush of time, and then you feel it come to a dead stop. I know you were experiencing this yesterday, did you not?

Response: *Yes, it was like there was an open space.*

It is not only an open space, it opens and functions like an eye. It closes, shut tightly and then it opens briefly. That is when you capture that brief moment where it opens, not only within the Adjutant Point itself, but also upon that lei-line. I have given you much to think about today Dear ones. Strength and focus; always strength and cooperation is best. If you have questions, you may ask them now.

Question: *So because the lei-line has the ability to traverse time, can an event that has already occurred that may have been devastating and has sent humanity on a different tangent, can that event be altered?*

They can be altered, but first let me teach you how to view events. When you enter into the lei-line and you begin to feel either the compaction of time or the slowing down of time, this will tell you how the eye is focusing and operating within the Adjutant Point itself. Do you understand?

Response and question: *I see, so this is almost akin to the All Seeing Eye that the other side uses?*

Indeed, it is. This is the meaning of it, for it is how events are viewed and seen, and then acted upon, or acted though, or acted by. Do you understand?

Question: *So in our tradition, the answer to the All Seeing Eye is the Adjutant Points of the Golden Cities?*

IT TAKES TWO TO VIEW

They are indeed and you will learn more about them as you continue in this line of accelerated teaching. First you feel that first compression, or that first release. I ask you to find a place within the lei-line to settle yourself down, let your Root Chakra touch the Earth, in that moment enter into meditation—any technique that works for you. Take three cleansing breaths and focus upon the Third Eye and your Crown Chakra. From begin to view . . . view events of the past, view events in the present, view events that are yet to come. This is best done as a minimum of two, never as one, for remember two become as ONE, one together as two is strength. Do you understand?

Answer: *Yes.*

Then share what you have viewed and seen. In the next lesson, should you choose this, I will teach you how to join your viewing together as ONE.

Question: *Is there an optimum amount of time for us to sit there and be connected to the lei-line?*

OPENING AND CLOSING

Again this is your sensing ability, for Dear ones, yesterday was optimum. Sometimes the eye opens for approximately forty-five to sixty minutes; sometimes it is closed for four hours. I will not say more, for it is important that you to learn to observe and to understand that it contains within it, its own pulsing energy. That, too, can predicate its opening and closing. Do you understand?

Answer: *Yes.*

I have given enough for this day, and I shall come forward when needed.

Response: *Thank you Hercules, this is most enlightening.*

He is now backing away.

THE GIFTS OF SHAMBALLA

Greetings Beloved chelas, I AM Saint Germain. I realize you have been given much to think about today—these are the eternal gifts of Shamballa. For you see it is true that during Shamballa much more is open and available to humanity, for those who have the "eyes to see and the ears to hear." Now, do you have any further comments or questions regarding the Step-down Transformer techniques?

Question: *So the Step-down Transformer technique, we can really apply it as individuals, but also as a group?*

Yes, and that is the next teaching that I wish to share with you. I have instructed you in the Group Mind and use of Group Mind, so you can use and apply the Group Mind for this as well. Also, as you well understand, you can also use and apply this at specific Adjutant Points and there you will receive a ten-thousandfold greater result. Now, you want to have a minimum of three to work with your Group Mind, two of course to enter into the lei-line, but three to enter into the healing force of the Group Mind. Create the Golden Orb as I have instructed you and then focus within that orb the eternal healing energies as they are applied to the West Coast of South America, the West Coast of North America, to the Philippines, and to the Aleutian Islands. Hold them in your eternal focus as a healing energy; remember the highest of the healing energies is always that great Golden Light, as it streams forth from the center of the Earth and from the center of the Sun. And now, unless there are further questions, I shall take my leave and shall return tomorrow if you are available.

Response: Thank you very much. Happy Shamballa.

Blessings and eternal life and Ascension to you Dear ones, I AM that Mighty Light of God that never fails, from the Heart of the Earth to the Great Central Sun. So be it!

Chapter Eleven

One-thousand Eighty-eight

Saint Germain

Greetings Beloveds, in that Mighty Christ, I AM Saint Germain, do I have permission to come forward?

Response: *Please come forward dear Saint Germain.*

In that Mighty Christ, I AM Saint Germain, and I stream forth on that Mighty Violet Flame of Mercy Transmutation and Forgiveness. As usual Dear hearts, we will continue now with our discourses upon Shamballa. It is important that we review the Temples of Ascension again, for you see Dear ones, Dear hearts, each of these is an individualized path to achieve the Ascension. But also Dear ones, they are ways that you can understand your spiritual practice and also your form of seeking Spiritual Liberation.

TEMPLE OF THE GOLD RAY AND THE GOLDEN CITIES

Now, I realize I did leave off with that Temple of the Gold Ray, and it is important to understand that those who have a strong leaning towards the Yellow Ray also have a strong leaning towards that Mighty Gold Ray of Freedom. The Temple of the Gold Ray rests upon the teachings of the Golden Cities and the use, not only of their Stars for ceremonial order, but also upon the Beloved Adjutant Points. The Golden City Stars and Adjutant Points increase the momentum and the energy of each ceremony and spiritual practice that you bring forward for your freedom and your liberation. As I have stated before, they also increase the use of the Group Mind and increase its ability to perform and bring forward a chosen Co-creation. The Gold Ray is a very important in this work, for you see the Gold Ray itself carries the freedom for humanity.

The Aquamarine Temple is still being contemplated here, and will be added at a later date—perhaps in the next one hundred to two hundred years.

ONE-THOUSAND EIGHTY-EIGHT ASCENSIONS

Now, as we all well know, this is the time of Shamballa when those Mighty gates are open for those who have the "eyes to see and the ears to hear," at night we reach you in your dreamtime and when I say *we*, we are the united Brotherhood and Sisterhood of Breath, Sound, and Light that serve the spiritual upliftment of humanity at this time. It is important for you to also understand that there are many who have actually reached their Ascension this year and many of them come forward in a graduation of sorts during this first week of Shamballa. I am very pleased to announce that over one-thousand and eighty-eight achieved their Ascension this year. Of course they all came from very different, diverse sources of religions and spiritual practices. Many of them from organized religion, for as I have said so many times, that it is the devotion in the belief system that allows one to achieve liberation into the realms of light.

BELIEF SYSTEMS AND THE RAPTURE

When I say this, I am speaking of the Blue Ray, for you see, this is where one believes with all their might, that their belief system actually catapults them into the Rapture of the Ascension. When I say one-thousand and eighty-eight, they have yet to achieve their Ascension from the Astral Plane, and there are many who reside in the Temples that are now activated in the Golden Cities. Many of these souls travel to the Golden City that is near them when they make their transition into the light. And when I say near them I speak of that which is close to their heart, for you see there is always one Ray which is favored.

RELIGIOUS PRACTICE AND THE GOLDEN CITIES

Those who practice Christianity and yearn to see their beloved Savior often travel to Malton and the heavenly forces that exist in its ethereal realms. Those who believe in Shiva, Vishnu, and the Grand Creator from the Hindu form of thinking often travel to Shalahah and the other Mighty Temples that arc themselves to the Green Ray, but to Gobean and that Mighty Blue Ray. Now, those who have given a devotion of practice to that Mighty Violet Ray often travel to my ashram in the Golden City of Wahanee. Now I will not go though all of the temples at this time, for we have talked about them in discourse in previous lessons.

USE OF THE VIOLET FLAME WITH OTHER SPIRITUAL DISCIPLINES

At this time it is important that we also begin to understand certain spiritual techniques. When I give you information about the Violet Flame, remember earlier when I stated that through the use of that Mighty Mantra

OM HU, you would align all the Rays in their service and understanding. This is because the Violet Flame has the ability to align and balance all of the other six Rays. One may practice the Violet Flame, however their devotion may still remain to the Pink Ray, or the Blue Ray, or even the White Ray. For you see Dear ones, Dear hearts, this Violet Ray (and Flame) has the ability to transconduct its energy among many different spiritual practices and disciplines. It is the same for the Gold Ray; however it is a much more highly refined focus. The Gold Ray does require understanding of Golden Cities, and the use of the Golden Cities to achieve your Ascension and enter into the Temples of Service, Light, Brotherhood, and Sisterhood. Now, Dear ones, I do ask if you have any questions?

Question: *Could you give some clarification on Hercules, if he was from Stienta or Gruecha?*

Hercules was one of the Master Teachers of the epoch of MU. He has existed for time immemorial; he was present during the time of Rama and also achieved Ascension during that epoch upon the Earth Plane and Planet. He identifies with the Blue Ray, for he walked this planet wearing many a blue skin. Throughout the many incarnations upon the Earth Plane and Planet we take on many races, we may have many different religions, or spiritual orientations, and we move from gender to gender—that is, from male to female, from female to male. We take on the body in an incarnation that best suits the cause that we will serve in that lifetime.

RELATIONSHIPS BETWEEN THE GOLDEN CITIES

Hercules, and when I refer to him, I am referring to a being who contains both aspects of feminine and masculine energies. However at times he does spilt his energies and then moves into his Divine Counterpart which you know to be Amazonia. In relationship to these Golden Cities, both of them work together. They carry an in-breath and an out-breath, and create a circulation of energies much like the figure eight. There are moments when you will feel Archangel Michael in Gruecha; there are times when you will feel Hercules and Amazonia in Stienta. So when I say Hercules of Stienta, Hercules is of Stienta, when I say Amazonia of Stienta, Amazonia is of Stienta, and likewise with Gruecha. We will find many of these relationships that exist between the Golden Cities. It is also important to know that Amazonia carries an energy that is most conducive to that of Beloved Mother Mary, and she has served for many cycles of life upon that Mighty Pink Ray. That is why she does have a countenance that serves the Three

Sisters in the Swaddling Cloth of South America. Because of this and her association with Stienta and also with Gruecha, there is a flooding of energy of the Blue Ray into the Beloved Three Sisters of Light of the Pink Ray. Do you understand?

Answer: *I do understand, yes.*

Do you have questions?

ENTERING DIVINE SERVICE

Question, Guest-student: *I ask for guidance if the students coming . . . is it a good idea for them to listen to these discourses?*

I asked for this specifically to be for the three of you with your Group Mind, with your thought, intention, and your most devoted service. It is something that after they come through their lessons and have achieved a level of initiation at the Hercules Adjutant Point, that it may be possible. However, I would still like for you to seek permission for that. I would also like to scan their energy to see that it is appropriate for them to enter into this level of service. For you see Dear ones, Dear hearts, one chooses in the inner realms to enter into Divine Service, and sometimes it is not appropriate to ask someone incarnating into these lower realms or lokas of expression to engage upon that service at that time.

For you see, each step in spiritual development is sensitive and often quite fragile. It is important that we build light bodies and that these students have an opportunity to actually practice the Violet Flame, not only for two years, but for at least seven years before they enter into this level of service. Sometimes we can bring about acceleration in their light bodies that will afford them to come to this level of service, so I hope you do understand.

Response: *I do understand clearly, it is something you are inspired to do and to step into that service.*

Indeed, now, if one were to come to you and ask you specifically that they would like to perform and assist in this service, then they likely have been touched by the Angels of Shamballa and the higher realms. Then they shall bring forward this service. You see, all must move forward in accordance to the Divine Plan and the Divine Will. Now when I say the Divine Will, what are we speaking of? We are speaking of the Holy Father, the Father Principle in all of spiritual teaching and understanding, but we are also speaking about the individual choice and how that individual choice must align itself to that which it chooses. For you see, one cannot choose that which they are not prepared for and ready to experience. Do you understand?

Response: *Yes.*

ESTABLISH DAILY PRACITCE

Choice is an example of, or shall we say, the outpouring of that Mighty Divine Will. When we ask for humanity to be touched by that Mighty Divine Will and align their actions to that Divine Will, we are asking them to bring forward their choice in that Mighty Divine Plan in accordance to the Divine Will. The choice, you see, is their actions, and how they work those actions out upon the Earth Plane and Planet. If one has not ameliorated their karmas to the degree that they then can actually effectuate such an act of service then it is a wasted motion, unfortunately. This happens many times. For sometimes chelas, when they are new to the path, take on far too much. It is important your students to enter into the path of the chela, and that they first establish daily practice. That daily practice should include meditation, decree and invocation of the Mighty Violet Flame a minimum of two times per day. This will place their energy bodies in the right time and the right place, that is the opening at twilight and also in the morning at sunrise. This is when the energies are at their peak, and I can come forward and assist them. It is suggested that in the morning they call forth my assistance, and there I shall be. In the evening have them call forward Beloved Kuan Yin, and there I know she shall give her service.

ORIGINS OF THE VIOLET FLAME

I speak of this with the authority and the knowledge of the Lineage of the Violet Flame. For you see Dear ones, the Violet Flame was brought forward, many, many light eons ago. When I say light eons ago, it is a practice that was brought far, from another planet. It has its origin beyond that of the Andromeda, but also that of beyond the DAHL. However, we will not get too far into this explanation of how it works in its historical provenance, but it is best to know that it originated in the form you are using today through spoken mantra, decree, and invocation through the light on the planet Venus. The step-down energies were afforded through the Pleiades, and when I speak of the Pleiades, I speak of all those beloved Seven Sisters of Light, for each of them contained an aspect of the Ray to balance out the Beloved Violet Flame as it existed on the Planet Venus.

From Venus, its provenance landed within the first building of that sacred site of Shamballa and there is has been eternally. The Great Lords of Light, even in the great destructions of Shamballa that occurred three times, carried and held in sanctity and protection the Violet Flame. They held it literally within their heart substance, and it leaped from their hearts to light the sacred Altar of Shamballa. You see this Mighty Violet Flame has the ability, not only to remove the negative karmas of the past but to ably place you upon the path of Ascension. If it is applied properly and understood in its purity, can instantly youthen—it is its Mighty Alchemy that many seek. I myself applied the Alchemy and the transmutative processes of the Violet Flame, and there I achieved my eternal freedom and Ascension. That is why it has the ability to transconduct itself across all of the Ray Forces. In the Pleiades, those seven Beloved Sisters danced within this light, and it found and anchored itself in the spectrum of the atmosphere of Venus.

THE TRANSCONDUCTING ENERGY OF THE GOLD RAY

Now it is also important to understand that the Gold Ray, too, can transconduct all the lights of the Seven Temples of Ascension, and all of the pathways of the Seven Temples of Ascension. It transconducts in a very similar manner to this Mighty Violet Ray. It is best to be used in adjunct with that Mighty Violet Ray. When you call forth the Gold Ray, it is best to always be within a Golden City and there you will receive its highest frequencies and energies that are easier for your light-field to consume. For you see Dear ones, Dear hearts, the light-fields themselves must be ready to receive the light, we have spoken of this for many discourses have we not? To prepare and strengthen the light-fields as they are ready to receive the light of Ascension, the light of freedom, that Gold Ray of eternal liberation. Now, I do still sense your questions, so proceed.

Question, Guest-student: *I would like clarification about sharing with the students the messages that have been brought through over the last few months.*

THE STUDENT OF LIGHT

It is important of course that they move forward in their training in the I AM America Teachings and they must establish their daily practice—that is of the utmost importance. Secondly, travel to Adjutant Points is also very important for each of the students and this is encouraged. For there they will strengthen their light-fields to be able to receive the new frequencies of light. It is also important that they continue in the timing and intention of their oral study. When I say oral study that is listening and reading the information as it has come forward, for there is a timing and intention in such. So, it is important that they continue onward with *Temples of Consciousness*, onward into *Awaken the Master Within*, and finally into *Soul Alchemy* and *The Twilight Hours*. These are all very important for them to know and understand, and of course as you both well know we have yet another book in front of us. Do we not? These are teachings that in there own timing and intent will reach that student of light through the I AM America Teachings. Now, do not worry for they are now overshadowed by the Beloved Four Pillars of Light and their growth and spiritual evolution will be entrusted within them. Realize that the Four Pillars of Light shall guide you, for this is the sponsorship of this school on Earth.

Response, Guest-student: *Thank you, I think this gives us direction and clarification . . . it sounds to me that they need to read those other books though their own process before what has been brought through most recently is revealed to them.*

In its timing and intent; however, we have also heard your requests about Group Mind and of course, I did already authorize that could be dispensed to them, did I not?

Response: *Yes.*

So that may be shared, for that spiritual technique is of the utmost importance. Questions?

Question, Guest-student: *Is sharing with them that they are on the Green Ray? Is that for them to know at this time?*

Since that information is secular in understanding—the Seven Rays of Light and Sound and the Seven Pathways of Ascension—it is best to not speak of that just yet, until they have the opportunity to firmly understand the seven approaches to Ascension. Do you understand?

Response: *Yes.*

THE NEW SHAMBALLA

You see Dear ones, "To do, to dare, and to be silent." They, too, shall come to their own understanding and the great and mighty healing that is in front of them. These three students will be entrusted with the building of the New Shamballa—that is a great order in front of them. However, they will know which way to go and they will be overshadowed by the Four Pillars of Light. When the time is right, Beloved Serapis Bey as well . . . are there any other questions?

Response, Guest-student: *No, I have no other questions. I will have to work with the World Map as you have given us guidance yesterday.*

Then I say to you, be blessed in your endeavor and know as you share these teachings that you too share our energies and our frequencies. You shall become as we once were, teachers of this material in your Mastery and also in your liberation.

Response: *So Be It. Thank you.*

Now, unless there are other questions, I shall take my leave from you. For you see there are many other events at Shamballa and you have been given your glorious assignment.

Response: *Thank you.*

I AM Saint Germain

Chapter Twelve

Tipping Point

Saint Germain and El Morya

Greetings Beloveds, in that Mighty Christ I AM Saint Germain and I stream forth on that Mighty Violet Ray of Mercy, Transmutation and Forgiveness. As usual Dear hearts, I request permission to come forward.

Response: *Dear Saint Germain, please come forward, you are most welcome.*

THE EARTH PLANE AND PLANET

Salutations and Blessed Shamballa. Dear ones, there is always so much work to be achieved on the Earth Plane and Planet is there not? For you see Dear ones, we are also overseeing the Earth at this time, and there is much planning going on at Shamballa at this time and the activities and the Earth Plane and Planet. The Great White Brotherhood and Sisterhood oversee the surface of the planet. As you well know there are many other kingdoms of creation that exist in your Inner Earth, and they too have there own levels of organization. But the Earth Plane and Planet, as we have always stated, is going through its mighty cleansing at this time and there is much that is happening upon the surface of the Earth. This is happening through the Collective Consciousness, but also an intercession that is happening through the Galactic Light that comes through that Great Central Sun. This, too, is affecting the kingdoms of creation of the Inner Earth, but those that are most affected are indeed that of the Outer Earth. Why is this so? Because of the Golden City Vortices. They, too, are calibrating this great light at this time and the Mighty Gold Ray is coming forth to raise humanity and many other kingdoms of the Earth Plane and Planet into their Ascension.

KINGDOMS OF CREATION

Yes, too, the many other kingdoms of creation, this including the Plant Kingdom, the Mineral Kingdom, the Devas and the Elemental Kingdoms, and the Animal Kingdom are all rising in vibration. They are all going through a type of Ascension Process and they will have the ability to transmigrate to other kingdoms of creation. You shall see this among your many household pets this year, and you will see that they are reaching out and into the Human Kingdom, as you rise from the human to the HU-man. They will rise to take your place as humans. Others will be those rising from the Plant Kingdom and Mineral Kingdom, into the Animal Kingdom and those of the Devas and the Elementals. They, too, have there own scheme of evolution and will rise in there own evolutionary process.

Spiritual Evolution is the rule of the Earth Plane and Planet. This is also the rule of the Inner Kingdoms of the Earth. Many will reach their Ascension and reside in the Ashrams of Light that exist and are guided by the Maha Cohan and the Seven Rays of Light and Sound. And those who have resided for the last twenty years in the retreats of the Golden Cities will also then make their Ascension into the light and move into new lokas of experience.

GALACTIC LIGHT AND CIVIL UNREST

As there is much that is happening upon this Earth Plane and Planet, it is important to understand that in this upcoming year there will be much civil unrest. This unrest will be happening throughout the whole planet, many countries will be affected by this Great Galactic Light. This light affects all the chakras of creation. First, it affects the lower chakras, then onward and upward until it affects the higher chakras of frequency, or, as I would, say the HU-man Chakras—the Throat, the Third Eye, and the Crown Chakra. These are the chakras that you work for developing of the evolved bodies of light that aid and assist your Ascension Process. This is somewhat true with other kingdoms of creation, especially those Kingdoms of the Elemental and the Deva. Of course, each animal has there own chakra system, and you will notice different changes in their (pets') behaviors, and this will also indicate how this great Galactic Light frequency is also affecting them.

FREEDOM OF CHOICE

The civil unrest that I speak of will be very rampant throughout South America and also Europe, both of these countries experiencing great tumultuous change. There will also be civil unrest in the United States. For you see Dear ones, the United States is in the process of the restoration of the true Republic that is "of the people" and "for the people."[25] Why is this so

---

25. A republic, in simple terms, is a political body led by an elected official, such as a president or consul, rather than a sovereign leader. It follows some type of charter (e.g. the Constitution), which directs the government to elect representatives who will advance national interests and support the right of self-determination. Though the terms *republic* and *democracy*, a system where majority rules, are often used synonymously, the general idea of these political philosophies differ in principle. A republic, in theory, serves the common good of its citizens whom are subject to the Rule of Law. America in its current state is a republic—consider the Pledge of Allegiance: "I pledge allegiance to the Flag of the United States of America, and to the Republic, for which it stands . . . "

important? Freedom is the basis of any evolving system, and if you look at the other systems of creations that I have just mentioned, they operate through one premise—freedom of choice. There is been much occurring on the Earth Plane and Planet that is destroying the choice of the human and making it almost impossible for the human to evolve into the HU-Man. It has been through the great decrees of light though many lightworkers and Ascended Beings for the Earth Plane and Planet that has allowed for many of the humans to rise and to understand the human evolutionary process—even you have been affected by this. The use of that Mighty Violet Flame is of critical importance.

LIGHT OVERCOMES DARKNESS

This civil unrest will be in many of the metropolitan areas, especially in your east coast and some upon your west coast. And there will be much civil unrest in Los Angeles and also in Seattle. These are areas that have been affected by the dark ones. Now, when I say this, I know you understand the difference between the Republic and the shadow government. It is also important for you to place your emphasis and focus upon light supreme, for you see Dear ones, the light always overcomes the darkness and we must place our focus (on the light) at this at this critical time. This is a Tipping Point—a Tipping Point for humanity at large, I have said that America shall be first to enter into the stream of Light, and hold the balance for the rest of the world.

HEART OF THE DOVE

Now, for those who would like to serve the light for freedom, they can travel to the central point of the United States to the Great Galactic Heart, in the Heart of the Dove.[26] This is a center of the Earth, it is functioning somewhat as an umbilicus, but because it functions as an umbilicus of Light, it will serve all of the chakras and the light centers of the Earth. Those who wish to travel to this area, the best time would be in the month of July. The planets will be in their best alignment at that time period for it (America) to receive and undergo the highest of transformation. This is something that could be suggested to your students, but it is best to gather a minimum of seven of them to go and to hold group focus through the creation of the Group Mind and then hold a focus for the rest of humanity for their freedom and independence at this time. Remember, this not only affects the United States, but it affects the entire planet. As you well know, you are connected

---

26. See Appendix X: The Heart of the Dove, page 343.

through that Mighty Galactic Web and connected to many other lokas of creation. Now, Dear ones, I shall open the floor for your questions.

Response: *When you say the month of July, is there a more specific date?*

Study the cycles of the Moon, and go during the bright Moon phase. Go in the first nine days of the bright Moon phase. Then you will see the greatest alignment to achieve this work of which I speak. [Editor's Note: Anyone can travel to the Heart of the Dove to perform this ceremony to assist the United States at any time. This particular timing was selected by Saint Germain as there were two important eclipses during this month, and the Ascended Masters could best potentiate the energies. When selecting a date for your service, follow Saint Germain's suggestion of the bright Moon phase.]

Question: *Since this is to help restore the Republic and to bring this upliftment to the whole world, which also affects the rest of creation, is this to be limited only to students?*

At this time, it is best that those who have been brought through the work of the Violet Flame and the Gold Ray. But, I also suggest that those who wish to assist them (the seven) at that time, to light a candle during those nine days and to hold a focus for the Light of God that never fails. Many can participate at a global collective level through this. However, it is important to keep those who are serving through this process to utilize the cover of the Indigo Cloak. You know well what I speak of, for the Indigo Cloak is always used in these types of activities, and it is important, "to do, to dare, and to be silent." I hope you understand.

MORE INSTRUCTION ON THE GROUP MIND

Now, it is important to practice your Group Mind and to call forth the Gold Ray to function through that Group Mind. Now, there will be further instruction that is detachment from Group Mind, so that the Group Mind hovers in its creation is kept at your chosen location. This is another technique, which I think is important for you to understand. Now, I would like to give more instructions upon this.

Response: *Yes, please.*

THE VITAL BREATH OF INDEPENDENCE

As you create that Mighty Orb of Light and it is infused with its own energy of Golden Light, there must come a disconnection. Now, as always, the creation of this Orb of Light is done through the higher chakra system— first through the Throat, the Pineal and then the Crown Chakras as a Trinity of energies. Project your energy, primarily through the Third Eye for its creation; infuse with Gold Light Supreme and then your call:

> Mighty Galactic Center,
> Come forth in your supreme light,
> Guide and direct this force of light,
> Through which I AM!
> Guide and direct this light
> For liberty and freedom.
> Guide and direct the United States,
> As a leader of our world.
> Mighty Galactic Light,
> Come forward and free humanity,
> Into the HU-man.
> So be it,
> It is now done.

As you focus into this call this allows the Golden Orb to function in its own Mighty Co-creation. Next, say aloud:

> Freedom I AM, Freedom I AM, Freedom I AM!
> Liberty I AM, Liberty I AM, Liberty I AM!
> Human to HU-man, Human to HU-man, Human to HU-man!
> I AM that I AM, I AM that I AM, I AM that I AM!

In that moment it receives its vital breath to function as an independent being of light to hover there in its galactic frequency. It is important that you close down its streams of light in a reverse motion in each of the chakras. This allows a frequency for these streams of light to disconnect, so it will focus (and function) upon its own. At that moment call forth my sponsorship:

> Beloved Saint Germain come forward!
> Beloved Saint Germain come forward!
> Beloved Saint Germain come forward!

Call upon me three times; each call instills a vital breath within the Orb of Light. You must follow this in its exact instruction as I have given it to you. Questions?

Response: *This will require some practice.*

THE ORB IS COMPLETE

Yes, and call upon me as I shall give my assistance. In its finality you are to stay for a total of fifteen to twenty full minutes at your location and practice an outward breath through the Sananda Mudra. This gives indeed, yet another vital energy to this Orb of Light that now we shall call a, "Subjective Energy of Freedom." The Orb is then complete.

I do have some guidelines prior to its creation. I ask that there is no consumption of flesh for seven days before creating this. This is of great importance, and on its day of Co-creation, I ask for you to use only the fruits of the Gold Ray. This creates, yet again, another frequency and energy that is of great importance.[27] Questions?

Response: *I will have to think about this before I have more questions. No further questions at this time.*

He is backing away. Beloved El Morya is coming forward.

Greetings stalwart chelas, initiates. I AM El Morya and request permission to come forward.

Response: *Please come forward, you are most welcome.*

EL MORYA'S INSTRUCTION ON ADJUTANT POINTS

Blessings and Shamballa to you, my Dear ones in the Golden City of Gobean. I am grateful and happy that you have discovered the Cooperation Point of my Beloved Master and friend Hercules. There are other instructions that I would like to give you upon the Adjutant Points. The outer Adjutant Points bring forward a manifestation into the physical plane. The inner Adjutant Points bring forward manifestation into some periphery of Third Dimension, but primarily function at Fourth and Fifth Dimensional levels of consciousness. It is best when you are working towards a Co-creation, and when you work upon one of the inner Adjutant Points, in this case the Point

---

27. See Appendix Y: Golden Ray Diet, page 345.

of Cooperation which is Fourth and Fifth Dimensional frequencies, that if you wish to bring that Co-creation into its outer activity that you travel to the Outer Child Point of that doorway and continue your focus. This brings about its (your Co-creation's) presence into the Earth Plane and Planet.

It is not always so necessary to travel to the outer, but if you wish to bring something into its physical manifestation this is highly suggested. Now you can also travel to the Star frequencies for they too coalesce the energies of both Third, Fourth, and Fifth Dimensional consciousness, so all can be used within a Co-creation. I have heard your decrees for abundance, and this is why I have brought this forward to you. Remember, that all money that comes forward to you, comes forward for the work of I AM America. Remember at all times that it comes through the auspices of the Great White Brotherhood, especially when you do this work. Remember that you are stewards of this work and I love you and bless you. Questions?

Response: *As I understand in the South Door, going back to the concept of manifestation into the Third Dimensional realm, that we would go to the outer points of the East and the West and I assume we do the Inner Child Point, but we still have the Outer Child Point to finish at the Southern Door.*

PILGRIMAGE FOR MANIFESTATION

In migratory work, this is the best pathway. However, for manifestation work it (migratory pathway) moves in the opposite direction. For you are working with migration to move from the physical to the spiritual; when you work in manifestation patterns, it moves from the spiritual to the physical plane.

Question: *So that means we would start at the western point?*

Sometimes it is better to start in the Star and then define your pathway through the Inner Child Points and the Outer Child Points. These are always used for manifestation; now, to be clear with you these are cardinal points, not intercardinal points. For instance, for a Northern Door application start in the Star, then move to the Inner Child Point of the cardinal, due North (direction). Then move to the Outer Child Point due North. In the Eastern Door, if there are issues you wish to bring into manifestation for relationships, you move from the Star to the Inner Child to the Outer Child. Southern Doors for (realizing) healing into manifestation, Star to the Inner Child, Outer Child. For illumination and enlightenment in the Western Door, follow the same pattern. This is perfect, for this will allow you to know even greater mysteries and knowledge of the manifestation process.

Remember, everything is based on energy-for-energy and the hermetic law, "As within, so without." Unless there are further questions, I shall take my leave and return to the glorious festivities of Shamballa.

Response: *No further questions, thank you.*

El Morya is backing away, Saint Germain is coming forward.

And now Dear ones, I have with me another Dear, Beloved One. Mother Mary stands to my right and she has a small message to give to you.

Saint Germain is backing away, she is coming forward.

Greetings my Dear ones, I AM Mary and I request permission to come forward.

Response: *Please come forward, you are most welcome.*

THE SEVENTH MANU

My Dearest ones, as you know I have remained so focused upon the Swaddling Cloth of South America, and if there are those beloved chelas who would still help to sponsor these new souls that are coming in, I still ask for that service. I call upon those of humanity who are awakened and ready to serve. As you well know, I have asked for the meditation and decree for the Swaddling Cloth at six am in the morning. This, you see, creates a wave of energy that reaches out not only from Earth but to the cosmos. Many of these souls that are coming in have never incarnated upon the Earth Plane and Planet. Through your Divine Call and divine work within the Swaddling Cloth of creation, they are readied to raise the vibration of Earth.[28]

Each of them enters through that first birth call into the Earth Plane and Planet, when the umbilical cord is severed from the mother, the vibration then is raised upon the Earth. One by one they come, each in their Golden Light, and they too shall stay as the Seventh Manu for many, many of thousands of years upon the Earth Plane and Planet. They shall help to raise the overall vibration of Earth. They will do this by increasing life spans upon the Earth Plane and Planet. They will also help to lead in some ways a great rebellion against the darkness. This great rebellion will emerge into a dance of Oneness into the Light. If there are those who will serve, please ask them

---

28. See Appendix U: *The Seventh Manu, the Swaddling Cloth of South America, and Mother Mary,* page 331.

Dear ones. Remind them of their service that they bring to the Earth Plane and Planet, for indeed service is one of the highest aspects of this work. I AM ONE with you and the Heart of Love. I AM Mary.

Response: *I will do this at 6 a.m., as you request.*

Saint Germain is coming forward.

Beloved Dear ones, unless there are further questions, I shall take my leave back to the festivities of Shamballa.

Response: *I have no further questions, but I will in the future.*

Blessings unto all of you,
And unto mankind,
Moving from the Human,
To the glory of the HU-man.
I AM,
Saint Germain.

Compassion
Painting by Nicholas Roerich, 1936.

Chapter Thirteen

Activation

Saint Germain, Sananda, Lady Nada, and Serapis Bey
with students of the I AM America Teachings

Greetings beloveds, in that Mighty Christ, I AM Saint Germain. And I stream forth on that Mighty Violet Ray of Mercy, Transmutation and Forgiveness. As usual, Dear hearts, I request your permission to come forward.

Response: *You are most welcome. Please come forward.*

Group Response: *Please come forward.*

THE GRACE OF SHAMBALLA

Greetings Dear students, chelas, initiates, welcome. Welcome and Shamballa, for this is the time of the Great Festivity of Light, the great time of the four weeks of celebration. Four weeks that are given (celebrated) at our refuge which is known as Shamballa; but, also four weeks that are given to Earth, to Water, to Air and to Fire. All of these, Dear ones, have their purpose and their intent and how they hold intention for humanity. For you see Dear ones, Shamballa has its provenance and history. This provenance well settled within your consciousness, but also one that extends to you at this time.

As you know, Dear ones, as you sleep at night, you attend classes and each of these classes have their own purpose and intent. For they raise the student into the chela, the chela into the initiate, the initiate into the arhat, and onward into the adept and the avatar. You see, Dear ones, Shamballa is also a time when we can give you just a bit more, for as you know, everything on the Earth plane and planet is based upon energy-for-energy.

I realize that you know this well. For all comes under the Law of Karmic Retribution and Hermetic Law. But through the grace of Shamballa, you are given five to ten maybe even upwards to twenty percent more chance to leverage your consciousness and the light of God that never, never faileth. Now, before I continue onward with more teaching, I shall perform an energetic adjustment of this room.

I'd like to explain. He is now in the center of the room. From the palm of his hand, you can see streaming Violet Light. He is swirling the light throughout the entire living room. He is now traveling upward and you can see a pillar of Violet Flame and this light covers this entire home.

FOUR PILLARS OF SHAMBALLA

Dear ones, it is with great joy that I AM here this day, and I also know and realize the great sacrifice that you have made to come here. For everything is based upon that Law of Sacrifice. This is beyond energy-for-energy. For anything of great purpose and great intent comes through the Law of Sacrifice.

You know Dear ones, Dear hearts, that this is so and the Great Avatars and the Great Adepts demonstrate this law. I will give you a little more history about I AM America, and its place within the provenance of the Shamballa Teachings. For you see, Dear ones, Shamballa has four other schools or disciplines. I AM America being one of these four. They act as a Four Pillars to anchor Shamballa into the Earthly Plane. One of course comes under the auspiciousness of the Lord of the World who was once known as Sanat Kumara, and (this office) is now held by Lord Maitreya.[29]

There is also the World Teacher (an office) known throughout time immemorial. Now, Lord Sananda fulfills this as the Christ Consciousness comes into its full realization. There is also the (office of) the Buddha and under Gautama Buddha are sponsored many forms of Buddhism including Tibetan Buddhism. I will not give more upon this topic as this is something that you can do your research upon and understand even more thoroughly. And the (fourth) final great pillar is the I AM America Teachings. This you see, Dear ones, is the work of the beloved Golden Cities.

It was long designed in the eye of Sanat Kumara and Lord Apollo for this to come at this time, this Great Age—Golden Age of Kali Yuga. You see, it was brought forward at this time so that there would be an opportunity for those when the galactic spectrum of light would be lower in its frequency, and those who had the eyes to see and the ears to hear along with the great devotion, could reach through the Law Eternal and in the glory of their Mighty I AM Presence, the Ascension Eternal.

Now, you well know these teachings, as you have studied them. And today, I shall like to also introduce to you my Beloved Brother, Lord Sananda.

He's backing away. Lord Sananda is coming forward.

---

29. See Appendix V: *The Four Pillars: Schools of Shamballa*, page 339.

Greetings beloveds, I request your permission to come forward.

Response: *Please come forward. Lord Sananda, you are most welcome.*

LORD SANANDA

Dear ones, Dear hearts of mine, I know each and every one of you so well ... each of you like a dear friend and comrade in this work of light. It is important to understand, too, that I have given of my energy to help support the Golden City project and I oversee it as Lord Sananda. Yes, I do attribute this to the Mighty Christ Consciousness that streams in, through, and around all of humanity. You can call upon it at any time for any miracle that you need or see fit. But right now, let's attend to the work at hand.

Sananda greets each of the chelas, and Len, and adjusts each of them energetically. Saint Germain comes forward to speak, and Sananda backs away.

THE GIFT OF ASCENSION

This, Dear ones, is your first level of initiation into these great mysteries of the I AM. You see, when it was decided that I AM America shall be not only a clearing-house for the new humanity, it was also decided that through the work of the Golden Cities, that the Ascension would be made possible for many upon the Earth Plane and Planet. This Ascension you see is initiated from this very moment. Say unto yourself:

"Mighty, I AM Presence!
I AM Free in the Light of the Ascension.
So be it,
It is now done."

Group response: *So be it. It is now done.*

This Ascension, you see, is your gift of eternal freedom. Focus upon your freedom, Dear students, chelas, and stalwart initiates. Now, I shall give more information about the I AM.

THE MIGHTY GOD, I AM

The I AM is that Mighty God force that is within your heart. It streams from the Causal Planes of Light with the Cosmic I AM Presence and with your individual I AM Presence. In your individualized incarnation process, you are an individualized aspect of that Mighty I AM. You have come forward through many different lifetimes to balance the different frequencies of light and sound that are known as karma and dharma. The I AM, you see, is your great inheritance, for you are Co-creators, ONE with the source, ONE with the great God, I AM. As you work to raise your frequencies, it is also important to understand that America itself is that Mighty Light that is coming forward at this time. For she holds the cup of freedom for humanity, and as we all know, those great shadow forces have been busy with their own agenda. We, too, carry our own agenda of light and sound! And the light of God never, never faileth!

A SERIES OF ACTIVATIONS

The I AM contains within a matrix of Light and Sound frequencies and when you call upon it you engender that Mighty Monad within the heart activating the Eight-sided Cell of Perfection and the Divine Flame. From this activates even a further initiation into that Mighty Flame of Freedom. The Flame of Freedom spans its width and its breadth, radiating energy, around that vibral core axis of energy—this is known as the Golden Thread Axis. You feel the pulsation of it through the top of your head through the Crown Chakra.

Right now, through this activation by Lord Sananda, you are all pulsing with much higher frequency and energy. This you see, Dear ones, is of no mistake and you know there is no mistake ever, ever, ever. You have been brought here with timing and an intention, and this great intention comes forward now, at this timing of great light. Dear ones, as I have an extra fifteen to twenty percent to help you at this time, I shall do so. Call upon me and there I AM. Call upon me and there is the transference of my light unto you. Call upon me in your great calls, decrees and fiats of that Mighty Violet Flame Supreme.

He's just backing away for a minute . . . more Violet Light is streaming into the room. Perhaps you can feel it . . .

Now, I would like to give you a brief instruction on breath. Close your eyes and feel within this room that Mighty Violet Flame as it pulsates. It is a swirling frequency, much like a Vortex. Please notify me as you feel this.

Group Response: *Yes.*

Take your first breath deep into your lungs, carry the Violet Flame through your breath and in, through, and around your vital Chakra Centers to the bottom, which would be known as the Grounding Chakra. There, you will feel this Mighty Violet Flame pulsing, and its energy is transmuting. Gently bring the breath upward to the next chakra. There, you will feel the cleansing activity of the Violet Flame. Now, gently feel again, the Violet Flame move to the Solar Plexus. If you need to release breath, do so, but breathe this Violet Flame in, through, and around your Solar Plexus.

Now, move up to the heart. Do you feel the burning sensation? Please notify me as you feel this.

Group Response: *Yes.*

Settle deeply into this great Chamber of the Heart, for this is the nexus of your spiritual growth and development. (This) is this open heart that gives freely of love, compassion, and ultimate Forgiveness to humanity. Now, move your breath into the Throat Chakra. It was the great teacher who said, "Before the eyes can see, they must be incapable of tears. Before the ears can hear, they must have lost their sensitiveness. Before the voice can speak in the presence of the Master, it must have lost the power to wound."

Stream the Violet Flame in, through, and around. Exhale. Now, let us move the Violet Flame energy into the pineal gland, the Third Eye. Hold (your breath) to a count of eighteen. Signal when you are complete.

Group Response: *Yes.*

Do you all feel that Violet Fire circulating through your Third Eye? Gently open your eyes. Observe the auric fields of those around you. You should notice an influence of the Violet Flame in, through, and around everyone sitting in this room. Now Dear ones, Dear hearts, close your eyes, take in the great breath, and raise it to the Crown Chakra.

Violet Flame, come forth in the freedom
Of I AM that I AM!
Mighty Cosmic Beings,
Torchbearers of the Universe,
Come forth in service
For my freedom and Ascension
In the light!
So be it.

Group Response: *So be it.*

BREATH OF THE VIOLET FLAME

Now, release. And upon the count of three, open your eyes. This is the use of the Alchemizing Fire as it has been taught throughout time immemorial. I know that many of you have not used this technique before. However, this is your initiation into the great breath of the Violet Flame. Some call it the great Breath of the Dragon. We call it the breath of the Violet Flame, for we know it shall set you free. Now, this technique can be used in Golden Cities at Adjutant Points and also, at Star locations.

As I have taught before, this will increase the efficiency of this technique ten-thousand-fold. So it is an important technique to know and to understand. Now, it is important to also know and understand that before you use this technique, or share this with another that you must have had at least one full year of use of the Violet Flame or acceleration (kundalini) through the Sacred Fire. Now, Dear ones, I shall open the floor for your questions.

Question: *Would you be kind enough to accelerate the Violet Flame in all those who have not practiced this for a year?*

That has been achieved, Dear one, when I entered this room.

Response: *Okay, thank you.*

Proceed.

Student, question: *How does one gain trust in a relationship once trust has been broken?*

"THE GREATEST OF THESE IS LOVE"

Trust is not built upon one thing and one thing alone . . . it is built on love.

Saint Germain is backing away. Lord Sananda is coming forward. Sananda walks up to the student and faces them directly. He asks for permission to enter their energy, and the student grants permission.

Dear one, the great wounds of the past are released through but one simple premise, love. Love has the ability to heal all wounds, to stitch them up firmly and to let them heal. Healing is what is required now for you, Dear one. Healing at every level . . . body, mind, soul, and onward into your energy frequencies. For you are my Dear one, and call upon me and I shall be there for you.

He's streaming light into your Heart Chakra. Now, he's backing away.

Dear ones, the greatest of all laws that I have taught is to love one another. For in love, is there not acceptance? Is there not the ability then to forgive?

In love, do we not detach, and then go that extra mile? When you are weary, call upon that Mighty Law of Love (to) stream in, through, and around you. Of all the Jurisdictions you have studied, the greatest of these is Love. Love anchors itself in the heart. It is what we keep our devotion focused upon, and love expresses itself as a "hand in action." This, Dear one, is what we know as service, and we realize that you have been giving a great service to another. Lift your Brother up in frequency and energy . . . this shall be done in great loving service.

He's backing away. Saint Germain is coming forward.

Are there questions?

Student, question: *Beloved Saint Germain. I'm so grateful and Shamballa.*

Greetings, beloved . . . Shamballa to you.

BUILDING THE NEW SHAMBALLA

Student, question: *Thank you. I am wondering to what extent these maps are accurate and these Adjutant Points of beloved Klehma. And if they are, if it is in the highest and greatest good that I move in particular, to the Southwestern Adjutant Point . . . the Child Point?*

Yes, Dear one, and it is with great appreciation that comes forward from my heart to you and there are many who applaud you for the efforts you have made. Yes, you must travel to all the Adjutant Points throughout Klehma. These you see, not only accelerates your own development, but you're setting in place a grid to build the New Shamballa. You will receive a great impact of energies that will come in the last week of Shamballa to give the impetus to continue with this work.

Now at that time, it is very important that you call forth your Mighty I AM Presence into protection:

Mighty I AM,
Come forth in protection,
As I build this new grid for Shamballa.
So be it.
It is now done.

Your maps are somewhat accurate, but as you well know, there is a continuous flux within the Golden City Vortices. We can only pinpoint them within a five to ten-mile flux. You realize this?

Student, response: *Yes.*

Right now there is a cleansing activity that is occurring in the Golden City Vortex of Klehma This will continue for approximately twenty days, so be aware of this within your travels. There might be some difficulties with the travel due to extreme weather, but I shall guide and direct you.

Now, he is backing away . . . there's great energy coming forward.

SERAPIS BEY

Greetings from the Temples of Ascension. I AM Serapis Bey. I request permission to come forward.

Group response: *Please come forward.*

I come forward this day based upon your great desire. Call upon me and there, I AM. Let your energy bodies be raised into the glory of Light and Ascension through this mighty work that you give to Klehma. Know, Dear one, that I AM there with you. Know, with every step you take, I too am there for we are ONE . . . ONE in unity, ONE with that mighty I AM. The service you give is not just for I AM America, but for all of humanity. For Shamballa, you see, will be that New and Mighty Jerusalem on Earth.

He's backing away. Saint Germain comes forward.

Questions, Dear ones?

Guest-student, question: *Is there a next step for my spiritual development? I feel I'm where I'm supposed to be at the moment.*

Dear one, indeed. For as I said before, there are no mistakes ever, ever, ever. You traveled to the Golden Forest with beloved Kuthumi. This was indeed your initiatory passage. And now, you are here in service, are you not, Dear one?

Guest-student, response: *I am.*

We thank you and applaud your work, and ask for you to continue to hold your energies and service for I AM America.

Guest-student, response: *I will.*

He's backing away. Lady Nada is coming forward.

Greetings, Dear ones. I request your permission?

Group response: *Please come forward.*

THE PATH OF SERVICE

I AM Lady Nada, and I come forward as a steward of that Mighty Yellow and Gold Ray of service. I, too, serve with beloved Lord Kuthumi. Dear one, remember when I handed you the yellow rose?

Guest-student, response: *I do.*

Service unfolds with wisdom. Wisdom, you see, is the highest power within your walk as a chela. For you well know that this (Yellow Ray) is your soul force and your soul Ray. This (as it progresses) in its unfoldment will align itself with Love, Wisdom, and Power. This comes forward not only as the activated Unfed Flame, but also in its great unity as a Flame of Service for Brotherhood. We have spoken at this as the Flame of Desire, but the Flame of Desire in its higher level is always "of service." So, Dear one, call upon me and I shall be there for your higher service.

She's backing away. Saint Germain comes forward.

Dear ones, if there are questions . . . proceed.

Student, question: *What is the highest and best service from a spiritual path?*

You are here, Dear one, in the cradle of that Mighty I AM, in the frequencies of the Violet Flame. Ascension is your birthright. Claim it! Questions?

Student, question: *What is the highest and best that I can pursue?*

At this moment, establish your daily practice to include the Violet Flame at least twice a day. We recognize and realize the great service that you bring forward through helping others. This you chose, before this lifetime. This you know, do you not?

Student, response: *Yes.*

There are yet several more souls that you are destined to meet in your job, but see it not as a job or employment, see it as a service that you give to humanity. Once this is completed, then I ask for you to focus entirely upon the Golden City Vortices and your path of Ascension, do you understand?

Student answer: *Yes. May I ask you a question?*

Proceed.

Student, question: *As for my path, how do I know when I meet these people in the course of my employment?*

You will know . . . I will send an indicator. There will be a whisp of either the Violet Light or someone will wear a piece of purple clothing.

Student, question: *Hello, Saint Germain. In Shalahah I learned that I was to help cleanse and heal Klehma, and to hold the focus for the New Shamballa in the Fourth and Fifth Dimension. How do I accomplish this?*

ADJUTANT POINTS AND THE STEP-DOWN TRANSFORMER

By traveling to each of these Adjutant Points and performing your Cup Ceremony. See yourself as that mighty Step-down Transformer. Now, let me give you this teaching. As you stand upon the Earth, you will feel it vibrating through the core of the center of the Earth upward into your feet and onward through your grounding chakra. Once you establish this pulse, then call forth your decree and Divine Service:

"I AM a being of light serving the Divine White Ray,
and the Golden Cities for Shamballa."

In that moment, this energy frequency will attend to itself, streaming through the Divine Heavens through your Crown Chakra and out through your Heart Chakra. Are you familiar with the Sananda Mudra?

Student, response: *No.*

Place your left hand over your heart, your right hand extended. Energy streams out of your palm of your right hand.

Student, question: *What are the next steps for me . . . I've just moved to Klehma, what are the next steps for my path there?*

As you well know, Dear one, Dear heart, we never tell one what to do. For this, too, is based on those mighty Laws of Karma. However, if you would like to enter into service, you can accompany this Dear one in her frequencies building the new Shamballa, and you two shall be over-lighted not only by me, but by Lord Sananda and Serapis Bey.

Student, response and question: *Thank you. May I ask another question?*

Proceed.

Student, question: *How can I best fulfill ascension as you describe, and to claim it in this lifetime?*

Focus upon that Mighty Violet Ray of Mercy, Transmutation, and Forgiveness. Practice it on a day-by-day basis through your bhakti of devotion and compassion. This is enough for you at this time, Dear one . . . then continue in your Divine Service to build the energy frequencies of Shamballa.

Student, response: *Thank you.*

And now, if there are no more further questions, I shall take my leave.

I AM the Violet Flame,
An ember in the heart.
I AM the Violet Flame,
To the Golden Retreat of Shamballa,
I depart.

Group response: *So be it!*

Chapter fourteen

Great Awakening

Saint Germain, El Morya, and Mother Mary
with students of the I AM America Teachings

Greetings, beloveds. In that Mighty Christ, I AM Saint Germain, and I stream forth on that Violet Ray of Mercy, Compassion, and ultimate Forgiveness. As usual Dear hearts, Dear chelas, students of mine, I request your permission to come forward.

Response: *Please, come forward. You are most welcome.*

THE GREAT INTERVENTION

Greetings, Dear ones. Blessings and Shamballa, on this week of fire. Today, Dear ones, Dear heart, we shall spend some time in review of the Sacred Fire and it's importance in this work. As you know, Dear ones, the Violet Flame is of vast import to chelas in this study and in this work. For you see the Violet Flame itself is very important in clearing the karmas of the past and also in assisting in that Mighty Freedom of Ascension. The Violet Flame, you see, was brought many, many eons ago from the Lords of Venus. They engendered this as energy within the atmosphere of the Earth itself to clear away the residue what was left over from the experiments of Lemuria and also of Mu. You see, Dear ones, at that time, there were great experiments happening upon the Earth Plane and Planet.

Now, I can go into depth into this if you so choose, but perhaps it is better just to understand that this was a time when the reptilian nature had hold of the planet itself. Many throughout the Galactic Service saw that it was time for a change upon the Earth. So the Great Intervention was decided to happen through the Lords of Venus.

As they came and intervened, they used the Violet Flame to clear the psychic residue. This allowed for the creation of a new type of body for the sons of man and humanity to take. You see, Dear ones, I am talking about levels of spiritual evolution. And this, you must begin to understand. Of course, there was a group of those who did make their Ascension in the time of Lemuria, but there were also many experiments that happened. And during this time period the DNA got a bit clouded. DNA was programmed to arrest the spiritual development of the mammal, and this brought with it, again, its own shadow. This shadow, you see, has always been the dark side that the human must deal with. And of course, there are many religions that have known and understood this.

LOVE, AND THE LORDS OF VENUS

The Great Sacred Fire began to clear the psychic residue from the atmosphere, and a new spiritual infrastructure was built within the human. This, of course, happened with the birth of the Atlantean. This brought about a new emotional body that was driven through the true understanding of love. Love, you see, Dear ones, is the basis of the Astral activity. And in the finer reaches of the Astral Plane of the human, one does experience the great and grand experiences of art and music, all surrendered to the balance of beauty and love. This love, you see, came originally through those Lords of Venus who engendered it in their temples. During this time of Atlantis, it raised into such a great level of purity that humanity themselves even carried the Violet Flame as a spiritual moniker in the human aura.

Now, I know that this is difficult to understand in this darkness that you have experienced of Kali (Yuga). But know, Dear ones, Dear heart, that the Golden Age is here. The Great Awakening has come.

THE PLEIADEAN BROTHERHOOD AND THE SACRED FIRE

As history transited from Atlantis and into the Aryan, another great disturbance happened, another great interference, and DNA was, yet again, tinkered with. This brought another (consciousness) downfall and the reptilian genetic came up (appeared) in higher, inner consciousness. At that time, yet another Brotherhood came forward. This Brotherhood came from the Pleiades, and engendered, yet again, another infusion of the Mighty Violet Flame of Light. At this time there was such an intertwining of the genetics that it called for (a second) Divine Intervention. This is why the Violet Flame is now called the Sacred Fire, for the Sacred Fire contains within it two aspects: the Blue Flame and the Pink Flame.

ACTIVE INTELLIGENCE OF THE EIGHT-SIDED CELL OF PERFECTION

At that time, it was decided that not only shall Love be the basis of this Mighty Violet Flame, but also that the Mighty Will of God, the Divine Spirit, would rest within each and every one of you. At the basis of this encoding, this Mighty Violet Flame rested (seated) into the Heart of Humanity. It seated itself into that Mighty Monad, and moved then through the Eight-sided Cell of Perfection. Now, mind you, the Eight-Sided Cell of

Perfection was the addition that was given for the time of the Aryan. This is the movement of that plane, and leads one into the rising of intelligence. For you see, it is the *active intelligence* that will drive the Aryan onward and to its understanding of Freedom and Ascension.

Now, these are the great historical underpinnings that I give you, but sometimes, it is better to obtain the overview and then we can work at the inner level. This history, you see, is important to understand how sacred the Violet Flame is indeed, what it can give you, and how it rests within the Law of Eternal Freedom. Now, before I proceed with more instruction, do you have questions?

Student, response: *Yes.*

Proceed.

Student, question: *Yesterday, I was instructed, or I was asked and I agreed to serve I AM America and the Shamballa lineage. Will you tell me how to do that specifically for I AM America, and for the Shamballa lineage?*

It is important for you to review all published materials. Of course, I realize that you have your spiritual practice as well. Through the review of all published materials and all other teachings I have given, you will gain a great insight and knowledge in how you can share this information with others. I shall give you further instruction on how you shall form your own school with your own students. Does this complete?

Student, response: *Yes. Thank you.*

Questions?

THE WHITE LIGHT OF THE ONE

Response: *Yes. As we know, those of the dark force take everything and turn it into its opposite. So the Aryan has always had the understanding in our culture that the Nazis use the Aryan as a supreme power in their perspective. To, in a sense, segregate people and take advantage. It occurs that we have the residue of this. I ask that the Violet Flame be applied to this also, so this understanding is not permeated any further through the consciousness of the planet.*

Now, understand that the Aryan is what is now left of the Atlantean that settled into the lands known as Egypt. It was there that the Egyptian teachings were taken even into a greater height and understanding of the

Atlantean. There was a migration that occurred from Egypt into Spain and onward into Central or Meso-America as you would understand. Onward to the Lands of Ameru, this is now America. Now, the Aryan, itself, was a teaching of the White Light. This, too, has been adulterated. And as you well know, it was taken into consideration through Akhenaton and the teachings of the ONE that were originally known as the teachings of Quetzalcoatl. This is an understanding of the Aryan of the ONE, of unity of ONE. For you see, in Atlantis, what brought it down was the quarreling and the warring between status and cast. This, too, has been a predicament for humanity. For you see, now all are engendered with this Mighty Monad. But indeed, it is how one cultivates this Great Seed of Divinity, is it not?

Response: *Yes.*

Questions?

Guest-student, question: *Where does Tibet come into this lineage? Was that from Egypt?*

This is the original land of Shamballa. And of course, it was preserved to some degree from the great cataclysms because of the height of the mountainous range. It carried the lineage of the lands of Brihaspati, and this is where those of the golden skin lineage came from, celebrated (Shamballa), and understood. Some of it, of course, was culturally related to Atlantis, but it also contained and held its own Star seed Consciousness. Now, if you would like to know more about this, please review the lineage as given to you by Lord Meru. Questions?

THE BEGINNING OF THE GOLDEN AGE

Student, question: *What is the lineage of our President Trump, and how is he being used to assist the Ascension Process?*

Your current president was once a great Raja of India. He himself remembers this and has also studied this lineage. However, at this time, he has been brought forward to engender a great change within the American mind. This will be the beginning of the Golden Age and will be remembered and referred to in a historical context. Questions?

Student, question: *Is the Wall that President Trump is building, what is that really being used to do?*

(The Wall) is to keep the shadow government out of conflict with America, as one (Americans) rises in consciousness . . . at a later date, of course, all will be united as ONE. However, the shadow government is far from ready for that, are they not?

Saint Germain is chuckling.

Student, response: *Thank you.*

Questions?

DISSOLVE THE SHADOW

Question: *Do you have a decree for us to dissolve the shadow government's power?*

Mighty I AM,
Flood the Earth with the Golden Ray.
May the Violet Flame come forward in tandem,
And serve this time of Light, Brotherhood, and Sisterhood.
So be it!

Response: *So be it. Thank you.*

Now, unless if there are further questions . . . I would like to proceed.

Response: *Please.*

Saint Germain is backing away. Master El Morya is coming forward.

Greetings, chelas. I AM El Morya of the Blue Ray. Do I have your permission?

Group response: *Please, El Morya, come forward.*

DIVINE FATHER AND THE WHITE FIRE OF ASCENSON

Welcome to Gobean. Greetings and Shamballa to all of you. It is that Mighty Blue Ray in action that serves Divine Father, and it is important to not forget Divine Father in all that you do, in all that you say, and in all of your spiritual activity. This Divine Will, you see, will carry itself throughout all of the workings of Gobean this year. And I realize that you will be traveling to more of the (Adjutant) Points for this Gobean activity. I AM here, Dear ones, to set-up energy for you to enter into this point and to prepare you and your light bodies to the reception of Ascension.

El Morya is backing away and he is flooding a White Light with Blue into the room.

Dear ones, this is known as the White Fire of Ascension, from Divine Heavenly Father. It is your destiny to reach this next level of spiritual evolution, and I will oversee this process for you. For you are now in the Ashram of Gobean, and my stalwart assistant will be with you for your journey to this Adjutant Point. This is yet another Ashram of Light that shall serve your Ascension. Of course, there are other energies through the Color Rays that come forward to assist and to help you, and these Color Rays assist each of your light bodies and your energy centers. For you see, Dear ones, you are in the process of developing that Eighth Collective Energy Body of Light. This also serves that Mighty Group Mind of which there are several lessons that have been dispensed to you through Master Saint Germain. I ask for you to learn them. Also, throughout this next year, remember, this Mighty Blue White Light that has been sent to assist your Ascension. It, too, is the White Fire of Ascension, and you can call upon it along with the Mighty Violet Flame.

> White Fire of Ascension,
> Consume all miscreation!
> White Fire of Ascension,
> Consume all past negative karma!
> White Fire of Ascension,
> Consume!
> White Fire of Ascension,
> Create the Ascension Body!

You see, Dear ones, this too will allow you an evolution of consciousness. Now, I shall open the floor for brief questions.

Response: *In previous discourse, you gave us the step-by-step process to create the Eighth Energy Body, the Ninth Energy Body, and the Tenth Energy Body.*

This is so. Do you have further need of instruction?

Response: *The students who are here were not present for that.*

Instead of repeating such discourse, for the sake of continuity and cooperation, they are allowed to listen to this instruction.

Response: *Thank you.*

He's backing away, and Saint Germain is coming forward.

Greetings, Dear ones. Now, yet another teacher would like to speak.

Now, he is backing away, and Mother Mary is coming forward.

Greetings, my Dear ones. Do I have your permission?

Group response: *Yes.*

MOTHER MARY'S MISSON FOR THE NEW CHILDREN

I have come forward this day on my mission of Mercy and Love, and gratitude for you, Dear ones. Dear children of mine. There is still such suffering upon the Earth Plane and Planet, and I enfold you in my care. I cover you in the Cloak of my Love, for you see Dearest ones, Dearest hearts, children of mine, you are all as ONE, ONE with me, one in the Cloak of Eternal Love.

Yes, I know there are many teachings that you must absorb but, remember me always. I AM Mary, and I love you and enfold you in my care. Also, it is important for me to ask, as I have asked before, "Will you do my work?" You see, there are the new Beings of Light who are coming forward at this time. And they too must be engendered in your care. Unfortunately, the great shadow, too, gives its resistance at this time.

We come forward for these Great Bearers of Light in the Swaddling Cloth to bring their energies as great Pillars of Consciousness. Each one of these new souls has never been incarnated upon the Earth Plane and Planet ever before. Many of them come from new planetary light streams. And as they come forward to the Earth Plane and Planet at this time, they will play a role in the the Golden Age of Kali Yuga. They will raise the consciousness for humanity, for they will understand not only the new technologies, but the new ways and spiritual understanding that will bridge the gap from the old ways to the new ways. Each day, if you will, review my teachings upon this sacred energy that can assist their growth and development, their incarnation into the Earth Plane and Planet.

Six am, every morning, work upon your meditation for these new beloved Dear ones. Yes, they are known as the Blue Children. Yes, they are known as the Indigo Children. Yes, they are known as the Seventh Manu. They herald and usher in a New Time upon the Earth—each one of them calibrating and working with the pure energies of the Galactic Center. I love you, and I enfold you in my care. I AM Mary.

Saint Germain is now coming forward.

Dear ones, now, I shall open the floor for more of your questions.

THE EVOLUTION OF THE ANIMAL KINGDOM

Student, question: *I have horses that are within my care. Should I know something about the horses and are they playing a role in my development and/or the development of the work at hand in Klehma?*

I've said many times that many of the animals are raising their consciousness. And in this time of Golden Light will take human embodiment. Spend time with them. Visualize the Violet Flame and the Golden Ray through their auric energies. This will help to engender them to receive the Monad. Do you understand?

Response: *Yes.*

You see, Dear ones, the Animal Kingdom is yet another scheme of evolution. They work upon entirely through Group Mind. Now, the human has been individualized, and contain their own auric field and that Mighty Will of choice. So these, Dear ones, have been brought to you for you to help and assist, and lead them onward at the close of their lifetime into human incarnation. Do you understand?

Response: *Yes.*

Questions?

INTRODUCING THE VIOLET FLAME TO OTHERS

Student, question: *I have a dear friend, who, like many people, are stuck in the paradigm of organized religion—specifically Christianity. What would be the best way to bring him and any other individuals, and possible future students and chelas to I AM America, and specifically to the Violet Flame?*

Teach them that this is the Mighty Law of Forgiveness as dear Sananda has taught. This, too, is contained within the beatitudes of Christian understanding. This should suffice.

Student, question: *Is there any scripture that I could go to that you can think of that would be speak to their heart in terms of helping them to practice repetitively the Violet Flame?*

I suggest that you research into the book of John, as well as in to the mighty work of Paul. Proceed.

Response: *Thank you.*

Questions?

ADJUTANT POINTS AND THEIR COLOR RAYS

Student, question: *I plan to retire shortly sometime this year. I would love to relocate somewhere. Where would be the best place that I could start?*

Please, stand up so I may scan your energies. May I have permission?

Student, response: *Yes, you may.*

The Green Ray is best suited for you. However, upon occasion, you can also move into the White Ray. Now, as we begin to understand the individualized presence of the Adjutant Points and their Color Rays which, by the way, we have taught change every twenty years. So any Golden City which radiates through the Green Ray, or any Golden City which radiates through the White Ray would be very good for you. I realize your attraction to Malton, and this too would be good. As you well know, I will not tell you exactly where to go or what to do, but I will make suggestions based upon your energy and frequencies. Does this help?

Student, response: *Yes, thank you.*

Now, I do sense there are several more questions, and I open the floor.

ALIGNMENT TO THE DIVINE WILL

Student, question: *I have been experiencing this pain in my lower back, and I've been trying to understand what the lesson is of it and also heal it. Is there anything that you can do to help me assist in the healing process?*

This is an alignment issue to the Divine Will. Of course, it is an engagement with the Will Chakras. Now, there are several energetic adjustments that can be done. It is known as the alignment of the Divine Will to the Divine Plan. This is also contained within the scope of the I AM America material. Now, I shall give you visualization. Please, sit down. Back up right. Close your eyes. Gently visualize the Blue Ray in, through, and around your energy system. Breathe with me now to the Root Chakra, and with your exhale say calmly and firmly,

> "I accept the Divine Plan,
> And I AM aligned to the Divine Will.
> I accept the Divine Plan,
> And I AM aligned to the Divine Will.
> I accept the Divine Plan,
> And I AM aligned to the Divine Will."

Now, do you feel the energy radiating in your heart?

Student, response: *All over my body.*

This is perfect. Proceed with this until your body reaches balance. Questions?

A GOLDEN PRAYER

Student, question: *So that I may fully focus on the work at hand in Klehma after leaving this class, I was going to drive to California to get ready to put my beloved property in California on the market. . . you mentioned potentially difficult weather?*

Yes, Dear one and because of Shamballa, I am allowed to tell you more for, you see, California itself is under attack by the dark ones. Of course, you know this, and have realized this for some time and have felt it through its energetic. Now, I suggest that you hold this beloved state in prayer but, yes, if you feel it is time for you to move forward, then it is time, is it not?

Student, response and question: *So it's appropriate timing for me to go there and be ready that location to get on the market to sell?*

As again, dear one, I will not interfere for these are *your* choices. However, it is important when you leave that you are ready to leave. Now, hold that precious state within the energy of the Golden Prayer:

> May the Golden Ray stream in, through,
> And around the state of California.
> May its heart be healed.
> May its Divine Intelligence come forward,
> In the glory of the Light,
> And sealed in perfection.
> So be it.

Group response: *So be it.*

Questions?

Student, response: *I have one further question.*

Proceed.

THE DAILY PRACTICE

Student, question: *Is there a way for me to increase my awareness of your guidance?*

Dear one, establish your daily practice of the Violet Flame two times per day. Also, recitation of Awakening Prayer is very important. You, Dear one, have been also given the great task of traveling to the Adjutant Points of Klehma. This is your Divine Service. We bless you, and keep you, and hold you in the great Love and Fire of Ascension.

Student, response: *Thank you.*

Questions?

Student, question: *When we're being the light bearers and holding the light, and when our bodies, our minds, or spirits become weary . . . what is your best technique to expand our energy field and grow our energy specifically so that we may continue to move forth in these teachings?*

The best is to silence the mind. Meditation is good; but, contemplative walks in nature, to understand silence and stillness is of vast importance. This, you see, allows the settling of the mind. For the mind would like to take over and run everything, does it not?

Student, response: *Yes.*

He's chuckling now.

Dear one, for you, the Adjutant Point of Clarity is quite good for you energetically, and I would suggest you spend time there alone and in nature. Does this help?

Student, response: *Yes, it does. Thank you very much.*

Unless if there are other questions, I shall take my leave and I will return at the appointed time. Blessings to you, Dear ones, Dear hearts. Shamballa. I AM Saint Germain.

Group response: *Thank you.*

Chapter Fifteen

The Aquamarine Ray

Saint Germain and the Elohim Sein
with students of the I AM America Teachings

Greetings, beloveds. I AM Saint Germain, and I stream forth on that Violet Ray of Mercy, Compassion and Forgiveness. As usual, Dear ones, Dear hearts, Dear students and chelas of mine, I request permission to come forward.

Response: *Please, Saint Germain, you are most welcome.*

GROUP MIND AND THE AQUAMARINE RAY

Good morning, and Shamballa. There is much work upon the Earth Plane and Planet . . . still much more to be achieved, and I am happy to be with you today. And today, I would like to give a brief discourse, upon the Group Mind. Of course, I was with you in your practice last night. I hoped that you sensed my presence. I shall give you further instruction upon use of the Group Mind—its import and impact upon the Earth Plane and Planet, and answer your questions.

Dear ones, Dear hearts, at the beginning of the Great Age of Kali Yuga, we gathered in the innermost retreats of Shamballa, knowing that this time of darkness would be difficult for humanity. We knew that consciousness could fall lower than animal states of consciousness, and we had great concern of this impact upon the ability for humanity to reach Ascension. It was then decided that we would sponsor not only those Golden Cities of Light and Sound, but also that a Great Ray Force would come forward. And this Ray Force would be that Green-Aquamarine Ray.[30] This Ray does indeed stream from the heart of the Great Solar Logos, that Mighty, Great Central Sun—also known as the Galactic Center. This you see has been used, not only by other planetary lifestreams, but is specifically used to bring in an era of the rising of consciousness, liberation, and ultimate Ascension in Light and

---

30. Please note that the Aquamarine Ray functions at three distinctive levels. Its first level is Green-Aquamarine, and the Green Ray assists and nurtures the development of consciousness and the Group Mind. The Blue-Aquamarine is the second level of this Ray Force, and this produces clarity and engenders the aspect of the Divine Will throughout its Co-creative interplay. The final stage of the Aquamarine Ray is the Gold-Aquamarine Ray. This produces higher states of evolution and consciousness and drives evolutionary abilities from the HU-man to Ascension. At all levels the Aquamarine Ray is a force of awakening from the establishment of Group Mind to HU-man development, freedom, liberation, and Ascension.

Sound. This has always been the use of the Gold and Aquamarine Ray. And even why at its lower levels, it sometimes can cause difficulties for developing nations, social structures, and cultures. At its mid to higher range, it does produce a Golden Age upon any planet that it is influencing.

This is being brought forward, now, in this Time of Great Testing. This time we know as the birth of a Golden Age. It is a time of Great Awakening. It is a time of transition, and it is a great Time of Change. But change, you see, is good, is it not Dear ones, Dear hearts? For change opens the door, and the fresh air can then move in. Dear ones, this allows you in your own sojourn and evolution the ability to evolve your own consciousness and achieve again, a new plethora of experiences with a range of development into the realm of consciousness.

THE CONCEPTION OF PERFECTION

The Green-Aquamarine Ray also has a great impact upon the development of Group Mind. Now, as I have taught before, the Group Mind is very instrumental in accelerating, not only this Ray Force into the human energies system, but also plays a great role in accelerating your Ascension Process. Now, this is not to say that you will be consuming (through the Ascension Fire) your physical body, and leaving. However, what this allows is a momentum of consciousness to lift you into the higher states of consciousness where you can then conceive, in the mind's eye, your vast and Eternal Divine Perfection.

THE GOLDEN ORB AND ASCENSION

The Golden Orb that you have co-created, you realize as I've stated before, that it is a living and breathing thing. It too, has consciousnesses. It too, can be accessed at any moment in time. And yet, indeed, it is timeless. You can pull upon this state of consciousness, the Golden Orb, to access timelines. The Golden Orb is free. Now this is what you need to understand . . . this Golden Orb that is created of your consciousness is also infused with the Gold and Aquamarine Ray, for it has been created in this frame of time, and also, because of the auspices of Shamballa, it has also been infused with the state of immortality. So it has the ability to raise you to the State of Ascension. What does this mean?

ARCHANGEL GABRIEL

The state of Ascension in Third Dimensional Density means that it functions beyond time. It also has the ability to access Akashic Records.

Each of you are connected to this Mighty Group Mind, and you can access this for any information you may need. Now I know in the beginning stages, you may question this. "Is this really working? Am I really receiving accurate information?" And this to assure you, Dear ones, call upon Archangel Gabriel, of the White Ray, then call forth, through your Mighty I AM Presence:

> "Beloved Group Mind,
> Activate now in truth and intent."

GREAT DARKNESS AND GREAT LIGHT

This gives you the access, then into this Mighty Golden Orb. The Golden Orb was taught in other times, that is, not upon the Earth Plane and Planet, but it comes from the Dahl Universe and was utilized at one time in the Pleiades. For you see, each planet in its own sojourn and evolution reaches these time periods of great darkness and glimpses of great light. The Golden Orb's purpose is for this time. I also want you to understand that the Golden Orb functions beyond the shadow of the dark governments, and it is held in the protection of Archangel Gabriel. There are also ways you can gain acceleration. This, through that Mighty Gold and Aquamarine Ray, and many of the Golden City Vortices, are now being activated with this Ray force. As you will begin to understand, this Ray Force will be sponsored and held, always in continuous activity throughout one of the Adjutant Points of everyone of the fifty-one Golden Cities.

GOLDEN CITY LEI-LINES

I will spend time in future discourse helping you to identify these locations so that you can understand them. Now, I understand today that you will be traveling to a great lei-line. This lei-line is one of the functional lei-lines of the Cardinal Directions, the Western Door of Gobean.

It, too, streams forward and its effect creates mighty pulsating vital energies that create and hold the third-dimensional aspects of Gobean that translate into Fourth and Fifth Dimensional frequencies. Now, not to get into too much education on this, for I realize you have received much already about this, but it is important to understand that this particular lei-line has a great influence of the Aquamarine and Gold Ray. Lei-lines, upon occasion, will have these great changes along with the great Adjutant Points and the Ashrams and Temples of Service.

GOLDEN CONSCIOUSNESS

Today when you are there, it is important that you enter into your Group Mind. All of you enter into meditation, and there you will find not only the information that you each seek, but also, you will feel the unity of your energy bodies. You will feel a great and grander consciousness that awaits you. You will feel a lessening of your burden and of your karma, and enter into the dharma —the realm of Golden Consciousness. Now Dear ones, I shall open the floor for your questions.

THE EVER PRESENT NOW

Student, question: *Hello Saint Germain, you were mentioning about timelines, and I understand that backward would be the Akashic and forward, would that be so we can move into the future through this Group Mind?*

Precisely! Now I would like to comment that time is not forward nor backwards, it is contained within the Ever Present Now. And you will have this experience as you access this level of conscious activity. Of course, we realize in the human condition, one must understand through their intelligence and activity, of that intelligence, a timeline of past, present, and future. This we clearly know and understand. However, in the reaches of your consciousness, today, you will be able to feel that Ever Present Now of eternal and immortal existence. Do you understand?

USE OF GOLDEN CITY STARS

Student, response and question: *Yes. Would it be best for all three of us to participate at a specific time and a specific day to practice our Group Mind?*

This is ideal. Of course physical proximity is best. However, if it cannot be achieved, first when you enter into a Star, this of course can always be achieved through that contact. And I would advise at least for the first time, to create your Group Mind at the Star. This of course can be achieved in your proximity to your Star, Gobean. From that and onward, you can then create your Group Mind through telepathic rapport. Do you understand?

Student, response: *Yes, thank you very much.*

I shall be present and call forth Archangel Gabriel. Questions?

Student, question: *We have another question that was not related to that, but it was about the new grid for Klehma and the new Shamballa and we were wondering if there was a specific doorway or direction to begin this journey that we would like to take.*

I would like to give you further instructions upon that, and request that you hold that for the moment, towards the close of this discourse.

THE ELOHIM, SEIN

Now, he is somewhat backing away and a new being is coming in. Let me explain this being. It is a great cosmic force, and looks like a Salamander of Light; it is aquamarine in color with gold all around it. It is vibrating and pulsating. Saint Germain will speak.

Dear ones, Dear hearts, and standing next to me I would like to introduce the Elohim Sien. Sien is the steward of this lei-line and also of the Outer Child Point. He, too, stewards the Ashram and the Beings of Light that serve there. He will come forward and give small discourse.

Saint Germain is backing away and the Elohim Sien comes forward.

Greetings chelas, students, may I have your permission to come forward?

Group response: *Yes, you have our permission.*

It is rare that I seek physicality or even communicate in such a manner, so my forgiveness first, I offer. Now, I will give you some information about this lei-line. This lei-line carries within it great peace and you will instantly feel your energy centers working in a cooperative manner. You see also, Dear ones, that it will accelerate you into Golden Age Consciousness every time you enter into its pulse and I ask you to always feel this energy first, for it is the birth of a New Time that is coming, swiftly and quickly upon your Earth Plane and your Earth Planet. You see Dear ones, I will also enter into rapport with you in conscious understanding, intelligence, and expression.

He's kind of floating above the room right now. He's actually doing a type of adjustment to our Crown Chakras.

MOVEMENT INTO GROUP MIND

With your permission please, let me move you all into Group Mind.

Group response: *Yes.*

Let me explain what is happening. He's reaching into our aura for each of our Golden Thread Axis, and forming ONE Group Mind between all of us.

Now, I ask of you to take but one cleansing breath, down to the bottom of your feet, and draw this vital breath up into the top of the head, your Crown Chakra. Now feel the pulsation into the ONE, into the Group Mind. This Dear ones, is Oneness. Now, the Oneness . . . and now the Oneship. Feel its pulsation. Feel the unity that comes forward in all expression, and in all human conditions.

Let me explain, he is going to disconnect us. And one by one, he is swirling, Violet Flame around the top of each cord.

I shall take my leave from your plane of expression, but know this: I AM always with you. Call upon me in any crisis, for I will bring a unifying affect to you. Peace, good will, and cooperation. So be it, in that Mighty Mind of the ONE.

Group response: *So be it.*

Saint Germain is coming forward.

This was a special dispensation given to you Dear ones, Dear hearts, for this time of Shamballa, so you can experience, all of you, one continuous flow of mind. There will be many more mysteries that will be dispensed to you upon your time in the lei-line as well as upon your entrance into the Cooperation Point. Now Dear ones, Dear hearts, I shall open the floor for the rest of your questions.

Student, question: *Beloved Saint Germain, Beloved Serapis Bey, it is with great joy that I receive every morsel of detail that you give to co-create together in a Divine Plan. I am grateful and I thank you.*

It is great joy for us to serve you, for we love you, and we bless you, and hold you in the Cup of Service.

THE NUMBER OF ADJUTANT POINTS

Student, question: *Thank you. My questions are, we are trying to clarify how many points. So if I may ask, in Klehma, are there two parental points in each doorway, two child point, inner and outer, and two Cardinal points in each doorway, that being twenty-four, plus the star, twenty-five, is it that there are twenty-five points?*

Dear one, Dear heart, let me explain. First we must deal with the cardinal directions for they will be infused with the Gold Ray of Service and that must come forward to humanity. Indeed, you are correct, we will dispense information upon inner Cardinal Points, but at this time the development must remain within the Cardinals.[31] Do you understand?

Student, response: *No.*

The vital lei-lines, which run North to South, and to East to West, these are the vital intersections of the Mother Point, the Father Point, the Outer Child, and the Inner Child . . . then onward to that Mighty and Magnificent Star. Do you understand?

Student, response: *Seventeen points total . . .*

Seventeen points total, for as was stated so many years ago, the seventeen, in scared numerology and geomancy, upon which this Time of Intervention functions for humanity. For Dear one, we must first establish through Unity Consciousness that Mighty Christ Consciousness has its root in Quetzalcoatl. Do you understand?

Student, response: *Yes.*

You are correct however, on the intercardinals; however, they too will become functional at a later date. Their influence is very subtle, and at this moment are presently held in latent development.

Student, question: *What is the order in which we visit the points?*

---

31. Please see Appendix W: *The Number of Adjutant Points*, page 341.

As you well know, there are many different Migratory Pathways and different spiritual pilgrimages. Do you request one for yourself?

Student, response and question: *Yes, and for the grid of Shamballa. Are they the same?*

The Golden Grid of Shamballa is established through starting first in the Northern Door, then head to the Southern Door, then to the East Door, and onward to the West Door, with conclusion in the Star. Do you understand?

Dear one, each migratory pattern will set up a series of geometric grids that interface with the Beloved Earth, Babjeran, and into your energy system. For you see, as there is the macrocosm there is the microcosm. This too carries through your chakra system, but is also carried through the subtle acupressure and acupuncture points upon the body—those that are known also as the meridians and the subtle nadis of light. Do you understand?

Student, response: *Yes.*

Questions?

Guest-student, question: *In today's journey to the lei-line, is there a specific set of instructions on how you wish us to proceed?*

Today it is important to enter into vital experience and to record every subtle nuance that you detect. Not only in conscious experience, but also in physical experience, for there will be many things that will remind you of your experiences today in this discourse. Do you understand?

Guest-student, response: *Yes I do.*

And now Dear ones, Dear hearts, unless if there are further questions I shall take my leave:

I bless you and carry you
In the Heart of the Mighty Violet Flame and Ray.
May the Gold Ray come forward and bless all of you,
And lead you into eternal freedom and liberation.
I AM victorious in the Ascension!
I AM, Saint Germain.

Chapter Sixteen

Golden Age of Co-creation

Saint Germain

Greetings beloveds, in that that Mighty Christ, I AM Saint Germain. I stream forth on that Mighty Violet Ray of Mercy, Compassion, and Forgiveness. As usual, Dear hearts, Dear students and initiates, I ask for your permission to come forward.

Response: *You are most welcome. Please come forward.*

CHANGE AND CONSCIOUSNESS

Dear ones, Dear hearts, there is still much work in front of us, is there not? For there is much work still upon this Earth Plane and Planet in this great Time of Awakening, in this great opening of the Golden Age. Yes, indeed, it is a Golden Age of Kali Yuga, but it is still a Golden Age. For you see Dear ones, there are frequencies that are moving quickly and rapidly from the Great Central Sun, onward to your own solar Sun—known as Helios and Vesta, and arced into that great central light of the Earth itself, and radiating upwards into each of the Golden Cities. It is also important to know that there are still many changes that could occur. Yes, during this great Time of Change, I have informed you of such, for indeed, we said this would be a time of great volcanic explosion. And many (volcanoes) are still destined to explode in this Time of Great Change and Great Awakening. For as I have said before, each one of these changes assists yet another change, and yet another change . . . and another change. These are indeed the changes related to consciousness. For you yourself know that when you change, what happens in your own world? All of your outer experiences begin to change, do they not? And the same is with the Collective Consciousness. For the Collective Consciousness is based upon every thought, feeling, and action of every man, woman, and child in human experience upon the Earth Plane and Planet.

"A CHANGE OF HEART"

There is also a Collective Consciousness that comes through each of the Kingdoms of Creation: the Plant Kingdom, the Mineral Kingdom, the

Kingdom of the Devas and the Elementals, and the Animal Kingdom. They, too, contribute to this great Collective Consciousness. But you see Dear ones, Dear hearts, the Divine Human is the great Co-creator. This Co-creator contributes (most) to this great Collective Consciousness. There are certain percentages that have been ascribed to this and it is said that the Mineral kingdom contributes five to six percent. The plant kingdom contributes ten to fifteen percent. We move into the Kingdoms of Elemental Life Force—the Devas and the Elementals . . . they, too, contribute, between ten to fifteen per cent. The Animal Kingdom takes the remainder of the balance up to fifty percent; but the human you see, Dear ones, Dear hearts, in their Co-creative ability, contributes fifty percent to the Collective Consciousness. This may be very difficult for you to know and to understand, and it is why we have always said that, "A change of heart can indeed change the world for you." The calibration of light that comes forward to the human at this time is of no mistake.

MANIPULATION OF CONSCIOUSNESS

Now, there were periods of time upon the Earth Plane and Planet, those epochs of Mu, Lemuria, and also Atlantis, when the DNA was altered. This DNA was altered in times of lesser light frequency, and it was done purposefully and intentionally so that the human could no longer carry this frequency and control the Collective Consciousness. Of course, there have been those dark ones who have frequented your Earth Plane and Planet, and they know and understand this. They have been able through their calculation and manipulation of the other Kingdoms of Light, to manipulate human Collective Consciousness so that it then would create in a way, shape, and form that pleased them and *their* Co-creation.

DOMINION AND CO-CREATION

This is the basic understanding of Collective Consciousness and how it works upon this Earth Plane and Planet. Now, in times of greater frequency of light, the human is activated not only through the Eight-sided Cell of Perfection, but through the development of the higher Light Bodies. These Light Bodies have the ability to take control at a Co-creative level over their environments. What does this mean? This means that they have control over those lower kingdoms. Now, as I have taught before, yes, indeed, all is a choice, is it not? And even in these kingdoms of creation, they too have their own schemes of evolution, their choice, and their will. But what I am speaking about is Co-creative Dominion with a Kingdom. You have experienced Co-creative dominion:

You farmers, who have plowed the field.
You foresters, who have cut timber from forests.
You potters, who have sculpted with clay.
You bakers, who have harvested wheat and made bread.

This form of dominion is applied through the Mighty Mental Body. This is the great gift that has been given to mankind and humankind, especially at *this* time. For this, indeed, is the Aryan (active intelligence). Remember, the Aryan is engendered through that Divine Eight-sided Cell of Perfection. This engenders the perfect Co-creation in alignment to the Divine Plan and the Divine Will, and knows of its Creator Source. This, of course, is the basis of hierarchal thinking. We have taught this as the Spiritual Hierarchy, and we have organized as such through that Mighty Great White Brotherhood of breath, sound, and light. We practice the Right-hand path.

LIGHT EMPOWERS THE I AM PRESENCE

Now, I have given you the contrast. I imagine there are many questions that are now coming up within you, but I would like to continue a bit further with this so you can begin to understand how important this great time of the Golden Age is.

Indeed, I have taught you that when you travel to the different Adjutant Points of Golden Cities that this expands not only your spiritual practice, but helps to develop those Mighty and Grand Light Bodies of Ascension. This begins to give you dominion . . . dominion over your own Co-creative Process. This is indeed very important and one must first Master this within their own world before it can extend out into greater Co-creation. What are we talking about? We are talking about the Mighty I AM and empowering that Mighty I AM through this extra calibration of light frequencies from the Great Central Sun. We can talk about every layer of new energy that comes in, and we can talk about each Adjutant Point, but more simply stated . . . we must talk about your union with the Mighty I AM Presence. This will bring about your Ascension in breath, sound, and light.

"EXPAND YOUR WORLD"

The Golden Age is designed to enhance your connection with your Mighty I AM Presence. There are moments when you will feel a subtle energy, see a wisp of golden light, or hear a sound frequency. These indeed are the presence of these higher vibrations or resonant frequencies that you can access and use. You see Dear one, as you began to expand your own world, you too are making a contribution to that greater Collective Consciousness and of course this is done through that Mighty I AM Presence. We well know that the I AM that I AM is connected to the Source of all Creation, and the I AM that I AM is created by the Source of all Creation. In this same way, you are fashioned, and made, and modeled as the heart of your Divine Mother and the will of your Divine Father, so therefore you too carry the I AM that I AM.

LIGHT AND YOUR DESTINY

This is the grand interplay that comes forward at this great time of the Golden Age. Now, why is it so important to understand not only the Golden Cities and these higher frequencies of light? For not only do they forge a deeper and a more viable connection to the I AM Presence, they allow an expansion that happens through timelessness. What do I mean by this? In the twinkling of an eye, one can indeed Ascend! In the twinkling of an eye, one can indeed unite with their Mighty I AM Presence! Why is this so? It is a great dispensation of light. This comes not only from the Great Central Sun, but from the lineage of the Great Galactic Suns.[32] These light frequencies will expand and exponentiate during this time of the Golden Age of Kali Yuga. Dear ones, it is your destiny at this time to become free ... free in the light ... free of the dark source that has tried to encumber your Earth for so long ... free of duality ... free of polarity. Move into your grander destiny as an Ascended Being of Light!

ASCENSION THROUGH THE VIOLET FLAME AND THE GOLDEN CITIES

We have explained the different forms of Ascension, and through your choice each of you in your own vital experience will know and understand the pathway that serves you best. However, at this time, I have given you two of the most important aspects and elements that you can apply. First is that Mighty Violet Flame of Mercy, Compassion and Forgiveness:

Mighty Violet Flame stream in, through, and around
All of my Light Bodies.
Help me to transmute and transcend
All negative karmic residue.
Grant me the eternal gift of Ascension.
Almighty I AM,
Almighty I AM,
Almighty I AM!

---

32. See Appendix Z: The Lineage of the Seven Galactic Suns, page 347.

You see Dear ones, Dear hearts, when you call upon this Mighty Violet Flame in its action and in its supreme activity, it is then able to begin to transmute the lower, dross energies. This karmic residue of the lower bodies no longer serves your vital experience in light and sound. Consume it through the Violet Flame.

Now, the second (aspect) that is important for you to understand is the use of the Golden Cities. For I've said in many discourses that the Golden Cities expedite your Ascension in the light and sound, and grant this Divine Victory. Your Victory can be achieved in this great time of liberation and ascent in light.

GREAT AWAKENING TO CO-CREATION

The Golden Cities, you see, were long, long planned. We knew in the great timing and intent that a time would come upon the Earth when these higher frequencies of light would appear and arc themselves into and onto the Earth. This, of course, changes many things, does it not? And as I said before, the Earth would go through a time of great cleansing. At this time you are indeed in this great Time of Change. Simultaneously comes a great Time of Awakening. You, too, are experiencing this Great Awakening. This is not just awakening to the external factors around you, or who is controlling what, or who is trying to control you; however, it is wakening to your great and grand gift of Co-creation. This you see Dear ones, is the gift. It is a gift that we have talked about in so many of our past discourses and now it is given freely to you in this time of Great Awakening. And now if you have any questions, please proceed.

Response: *Is there a decree that can be utilized to help people connect to their I AM Presence?*

In the name of I AM that I AM,
Mighty I AM Presence,
Come forth in full awareness!
Transcend all limitation of my thoughts and beliefs.
Transcend all past negative karmas that I may hold
Within my energy fields.
Mighty I AM, stream forth through
The law of I AM that I AM!
Stream forth in enlightenment
And Golden Light.
So be it.

Response and question: *Thank you. In proceeding to the Adjutant Points of the Golden Cities, is there a preferred migration starting point and finishing point for the Ascension?*

MIGRATION PATHWAY FOR ASCENSION

We have discussed this in past discourses and as I have suggested before, it is best to always start an Ascension Migration in Southern Doors. For you see Dear hearts, Southern Doors instigate healing processes. These healing processes can be of many different levels. There can be healing processes associated with thought, healing processes that are associated with feeling, and also healing processes that are associated with your physical bodies. Each of these play a great role in the grand creation of life, Do they not?

Answer and question: *Yes. The next question, is there something specific that you need Lori's students to be doing for this particular, date in July of this year?*

THE ENERGIES OF THE HEART OF THE DOVE

As in past discourse, it was suggested that they travel to the Heart of the Dove. However, their experiences with Group Mind must first ensue in a Golden City Star. It is possible, if they have advanced enough in the technique of Group Mind, that from the Star frequencies, they can tap into the Heart of the Dove. At this time it is important to understand the energies of the Heart of the Dove and if you'd like, I can give you more discourse upon that.

Question: *Would you please?*

THE AVATAR, BABAJI

The Heart of the Dove, Dear ones, Dear hearts, while it has some similarity to a Golden City Vortex is not a Vortex. It is a great location upon the Earth Plane and Planet that serves as a Center to the umbilicus of Mother Earth herself. Therefore, it is very sensitive. It is sensitive to all Co-creation processes. That is why the Great Avatar of the birthless, deathless body, Babaji oversees this particular point upon Babajeran. It is of no mistake that he has been appointed to this great retreat, of light and physical life. For you see Dear ones, this (Center) contains within it a type of chi, orgone, or prana that reinvigorates the physical body.

RESTORATION AND REJUVENATION

The Heart of the Dove restores not only the physical body, but also creates an order within the Light Bodies. This reinvigorates them for the Ascension. This, too, is another migration that can be used in adjunct to the Golden City Vortices. The Heart of the Dove functions through the grand principle of purity. It contains a higher substance (essence) of light frequencies and indeed it can increase (your body and Light Bodies) in frequency and in light. This is a further increase in energies that you may receive through traveling to Adjutant Points, and it (the Heart of the Dove) purifies the Light Bodies.

This purity is like an energetic adjustment. Not only is it an alignment and a balance, but it also allows you to proceed in the purity of light. This will help your Co-creative activities. It can be seen as a healing, but it is more than that Dear ones. It is like a restoration. It is a great gift that has been given to those who are beginning to develop, "the eyes to see and the ears to hear." This, of course, has a positive effect upon Collective Consciousness, for as each one achieves their Victory, does not everyone?

Answer: *Yes.*

PORTAL OF PURITY

It is also important to understand its energies will gently guide you from Oneness, to the Oneship, and into the ONE. It is best for the students to currently stay in the frequencies of the Stars, but sometime in their future endeavors I would suggest that they do attend and visit this great Retreat of Light. I refer to the Heart of the Dove as a retreat, and indeed it is shielded (protected) and held in a pure form of consciousness. For you must understand Dear ones, Dear hearts, that there are actual (genuine) portals that do exist upon the Earth Plane and Planet. The dark forces have known this for time immemorial, and have used them not only for time travel but also so that they can shift into different dimensions and receive a greater sanction of light. Do you understand? This, of course, is something that we will discuss in length, and beloved Hercules holds this teaching. He has given you some of the basis of this, but in this particular portal golden light is held in eternal protection. It has been held in its purity and sanctity since the latter days of Atlantis.

It was held in this purity so that it could be utilized at this time. For I know there are those who have a more difficult time sensing the frequencies and energies of the Golden City Vortices. This sensing requires a certain amount of the transmutation of karmic residues held in the lower Light Bodies. But remember, Dear ones, Dear hearts, when I first said to you that Beloved

Mother Earth, Babajeran, has offered herself to cleanse the lower bodies of mankind? Travel to the Dove . . . with this in mind, cleanses not only the lower bodies but restores the sanctities of the higher bodies. Questions?

RESTORATION OF LIBERTY AND FREEDOM

Answer and question: *Yes. Lori has one student who is intending to travel there on that specific date and her name is Joan. Is there anything specific for her?*

It is important that she adhere to the dietary requirements and I also would like to interject that she must increase his use of Violet Flame before his departure to a minimum of three times per day. It is also important for you to see Dear ones, Dear hearts, that my requests for (travel to) the Heart of the Dove was for the restoration of liberty and freedom in the United States. This I gave understanding the great timing and intention through the solar and the lunar eclipses. For you see Dear ones, we (the Brotherhood) use energies during these times to set in motion shifts and changes within, for lack of a better term, Akashic Records. Now, do not be confused. Of course when I say Akashic Record, you're thinking only of the past, but there are also what we would say predicated timelines that we, too, travel upon. We understand the potentials, and then ameliorate and avert certain events for the United States . . . a time of shadow, or a time of light? A time of darkness, or a time of great potential?

A PLEDGE OF LIBERATION

Every day hold the United States in that Great Cup of Freedom and understand that she (the United States) holds, indeed, the light for the world.[33] When I say light, what do I speak of? I speak of liberty and freedom and true justice for all. As children, I know that each of you once stood in front of your flag, with your hand over your heart while you recited the Pledge of Allegiance. I instruct you to continue to do this every day. For you

---

33. In the *I AM America Prophecies*, Saint Germain claims that the people of America have a unique destiny in the New Times. America contains within it a unique anagram: A M E R I C A = I A M R A C E. The I AM Race of people is a unique group of souls who lived in America as Atlanteans. But their destiny has evolved since those ancient times. Instead of sinking on a continent destroyed by the misuse of technology and spiritual knowledge, their active intelligence continues to develop in modern times. Their service is focused on the Brotherly love of all nations. In the I AM America Earth Changes Prophecies Saint Germain states, "America will be the first to go through the changes, and then give aid to the rest of the World." Interpretations of this Prophecy explain why American is possibly the chosen land—the first society to experience dimensional change. Members of this regenerated, enlightened society will share and teach the benefits of this new understanding with the rest of humanity.

see Dear ones, what are you creating in that moment with that great and mighty pledge? ... A Group Mind for your Ascension. [34] This, indeed, is the grander work of democracy.[35] Now, you may well know that democracy is not a perfect system for the human. However, the most perfect system is spiritual liberation! The human is a grand Co-creator, and as a Co-creator, he or she is always seeking this intention. Do you understand?

Response: *Yes.*

IMMORTAL LIGHT

The Heart of the Dove is indeed held in protection and in the sanction of Immortal Light. It is a connection to your great Solar Sun, Helios and Vesta, and it is also connected to the Great Central Sun, and the Galactic Suns. This is why it is a time portal, and the Heart of the Dove's frequencies and energies of light can also be used, now, to help purify those lower bodies. This promotes a type of cleansing, and then your contribution to Collective Consciousness and to the Group Mind that you create has a higher frequency and sympathetic resonance. I gave you exact instructions to be used, and it is important to use them first in the Star, and on the appointed day, if you are so inclined, travel to the great Heart of the Dove. If you are unable to do so, then travel to the great and mighty Stars, for all is interconnected. Is it not?

MENTAL OBSTACLES

Answer and response: *Yes, I personally am very desirous of going to the Heart of the Dove. I just need to have the obstacles that are presented in front of us to be transmuted.*

Remember, as a member of this lodge, every obstacle in front of you is not a physical obstacle. The obstacles that are always in front of one are mental

---

34. The I AM Activity and Saint Germain Foundation promotes the use of this Ascended Master Pledge of Allegiance: "I pledge Allegiance to God, the Beloved Mighty I AM Presence, to the Flag of the United States of America, and the Republic for which It stands. One Nation, under God, Indivisible, with Liberty and Justice for all. America, we love you! America, we love you! America, we love you! And our love is great enough to hold you eternally Victorious in the Light!"

35. Francis Bacon, a prophet of the Golden Age, envisioned a New Age for humanity through his utopian essays, *New Atlantis* and *Novum Organum*. Francis Bacon called for a New Age to emerge through a United Brotherhood of the Earth—Solomon's Temple of the Future—built through the Four Pillars of history, science, philosophy, and religion. Bacon theorized that the Four Pillars would eventually mature through the political development of Democracy. From this notion, current forms of Democracy are prenatal in form, whose ideal structure would emerge in the future after a span of three-hundred years. Today, the progressed foundation of a developed Four Pillars reappears in Saint Germain's four United States Golden Cities as: Peace, Realization (fruition), Freedom, and Prosperity. The Fifth Pillar is Ascension, achieved through the Balance and Harmony of the subsequent Four Pillars. Gobean: History transforms to Peace. Malton: Philosophy transforms to Realization. Wahanee: Religion transforms to Freedom; Shalahah: Science transforms to Prosperity.

indeed, and can be overcome through the use of thought. For you know, Dear one, Dear heart, thought is the grand creator.

THE STRENGTH OF THE GOLDEN CITIES

This is why I've given the suggestion that you can (also) travel to those mighty Star frequencies if you are attuned to, you can also travel to various Adjutant Points, for they, too, hold great light. In their order of activation Gobean is the strongest of all of the Golden Cities, followed by Malton, and Wahanee, Shalahah, and Klehma. (All of these Golden Cities are located in the United States.) Of course that grand Step-down transformer Gobi carries the frequencies of Shamballa.

THE FOUR DOORWAYS

Each of the doorways contains their great frequencies of light, and Southern Doors often hold a higher frequency of light. At this time for humanity, they bring about energetic healing at many levels. Eastern Doors also hold high frequencies and energies of light. Northern Doors and Western Doors can sometimes be more difficult and harder to achieve desired results because of their alignment processes. However, as we advance further into the Golden Age, we will see more evening of these energies. The Stars hold the function of the light in its purest form. Any of your students could serve as a Step-down Transformer of Light in any of these points, and this is a mighty service. Do you have questions?

THE TWELVE JURISDICTIONS

Question: *Yes. Is there a decree to put forward to complete your Co-creations?*

Please explain.

Response: *Well, since Co-creation is of the mind, the mind has a tendency to travel to places it doesn't need to. The mind has a tendency to wander, and that focus requires a tremendous amount of practice. Not everyone has a sustained focus developed.*

Indeed, Dear one. Now, this was also our great concern when we first released the I AM America Map and the great Prophecies of change. What you are addressing in this question is the great need for the Twelve Jurisdictions. I suggest that you review all twelve of these teachings and there you will find the decree that you seek.

Response: *Thank you. I apologize for not remembering.*

Questions?

INTEGRATION AND INITIATION

Question: *Is there anything specific that Luke must do in Malton?*

It is important to enter into that great and Mighty Star of Malton. For there he shall feel a balancing effect of all of the energies of his Light Bodies. And this will be felt by his beloved partner as well. There are other frequencies in the Southern Door that will be a great import. When you traveled to that Mighty Southern Door, you received great initiations through brother Kuthumi.

Response: *Yes.*

AMPLIFY YOUR DISCIPLINE

If it is possible, and if they so choose, traveling to the Southern Door will assist and help the overall process of integration. This is what you sought in your great journey there. Is it not?

Answer: *Yes.*

And so it is Dear ones. Remember that Golden City Adjutant Points calibrate and expand and amplify your spiritual work and practice. Sometimes it is as much as one thousand-fold. Sometimes it is as much as ten thousand-fold. This depends on the disciplines and the energy frequencies of the chela. Do you understand?

Answer: Yes.

Concerning the Heart of the Dove . . . if each of the students will apply as I have taught how to call upon me on that day, our frequency shall all join together in Group Mind at the Heart of the Dove. So be it! Questions?

Response: *I have no further questions.*

Dear ones, I shall take my leave from you, but I remind you that I AM very happy to come forward for more discourse upon this topic.

Response: *Thank you.*

I AM a being a Violet Fire,
Cleansed in the sanctity of God's desires!
Almighty I AM.
Almighty I AM.
Almighty I AM,
Saint Germain.

Response: *Hitaka.*

Epilogue

Our spiritual pilgrimage to the Heart of the Dove was completed during the time frame that Saint Germain had suggested, and in typical Ascended Master fashion, it was achieved with the Mastery that comes through spiritual practice, the order of the Divine Heavens, the devotion of both chelas and initiates, and of course a last minute dash of the miraculous.

Before we had a chance to transcribe this work, Len and I listened and relistened to the recorded lessons from the Master Teachers to begin to understand the detailed instruction on the Group Mind. This was especially important as it pertained to Saint Germain's request to travel to the Heart of the Dove—a spiritual journey suggested to assist the Ascended Masters' continued support and spiritual aid for humanity's personal liberty and freedom.

If you are not familiar with Ascended Master requests for specific spiritual journeys or pilgrimages, these trips are quite common in Eastern Spirituality and in Mystery Schools. Master Teachers recognize and know that they are limited to how much they can help or intervene for various physical and spiritual causes. This is because they, too, acknowledge and understand the karmic laws of spiritual growth, and they cannot and will not interfere with our free will or choice. These great ones are also familiar with another eminent law that must be heeded when assisting humanity's spiritual development and evolution: the knowledge of *energy-for-energy*.

Energy-for-energy is the metaphysical premise that in order for a person to fully comprehend and appreciate spiritual knowledge, the soul-freeing wisdom must not be spoon-fed. It is the notion that an equal effort by the student, aspirant, or chela must match the energy dispensed by the Master Teacher. In channeling sessions this is sometimes referred to as the *Law of Reciprocity*—or, in the Bible, "Give, and it will be given unto you." Those sitting for a trance session make an effort to raise their energy, and often do so through the vibration of song or decree, as the spiritual teacher lowers their energy for the teaching. This example of energy-for-energy maintains karmic balance and assures that spiritual growth is both structured and exponential.

If you are familiar with the Ascended Masters' service for humanity, you may understand that there are many forms of assistance that they readily give that may not be specifically educative in nature. For example, some Ascended Beings radiate vital, evolutionary energies to Earth that in turn assist our spiritual development and evolution. These energies may activate and empower consciousness or light grids, heal or protect our Earth at levels that we are not yet aware of, or help to change, mold, or empower societies and culture in ways that benefit the whole of humanity. Sometimes Ascended Beings and Masters can achieve this without our interaction. However, more often than not, the law of energy-for-energy must be followed and a physical human interface is required. In these types of activities Ascended Beings often work at a spiritual level with selected chelas and initiates to intentionally step-down frequencies, energies, and activities to the Earth Plane. This allows the spiritual plan of the Master Teachers to quickly reach fruition in the physical plane, especially with those strategies designed to assist humanity.

Undoubtedly, this was the case concerning the spiritual pilgrimage to the Heart of the Dove. Certainly, there would need to be some workarounds as my students had not yet learned about Group Mind. This would also include them working remotely with one another, as each of them would be assigned to certain Golden City Stars. So training and practice was imperative. We were also given the specific guideline of the *Indigo Cloak*. This is Ascended Master code for, "keep this as private as possible." Announcing this to our list was out, as it seemed that this particular mission was intended for advanced chelas only.

Apparently, Saint Germain considered this energetic infusion from the Hierarchy of Light to be important for North America, and specifically for the United States. During the last ten years, many of the *I AM America* prophecies shared by him and other Spiritual Teachers were rapidly beginning to manifest. Fortunately the more drastic Earth Changes seemed to be held back, or hopefully were somewhat ameliorated by the presence of the Golden Cities. Yet, the underbelly of our culture is polarized and every day this division is becoming increasingly angry and perilous. The Masters' intervention promised that the restorative, empowering energy of liberty would once again alight in America, and this power could readily carry healing energy throughout the world. If there was ever a time that our country and our world could use the light of healing, it was now. Could our presence in the light and energy calibrating center of Earth, the Heart of the Dove, in some small way assist this great cause? Surely, we must try.

After listening to Saint Germain's instructions over and over, Len and I both made the decision that the audio recordings would need to be released to the students so they could hear this instruction in its authentic form. We knew this would be a different dynamic for the students as the bulk of their study was primarily through discussion groups based on published materials. Now, they would be receiving both the information and the *shatki* of the channeled session—the vital energy released in a trance session that cannot be conveyed in a transcript.

The students readily organized weekly calls to discuss the new audios and each lesson's accompanying spiritual exercises. In two months, it appeared that they were beginning to grasp the technique and their first attempts in achieving Group Mind were successful. I had researched the Vedic Stars and found both the eclipses and stellium that Saint Germain had referred to, and chose the date of Monday, July 15th for our event at the Heart of the Dove. Overall the stars were difficult; but the Moon was somewhat benefic that day, in a Laksmi's Blessing configuration with Venus, and Jupiter would cast a benefic aspect to both Mercury and Mars. It was also important to remember that while the Astrology was perhaps not the best for humans, Spiritual Masters often use very trying energies and potentiate them for great good. Paramahansa Yogananda conveyed this important precept when he stated, "Seeds of past karma cannot germinate when roasted in the fires of Divine Wisdom."

I had spent weeks poring over topographical maps of Kansas and Missouri. According to the *I AM America Map*, the Heart of the Dove had been placed north and slightly west of Kansas City, Kansas. This location was identified by the Avatar Babaji. He claimed that an intergalactic portal exists there, and though not a Golden City, this location was an umbilicus connection between Mother Earth and our Creator Galaxy. Because of this, the area could experience time anomalies and in the future it is prophesied that this is where seamless travel between other galaxies is possible. More importantly, this area represents a central creation focus for our Earth, and the Masters claim it to be pure, untainted, and uniquely restorative. Babaji, the immortal birthless and deathless Avatar, asked that a symbolic heart be placed on the *I AM America Map* to mark its location and he claimed, "This is where my heart is." His prophetic words are mystical, metaphoric, and literal.

Years ago Saint Germain described the energetic movement of this portal like the, "wings of a dove in flight." Small towns with names like *Hiawatha* and *Seneca* were in the possible span of the Dove's massive wings, yet I searched for something unique, either in landform or by human definition. Throughout the years of hunting for Adjutant Points I learned that more often than not, these interdimensional points often include some nearby public park. This, of course, is the Divine Plan of the Ascended Masters, who undeniably aspire for each Golden City Adjutant Point to be utilized by humanity at every possible level: spiritually, mentally, and physically. I recalled that a student who had recently traveled to the area had mentioned a beautiful park for meditation, the *International Forest of Friendship* located in Atchison, Kansas.

Nestled among the rolling hills of northeast Kansas, the park was a bicentennial gift to America, comprising trees from every state and thirty-six countries. Interestingly, the park is dedicated to a theme of world and space

Golden Cites & the Masters of Shamballa

"friendship and flight," in perfect alignment with the Ascended Masters' provenance of the time portal and galactic travel. Surely, this is the location. We immediately purchased airfare, and made arrangements for our trip. All of the students made arrangements to travel to their respective Golden City Stars for our July 15th convergence in Group Mind.

Two weeks before our trip, Len noticed a rash forming on his neck. It first appeared as a bad sunburn, but since he had been outside for several days repairing a fence on our property, we thought nothing of it. Two days later, we took notice—he had developed a full-blown case of shingles, and was experiencing severe pain. We had no choice but to cancel plans for our trip and wait for Len to heal. Care packages from friends and students arrived in the mail: high potency essential oils for pain, healing ointments, and bags of dried chaga wildcrafted mushrooms for tea to clear the virus. Fortunately in about ten days, he was feeling a bit better, though heartbroken that we had cancelled our trip. I assured him that we could still easily access the Heart of the Dove through performing the Group Mind in a Golden City Star. In fact, I had already made arrangements with the students to remotely meet us at *Wenima*, our land in the Star of Gobean. "Besides," I firmly added, "if the Masters want us there, they will make it very clear we are to be there." Three days before July 15th, an ample donation arrived in the mail. We needed no more prompting and unequivocally knew we were to be there. Within hours we were packed and driving to Kansas.

After nearly three days on the road, we left the interstate near Topeka, and drove northeast. Within ten miles from Atchison, I could feel the subtle, yet gentle, whirling energy. Not the tornadic pull that one feels when entering a Golden City Vortex, but a steady, almost pulsing arc with each wave of the massive wings of the Dove in flight. As we entered into Atchison, we easily located the park and drove into the parking lot. I grabbed a few items, slung my shofar across my shoulder, and walked up a paved pathway to the park's eight-sided gazebo.

Sitting calmly and patiently waiting for us was Joan, the one member from our small group who had decided to not cancel the trip. "I feel I need to be there," she assured me on the phone before her departure. She had been studying with me for several years, and though I felt assured that she could handle the energies of our Group Mind, she was genuinely happy to see the two of us. The three of us sat together and centered our energies. Five minutes before our Group Mind would converge, I blew the shofar. The shofar is the ancient Hebraic musical horn used in many religious and spiritual ceremonies. It is claimed to carry the alchemic sound that opens God's heavenly portals to stream their transcendent energies to Earth. The shofar had been given to me by my friend Susan Hall, who owned one that sat as a centerpiece on her coffee table. During a visit I picked it up and placed it to my lips. My school days' trumpet ability magically rekindled, I blew a majestic tone that filled her living room. "No one's been able to play that!" she exclaimed. A month later, she presented me with my own, beautiful, smoothly curved shofar. I have since used this on many spiritual journeys, and especially when visiting Golden City Adjutant Points. I've learned its traditional, mystical sound that is described in the Old Testament: the *Shevarim*, composed of three connected sounds; the *Teruah*, a series of nine short notes, played almost staccato; and the *Tekiah* which mirrors the above sounds, only played a bit slower and producing longer notes. As the shofar resounded throughout the park, one could literally feel the Nature Devas of the trees respond, and the Elemental Kingdom awaken.

We seamlessly entered into the Group Mind, and our large golden orb of light descended into the park. Upon its landing, a column of golden light appeared, literally bridging heaven and Earth. Emerging through the light I first saw Beloved Babaji, who walked alongside Divine Mother. Divine Mother presented herself as a glorious being with dark eyes and hair, a generous smile, and she was dressed in pinks and corals. Then dozens of Spiritual Masters began to appear in the park, and before long literally hundreds of them manifested. I recognized each of the fifty-one Hierarchs of the Golden Cities and saw many more that I did not know. Each was attired in their finest seamless garments, beautiful cloaks and long gowns, tailored suits and saris, with many wearing the traditional dress of the world's religions and spiritual traditions. Saint Germain carried a silver, jewel-encrusted sword at his side, and he escorted Portia, clad in an ethereal lavender gown. The brothers El Morya and Kuthumi were both present. El Morya wore his customary turban with a large, blue sapphire affixed to the middle. Kuthumi presented in humbler fashion, yet wore a large rosary that featured a Christian Cross fashioned of gold and red rubies. The great beings of light manifested through all of the beautiful and stunning Seven Rays of Light and Sound until the entire park was packed to its outer edges. The light was almost overpowering, yet I viewed it in awe and fascination. As I emerged out of meditation, I noticed that a butterfly had landed between my palms, sitting so quietly I could almost feel its pulse. My gentle movement stirred her, and she took flight. More than twenty minutes had passed in what had seemed like a mere five minutes!

For about a half hour I strolled through the park, partially exploring but mostly basking in the refined, spiritual energy emanating from the heavenly event. To the west of the gazebo, I crossed a stream and entered into a forest and immediately felt the presence of Babaji. Locating a perfect, yet somewhat obscure location in Babaji's Forest, Len, Joan, and I joined together in a Cup Ceremony and offered Babajeran a devotional drink of water. After the ceremony, we gifted Joan with a Cup. She is now our official Cup Bearer for the *Heart of the Dove*.

After our ceremony, Joan and I leisurely walked back to the gazebo to take a few pictures. Since Atchison, Kansas, was the birthplace of Amelia Earhart, a bronze statue of her image stands just slightly east to the gazebo. On the base of the statue a familiar passage is engraved, "Let there be peace on Earth, and let it begin with me." We walked a bit further to the *Moon Tree* that stands next to where the celestial column of light streamed. We were dismayed to discover a monument placed at the foot of the tree, with the engraving, "To the Stars through difficulties." I immediately thought of the students who had diligently traveled to the Golden City Stars and our now cumulative journey of thousands of miles to assist the Masters' Divine Mission of liberty.

In Latin, the popular phrase to the stars reads, *Per aspera ad astra*, but in simpler, everyday terms it means, "nothing worthwhile is ever achieved without effort."

Babaji's Meditation Forest
International Forest of Friendship. Atchison, Kansas.

The Moon Tree
(Above) Up the Moon Tree at the International Forest of
Friendship. Atchison, Kansas. (Right) A marker beneath
the Moon Tree, inscribed: *To the stars through difficulties.*

Lilac Irises
Claude Monet, 1914-1917

Author's Acknowledgment

I would like to thank Rosalie Mashtalier for her numerous contributions to this work that assisted *Golden Cities and the Masters of Shamballa*'s manifestion to our physical plane. Rosalie spent months transcribing the original channeled tapes that now comprise the lessons of this book. She assisted at important junctures during the reception of this material, and supplied the much needed and updated recording equipment for the channeled sessions. She was always ready to lend a helping hand during our spiritual journeys together and handled many small but essential tasks, like carrying my shofar through airport security, driving on rural Arizona backroads during a snowstorm while I mapped out yet another hidden Adjutant Point, and arriving at our home with a Costco mountain of groceries that literally filled my frig for weeks. Above all, I thank her for her friendship and the willingness to help and support my work with *I AM America*. This reflects her unfailing love and devotion to the Dear ones, our beloved mentors, friends, and gurus—the Ascended Masters.

Sunset at Giverny
Claude Monet, 1886.

Spiritual Lineage of the Violet Flame

The teachings of the Violet Flame, as taught in the work of I AM America, come through the Goddess of Compassion and Mercy Kuan Yin. She holds the feminine aspects of the flame, which are Compassion, Mercy, Forgiveness, and Peace. Her work with the Violet Flame is well documented in the history of Ascended Master teachings, and it is said that the altar of the etheric Temple of Mercy holds the flame in a Lotus Cup. She became Saint Germain's teacher of the Sacred Fire in the inner realms, and he carried the masculine aspect of the flame into human activity through Purification, Alchemy, and Transmutation. One of the best means to attract the beneficent activities of the Violet Flame is through the use of decrees and invocation. However, you can meditate on the flame, visualize the flame, and receive its transmuting energies like "the light of a thousand Suns," radiant and vibrant as the first day that the Elohim Arcturus and Diana drew it forth from our solar Sun at the creation of the Earth. Whatever form, each time you use the Violet Flame, these two Master Teachers hold you in the loving arms of its action and power.

The following is an invocation for the Violet Flame to be used at sunrise or sunset. It is utilized while experiencing the visible change of night to day, and day to night. In fact, if you observe the horizon at these times, you will witness light transitioning from pinks to blues, and then a subtle violet strip adorning the sky. We have used this invocation for years in varying scenes and circumstances, overlooking lakes, rivers, mountaintops, deserts, and prairies; in huddled traffic and busy streets; with groups of students or sitting with a friend; but more commonly alone in our home or office, with a glint of soft light streaming from a window. The result is always the same: a calm, centering force of stillness. We call it the Space.

Invocation of the Violet Flame for Sunrise and Sunset
I invoke the Violet Flame to come forth in the name of I AM that I AM,
To the Creative Force of all the realms of all the Universes, the Alpha, the Omega, the Beginning, and the End,
To the Great Cosmic Beings and Torch Bearers of all the realms of all the Universes,
And the Brotherhoods and Sisterhoods of Breath, Sound, and Light, who honor this Violet Flame that comes forth from the Ray of Divine Love—the Pink Ray, and the Ray of Divine Will—the Blue Ray of all Eternal Truths.

I invoke the Violet Flame to come forth in the name of I AM that I AM! Mighty Violet Flame, stream forth from the Heart of the Central Logos, the Mighty Great Central Sun! Stream in, through, and around me.

(Then insert other prayers and/or decrees for the Violet Flame.)

Awakening Prayer

Great Light of Divine Wisdom,

Stream forth to my being,

And through your right use

Let me serve mankind and the planet.

Love, from the Heart of God.

Radiate my being with the presence of the Christ

That I walk the path of truth.

Great Source of Creation,

Empower my being,

My Brother,

My Sister,

And my planet with perfection

As we collectively awaken as one cell.

I call forth the Cellular Awakening.

Let wisdom, love, and power stream forth to this cell,

This cell that we all share.

Great Spark of Creation awaken

the Divine Plan of Perfection.

So we may share the ONE perfected cell,

I AM.

Study for the Pilgrim of the World on His Journey
Thomas Cole, 1848.

The Golden City Hierarchs of the Shamballa Lineage

ADJATAL
Lord Himalaya

This Golden City of the Blue and Gold Rays is overseen by Lord Himalaya, *right*, and promotes Spiritual Awakening. The Golden City of Adjatal is located in Pakistan, Afghanistan, and India; the historical Khyber Pass (the ancient Silk Road) is located on the western side of this Vortex city. Adjatal is a twin to the Golden City of Zaskar. Adjatal means, *The Big Rainbow*, and derives its meaning from the Suabo-Indonesian word *adja* ("big") and the Pashto-Pakistanian word *tal* ("rainbow").

AFROM
Elohim of Purity: Claire
Goddess SeRaya, the White Buddha

A Golden City of the White Ray that is located mainly in Hungary and Romania. Its stewards are Claire—the Elohim of Purity, (also known as *Svarog*, a form of Apollo), along with the Goddess SeRaya, also known as the *White Buddha*. (Both, pictured right.) Afrom assists Earth's Ascension through the spiritual attribute of purity. This Golden City name means, "A Devotion." This meaning originates with the word *from*, which in German, Norwegian, and Swedish means "pious" or "devoted." The Ascended Masters claim this Golden City also means "to affirm."

AMERIGO
Godfre

Ascended Master Godfre serves in this Golden City, located in Spain. Amerigo facilitates the spiritual ideal of, "God in All," through its alignment to the Gold Ray. This European Golden City is Spanish for "I AM Race." (Godfre pictured left with Saint Germain.)

ANDEO
Archeia Constance & Goddess Meru

The thirtieth Golden City located in Peru, Columbia, and Brazil, South America. Its qualities are consistency; its Ray Force is Pink and Gold; and its Master Teachers are the Goddesses Meru and Constance. The Golden City of Andeo is also known as the *City of the Feminine.*

The Golden City of the South American Andes is likely named for this mountain range; however, the source of this Golden City of the Feminine is rooted in the Albanian word *anda*, which means "strong desire," and the Huli (New Guinea) word *andia*, which means "mother." Andeo's meaning translates into this phrase: "the Mother of Desire." (Beloved Constance, above left, Goddess Meru pictured, left, with Lord Meru.)

ANGELICA
Elohim Angelica

The Golden City of Angelica is guided by the Elohim Angelica and is affiliated with the Pink Ray. It is located in Queensland, Australia, and is paired to the Golden City of Clayje. The Native American Algonquian word *ca* means "at present" or "present"; therefore, Angelica's full meaning is "Angel Present," or "Angels at Present." (Angelica pictured right, with the Elohim Orion.)

ARCTURA
Elohim Arcturus & Diana

The thirty-seventh Golden City is located in China. Arctura's stewards are the twin Elohim Arcturus and Diana of the Violet Ray. This Golden City is associated with freedom, precipitation, and the rhythm of universal harmony.

Arctura means "the brightest," and is named after the planet Arcturus. (Elohim Arcturus and Diana, pictured right.)

ARKANA
Archangel Gabriel

This Golden City is overseen by Archangel Gabriel, *right*, of the White Ray. Located in East Siberia, Russia, this sacred Vortex radiates and transfigures the HU-man for Ascension. The nineteenth-century language of peace—Esperanto, and the Polish language both state that the word *arkana* means "Mystery."

217

ASONEA
Peter the Everlasting

The Twelfth Golden City of the Americas is located in Cuba. Its qualities are Alignment and Regeneration; its Ray Force is Yellow; and its Master Teacher is Peter the Everlasting, *left*. This Golden City of ancient Atlantis derives its meaning from the pristine Ason River of the Cantabria province in Spain and its mythological race of supernatural undines—the *Xanas*.

BRAHAM
Goddess Yemanya

The fourteenth Golden City of the Americas is located in Brazil, South America. Its quality is nurturing; its Ray Force is Pink; and its Master Teacher is the Goddess Braham or Yemanya, progenitor of the New Manu. Braham literally means *the nurturer* and this Golden City is the second of the Three Golden City Sisters of South America. Braham is the feminine version of *Brahma*, and this Golden City meaning is the "Mother of the New Manu." (Goddess Yemanya, pictured above left.)

BRAUN
Mighty Victory

Mighty Victory overshadows and radiates the Yellow Ray of glory and achievement in this Vortex. The fifteenth Golden City is located in Germany, Austria, and the Czech Republic. Braun means, "the shining, strong one." (Mighty Victory, pictured right.)

CLAYJE
Elohim of Divine Love: Orion

This is known as the *Golden City of Many Planets* through its divine quality of Universal Oneness. Clayje is the forty-seventh Vortex and is associated with the Elohim of Divine Love—Orion, and the Pink Ray. Clayje covers the entire island of Tasmania in Australia, and is a Twin Golden City to Angelica.

Dialects from the Netherlands create this Golden City's name through the word *kla*—"clear." The word *je* in Bosnian, Croatian, Serbian, and Slovak languages means "is." The combination of these words constructs this Australian Golden City's meaning: "Is Clear." (Orion is pictured with Elohim Angelica and the Golden City of Angelica.)

CRESTA
Archangel Crystiel

The fifty-first and final Golden City to be activated serves the uplifting and evolutionary Gold and Aquamarine Rays. Beloved Archangel Crystiel is the hierarch of this sublime Vortex of eternal protection, healing, and clarity for humanity, located in Antarctica on Eternity Range. In Spanish, Italian, and Brazilian Portuguese the word *cresta* means "the ridge or peak."

CROTESE
Master Paul

The sixteenth Golden City of the Americas is located in the Heartland countries of Costa Rica and Panama, Central America. This Golden City's qualities are divinity and the Heart of Love; its Ray Force is Pink; and the resident Master Teacher is Paul, *left*. This Golden City means "the Attentive Cradle." Its meaning is derived from the French *cro*—"cradle," and the Etruscan *tes*—"to care for or pay attention."

DENASHA
Lady Master Nada

The Golden City of Denasha is primarily located over Scotland, and the Ascended Masters assert this Vortex holds the energies of Divine Justice for all of humanity. Denasha the Sister Golden City to Malton (Illinois and Indiana, USA) and both Vortices mutually distribute energies to the Nature and Elemental Kingdoms throughout the New Times. The Master Teacher is Lady Nada, and the Ray Force is Yellow. This Golden City derives its meaning from the modern English name *Denesa*, which means the "Mountain of Zeus." This mythological Greek father of both Gods and men is also known in Roman myths as Jupiter, an ideal symbol for this European Golden City of the Yellow Ray. (Lady Nada, pictured above.)

DONJAKEY
Elohim Pacifica

This Golden City currently presides over the Pacific Ocean and the prophesied new lands that rise in the New Times—*New Lemuria*. The Elohim Pacifica, *right*, guards and protects this Golden City of both the Gold and Aquamarine Rays. This Golden City's name comes from the Italian word *don*—"gift," and the Indonesian word *key*—"tree." Donjakey means "Gift of Trees," and is associated with new species of flora prophesied to appear on Earth in the New Times.

EABRA
Lady Portia

The seventh Golden City is located in Canada in the Yukon and Northwest Territories. Its qualities are joy, balance, and equality; its Ray Force is Violet; and its Master Teacher is Portia. (Lady Portia pictured right.) Eabra means "The Feminine in Eternal Balance." This name is a derivative of several words, namely *bra* or *bodice*, which means "the pair" or the "wearing of pairs." *Ea* has several meanings: in Frisian (German) *ea* means "ever," in Romanian *ea* means "she." The word *pair* numerically indicates two, a number associated with femininity and balance. Eabra's twin Golden City is Wahanee, located in the United States.

FRON
Beloved Desiree

Beloved Desiree, *right*, of the Blue Ray guides and overlights this Golden City located in Western Australia. This Vortex is fiftieth in the activation pattern, and assists aspirants, chelas, and developing HU-mans to spiritually focus upon their inner balance. The meaning of this Australian Golden City is "throne" in Albanian. In the Creole language, *fron* means "pious" and "devoted." The combination of these definitions creates Fron's meaning: "the Devoted Throne."

GANAKRA

Elohim Vista

The seventeenth Golden City is located in Turkey and is overseen by the Elohim Vista of the Green Ray. Ganakra is known as the "All Seeing City," and is affiliated with the qualities of Divine Focus and concentration. The ancient Turkish City of Ankara means "anchor" in Greek; in Portuguese *gana* means "desire"; and *kra* is a Creole word for "mind." Ganakra's combined meaning is "Desires Anchored by the Mind," or "Desires of the Mind." (Vista, pictured left.)

GANDAWAN

Master Kuthumi

The Ascended Master Kuthumi oversees the Golden City of Gandawan, also identified as the *Infinite Garden.* This Golden City of the Ruby and Gold Rays is located in Africa. (Kuthumi, pictured left.) From the Sanskrit word *Gondwanaland* means "Forest of the Gonds." Located over the Sahara Desert, this Golden City represents this ancient culture that claimed to survive in present-day India. Contemporary Gond legends mirror the emergence stories of Southwest Native American tribes, and the Gond Gods surfaced from a cave and were adopted by the Hindu Goddess Parvati (Divine Mother) and were assisted by their tribal Goddess Jangu Bai. According to myth, the Gonds emerged from their cave in four distinct groups.

GOBEAN
Master El Morya

The first United States Golden City located in the states of Arizona and New Mexico. Its qualities are cooperation, harmony, and peace; its Ray Force is Blue; and its Master Teacher is El Morya, *right.* The Ascended Masters claim Earth's first Golden City for the New Times means to "go beyond." However, Gobean's etymology suggests the meaning: "Go Pray." This phrase is derived from the word *bea* or *be,* which in Frisian (German) and Norwegian means "prayer." Gobean receives vital energies from the Golden City of Gobi, *see below.* El Morya's Golden City of the Blue Ray is a Twin Golden City to Fron, located in Australia and overseen by Lady Master Desiree.

GOBI
Archangel Uriel & Lord Meru

Steps-down the energies of Shamballa into the entire Golden City Network. This Golden City is located in the Gobi Desert. It is known as the City of Balance; its Master Teachers are Lord Meru and Archangel Uriel. (Pictured right, Archangel Uriel; below, Lord Meru.) Named for the Great Desert of China, Gobi in Mongolian means "the waterless place." Ascended Masters claim the Golden City of Gobi is a Step-down transformer for the energies of Earth's first Golden City—Shamballa. Gobi's esoteric definition comes from the Chinese translation of "go—across," and *bi* in Indonesian (Abun, A Nden, and Yimbun dialects) means "star." The Golden City of Gobi means "Across the Star," or "Across the Freedom Star." ("Freedom Star" is a reference to Earth in her enlightened state.) Gobi aligns energies to the first Golden City of the New Times: Gobean.

GREIN
Lady Master Viseria

Viseria, the Goddess of the Stars and Divine Compliment to Soltec serves in Grein, the Golden City of New Zealand's South Island. The Vortex radiates the energies of the Green Ray and is associated with Divine Consecration, and service to humanity's upliftment through scientific development. *Grein* is an Icelandic, Norwegian, and Swedish word which means "branch." The Ascended Masters maintain that the New Zealand Golden City of Grein means "the Green Branch"—a symbol of the peaceful olive branch. (Viseria, pictured above.) The Golden City of Grein is a Twin Golden City to Pashacino, a Canadian Golden City overseen by Soltech.

GRUECHA
Elohim Hercules

Gruecha is Norway and Sweden's Golden City of the Blue Ray. The Elohim Hercules serves in this sacred refuge, and its qualities produce spiritual strength through the principle of truth. This Golden City name is a Norwegian word and means "Hearth." (Hercules, pictured left.) Hercules is also a Solar Being, and is one of the Galactic Suns who serves with his divine counterpart, Amazonia, (also known as Amazon). The Golden City of Gruecha is a Twin Golden City to Stienta, located over Iceland.

HUE
Lord Gautama

This Golden City is also known as the *City of Many Spiritual Paths*, and is aligned with the Violet Ray. Hue's steward is Lord Gautama and its sacred quality is earnestness. It is located in Siberia, Russia. According to the Ascended Masters, the word *hue* invokes the Sacred Fire, the Violet Flame. In Tibetan dialects, however, the word *hue* or *hu* means "breath." (Pictured above, Lord Gautama.)

JEAFRAY
Archangel Zadkiel & Holy Amethyst

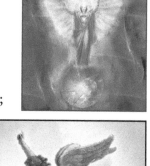

The eighth Golden City is located in Quebec, Labrador, and Newfoundland, Canada. Its qualities are stillness and the celebration of the Violet Flame; its Ray Force is Violet; and its Master Teachers are Archangel Zadkiel and Holy Amethyst, *both right*. The Golden City of the Ever Present Violet Flame meaning's translates to "Yesterday's Brother." This is based on the Gaelic word *jea*, which means "yesterday"; the word *fra* is English for "Brother" (friar). Since Archangel Zadkiel and the Archeia Holy Amethyst serve in this Vortex retreat, "Yesterday's Brother" is a reference to the work

of Saint Germain—as Sanctus Germanus (the Holy Brother)—and the many other archetypes of consciousness who tirelessly work for humanity's freedom and Ascension through the use of the transmuting fire.

JEHOA
Kuan Yin

The seventeenth Golden City of the Americas (I AM America) is prophesied to appear over new lands that rise in the Time of Change. The Golden City of Jehoa is located over the Lesser Antilles Islands of: Guadeloupe, Dominica, Martinique, Saint Lucia, Barbados, and Grenada. Its qualities are compassion, acts of love, and gratitude; its Ray Force is Violet; and its Master Teacher is Kuan Yin, *left*. It may be that this Golden City's name is based upon the Tetragrammaton YHWH; however, the etymology of this sacred haven of the Caribbean is based on the Russian word *YA*—meaning "I AM"—and *hoa*, which means "friend," from the Tahitian, Hawaiian, Maori, and Rapa Nui (Easter Island) languages. This translation elevates the various interpretations of Jehovah, the jealous God, into the uplifting phrase, "I AM Friend."

KANTAN
Divine Mother & Archangel Raphael

This Golden City is located in Russia and China and serves the Green Ray. It is affiliated with spiritual regeneration, dedication and assimilation of the Divine Feminine. Archangel Raphael, *pictured left*, and Divine Mother serve this Golden City. This fortieth Golden City of China and Russia derives its name from the English (Cornish) word *kan*—which means "song," and the Korean word *tan*, meaning "sweet." The full meaning of this spiritual Vortex is the "Sweet Song."

KLEHMA
Serapis Bey

The fifth United States Golden City is located primarily in the states of Colorado, Kansas, and Nebraska. Its qualities are continuity, balance, and harmony; its Ray Force is White; and its Master Teacher is Serapis Bey, *pictured right.* The meaning of the fifth Golden City of the United States is based on several Native American words. The first syllable *kle* (pronounced clay) comes from the Navajo word *klê-kai*—which means "white." The second syllable *ma*, is a derivative of the Shoshoni word *mahoi*—around, or encircling. Klehma's esoteric definition is the "Circle of White."

KRESHE
Lady Amaryllis & Lord of Nature

This Golden City is overseen by the Lord of Nature and Lady Amaryllis—the Goddess of Spring. Kreshe is associated with the Ruby and Gold Rays and is located Botswana, Namibia, Angola, and Zambia. Kreshe is in perpetual service to elemental life. This African Golden City is known to the Ascended Masters as the "Silent Star," an esoteric reference to Venus. *Kres* is also a Celtic word for "peace." (Above right, Lady Amaryllis; right, Lord of Nature.)

LARAITO
Lord Lanto & Lara

Beloved Lord Lanto, and the Goddess Lara—a form of the Buddhist Goddess Tara, *Lanto pictured left and Lara below,* share their Divine Service in this Golden City of the Yellow Ray. This sacred Vortex is located in Ethiopia and is affiliated with spiritual understanding and illumination. This Golden City's meaning is "Our Home." Laraito's definition comes from the Brazilian, Portuguese, and Spanish word for home—*lar. Ito* is a Tanzanian word for "ours."

MALTON
Master Kuthumi

The second United States Golden City is located in the states of Illinois and Indiana. Its qualities are fruition and attainment; its Ray Force is Gold and Ruby; and its Master Teacher is Kuthumi, *left.* The Ascended Master Kuthumi's Golden City meaning is derived from the Phoenician word *maleth*—which means "a haven."

MARNERO

Mother Mary

The eleventh Golden City of the Americas is located in Mexico. Marnero means *virtue*; its Ray Force is Green; and its Master Teacher is Mother Mary, *right*. The first syllable of Marnero—*mar*—is a Spanish, Italian, and Portuguese word which means "sea" or "ocean." The remainder of the name—*nero* translates into *ner*, a Hebrew word for "candle." The Golden City of Marnero's meaning is the "Ocean of Candles."

MESOTAMP

Mohammed

The eighteenth Golden City is overseen by Mohammed and the Yellow Ray. This sacred site radiates spiritual happiness for humanity. The Golden City of Turkey, Iran, and Iraq is likely linked to the ancient word *Mesopotamia*, which means the "land between rivers." The higher meaning of *Mesotamp*, however, is linked to the New Guinea word *meso*—"moon," and the Turkmen word, *tam*—"house." Mesotamp's meaning translates into the "House of the Moon." (Pictured right, *The Ascent of Muhammed to Heaven*.)

MOUSEE

Kona

This Golden City is located in the Pacific Ocean, northwest of the Hawaiian Island of Kauai. Mousee is served by the Ascended Master Kona, *left*, and the Gold and Aquamarine Rays. Mousee's attribute is "the eye of spiritual fire," and assists Earth's aquatic beings to instigate or achieve Ascension. This Golden City for the New Times means the "Ocean of Fish." This spiritual haven, prophesied to appear near Hawaii, combines the New Guinea word *mou*—"fish," and the Afrikaan word *see*—"sea" or "ocean." New flora and fauna is prophesied to appear as Earth enters the New Times.

NOMAKING

Minerva & Cassiopeia

Located in China, this Golden City of the Yellow Ray is overseen by Cassiopeia, the Elohim of Wisdom, and Minerva, the Goddess of Wisdom. This is the thirty-eighth Golden City in activation and is affiliated with the spiritual qualities of wisdom, illumination, the power of attention, and perception. (Pictured above left, Goddess Yum Chenmo, a form of Minerva; Cassiopeia; left.) This Chinese Golden City means "Name of the King." Its meaning is based on the word *noma* (or *nama*) and in many languages ranging from Italian to Sanskrit simply means "name."

PASHACINO
Soltech

The sixth Golden City is located in Alberta and British Columbia, Canada. Its quality serves as a *Bridge of Brotherhood* for all people; its Ray Force is Green; and its Master Teacher is Soltec, *right.* Pashacino means, "The Passionate Spirit." This Canadian Golden City's meaning is derived from the English word for "passion"—*pash*, and the Kurdish and Turkish word for "spirit"—*cin*. Pashacino is a Twin Golden City to Grein, the Golden City of New Zealand.

PEARLANU
Lady Master Lotus

Lady Master Lotus serves in the Golden City of Pearlanu, located on Madagascar. This is the twenty-fifth Golden City, is affiliated with the Violet Ray, and the transmuting quality of forgiveness. (Pictured right, Lady Master Lotus.) Madagascar's Golden City's meaning is based on the Malagasy (the national language of Madagascar) word *lanosina*, which means "to be swum in." Pearlanu's meaning translates to "Swimming in Pearls."

PRANA
Archangel Chamuel

The Golden City of India is overseen by its hierarch, Archangel Chamuel. It is affiliated with the Pink Ray and serves through adoration and the continuous heart. (Right, Archangel Chamuel.) Prana means, "life giving energy."

PRESCHING
Archangel Jophiel

Archangel Jophiel, *left*, of the Yellow Ray serves in this Golden City located in North Korea. It is the thirty-eighth sacred Vortex and is known as, "The City for the Angels." It is also associated with the enduring love of ordered service. This Chinese Golden City's meaning is linked to its topography. *Pres* is an English word which means "meadow," and *ching* is a Native American (Cahto) word for "timber and forest." Presching means the "City of Meadows, Grasslands, and Forests."

PURENSK
Faith, Hope, & Charity

The Divine Beings of Faith, Hope, and Charity serve the Blue, Yellow, and Pink Rays of the Unfed Flame in this twenty-first Golden City. Purensk radiates the spiritual gifts of Love, Wisdom, and Power. It is located in Russia and China. (Pictured left: Faith, Hope, and Charity.) This Golden City means "Pure Intelligence" or the "Pure Message." This Russian and Chinese Golden City derives its esoteric meaning from the Danish, English, German, and French name *pur*—"pure," and the Turkish word, *esk*, for "intelligence" or "message."

SHALAHAH
Lord Sananda

The fourth United States Golden
City is located primarily in the states
of Montana and Idaho. Its qualities
are abundance, prosperity, and healing;
its Ray Force is Green; and its Master
Teacher is Sananda, *right*. In Sanskrit,
Shalahah means a "Sacred Place
Indeed!" The syllables break down with
these meanings: *shala*—"sacred place",
"sanctuary"; *hah*—"indeed." Shalahah's
Twin Golden City is the Golden
City of Sheahah, located in Australia,
information below.

SHEAHAH
Elohim Astrea

Located in Australia, this Golden
City is the forty-ninth in the Golden
Cities activation series. Its steward
is the Elohim Astrea, *right*, the twin
force to the Elohim of Purity—
Claire. Sheahah is associated with the
White Ray and its spiritual qualities
are transmutation and purity. This Vortex is affiliated with the Golden City
of Shalahah, located in Idaho and Montana, United States. The Ascended
Masters claim that the meaning of this Australian Golden City is, "I AM as
ONE." The etymology of this Vortex meaning is undoubtedly related to the
Feminine Energies prophesied to dominate and direct the New Times. The
syllable *aha* in Tanzanian and Uganda means "here"; in Czechoslovakian *aha*
stands for "I see." Therefore Sheahah's hidden meaning is actually prophetic:
"She is here," or "She, I see."

SHEHEZ
Tranquility

Shehez's steward is Tranquility, the Elohim of Peace, and is the nineteenth Golden City. Located primarily in Iran and Afghanistan, this sacred site radiates the Ruby and Gold Ray. Its spiritual qualities are peace, serenity, and calm. (Pictured right, Tranquility—a form of the *Goddess of the Dawn*.) This Golden City located in Iran and Afghanistan is a Persian word that means "large," or "grand."

SIRCALWE
Group of Twelve

The Group of Twelve, also known as an ever-changing and anonymous group of Ascended Masters of Light, serve this Golden City of the White Ray. Located in East Siberia Russia, Sircalwe is known as the *Circle of Life*. The Russian Golden City of the White Ray derives its sacred name from the Turkish and Chinese languages—*sir*, which means "secret"; and the Elfish language of Middle Earth—*cal*, meaning "light." The word *we* in the English, Korean, and Italian language is defined as "ours." These languages combine to give this Golden City Vortex name its meaning: "Our Secret Light."

STIENTA
Archangel Michael

The eleventh Golden City of the Blue
Ray is served by Archangel Michael,
right, and is located in Iceland. It is
known as the *City of Inner Vision.* This
Golden City's name means "the path" in
Norwegian. The Golden City of Stienta
is a Twin Golden City to the Golden
City of Gruecha, located in Norway and
Sweden.

TEHEKOA
Pachamama

The fifteenth Golden City of the Americas is located in Argentina, South
America. Its quality is devotion; its Ray Force is Pink and Violet; and its
Master Teacher is Pachamama, *above,* the Third Sister of South America.
Since this Golden City represents one of the Three Sister Golden Cities of
South America, its meaning springs from the lost Moriori language and the
Hebrew word *Teku'a*: "the City of Tents," "secures the tents." These meanings
merge and Tehekoa means the "Wise Woman who Secures the City."

UNTE
Archeia Donna Grace

Known as the City of Grace, this Golden City is served by Donna Grace, the Archeia of the Ruby and Gold Rays. It is located Tanzania and Kenya and cultivates the spiritual principle of ministration and service to humanity. (Pictured left, Donna Grace.) This Golden City means in Brazilian, Spanish, and Portuguese "to anoint."

UVERNO
Paul the Venetian

This Canadian Golden City serves the Pink Ray. Also known as the *Song of God*, the Golden City Vortex is located primarily in Ontario, and Manitoba, Canada. Uverno is overseen by Paul the Venetian, *right*, an ascended being associated with music, art, and literature. This Canadian Golden City translates in Slovak to "trust well."

WAHANEE
Saint Germain

The third United States Golden City is located primarily in the states of South Carolina and Georgia. Its qualities are justice, liberty, and freedom; its Ray Force is Violet; and its Master Teacher is Saint Germain, *right*. This Golden City derives its name from *Wahabu*, the Nigerian name for the "God of Love." The etymological meaning of the final syllable *nee* in English, Italian, and French is "born." Wahanee's esoteric meaning is the "God of Love is born."

YUTHOR
Hilarion

The tenth Golden City is located in Greenland. Its quality is abundance of choice; its Ray Force is Green; and its Master Teacher is Hilarion, *right*. In minimalist language, *Yu* means "union." *Thor* is the Scandinavian God of Thunder— "Power." The Golden City of Greenland's hidden meaning is the "Power of Union."

ZASKAR
Reya

Located in Tibet, this Golden City is overseen by Lady Master Reya, *left*, a form of the Goddess Parvati. Zaskar radiates the energies of the White Ray and is affiliated with the guiding spiritual principle of simplicity. This Golden City of the White Ray derives its meaning from the Czech and Slovak word *zas*—"again," "over again"; and the Basque word *kar*, which means "flame." This Chinese Golden City means the "Repeating Flame."

HEART OF THE DOVE
Babaji

The *Heart of the Dove* is not a Golden City; however, this United States location plays an important role for humanity's spiritual development in the New Times. Also known as the *Center of Fire*, this energy anomaly is prophesied to exist Northwest of Kansas City, Kansas and Missouri. Master Teachings claim an umbilicus connection between Earth and the Galactic Center exists, creating time anomalies and the potential for time travel in the New Times. The *Heart of the Dove* is also prophesied to become a spiritual center for learning and self-actualizing the Christ Consciousness, and is sponsored by the immortal Avatar Babaji, *above*, who claims that, "This is where my heart is." Energies at the Heart of the Dove are restorative and rejuvenating.

Activations & Subtle Energies of the Golden Cities:

Golden City Vortices are activated in two-year periods during the New Times. Located in Arizona, Gobean, the first for the Time of Change, developed in the late 1970s and continued its growth into the early 1980s. Once the new energies began to flourish on Earth, the Ascended Masters, Archangels, and Elohim, in 1994, initiated a sequential, two-year awakening of the remaining Golden Cities throughout the world.

1. Gobean: 1970-1980s (United States)
2. Malton: 1994 (United States)
3. Wahanee: 1996 (United States)
4. Shalahah: 1998 (United States)
5. Klehma: 2000 (United States)
6. Pashachino: 2002 (Canada)
7. Eabra: 2004 (Canada)
8. Jeafray: 2006 (Canada)
9. Uverno: 2008 (Canada)
10. Yuthor: 2010 (Greenland)
11. Stienta: 2012 (Iceland)
12. Denasha: 2014 (Scotland)
13. Amerigo: 2016 (Spain)
14. Gruecha: 2018 (Norway, Sweden)
15. Braun: 2020 (Germany, Poland, Czechoslovakia)
16. Afrom: 2022 (Hungary, Romania)
17. Ganakra: 2024 (Turkey)
18. Mesotamp: 2026 (Iran, Iraq)
19. Shehez: 2028 (Iran, Afghanistan)
20. Adjatal: 2030 (Pakistan, Afghanistan)
21. Purensk: 2032 (Russia, China)
22. Prana: 2034 (India)
23. Gandawan: 2036 (Algeria)
24. Kreshe: 2038 (Botswana, Namibia)
25. Pearlanu: 2040 (Madagascar)
26. Unte: 2042 (Tanzania, Kenya)
27. Laraito: 2044 (Ethiopia)
28. Marnero: 2046 (Mexico)
29. Asonea: 2048 (Cuba)
30. Andeo: 2050 (Peru, Brazil)
31. Braham: 2052 (Brazil)
32. Tehekoa: 2054 (Argentina)
33. Crotese: 2056 (Costa Rica, Panama)
34. Jehoa: 2058 (Caribbean)

35. Zaskar: 2060 (Tibet)
36. Gobi: 2062 (Gobi Desert, China)
37. Arctura: 2064 (China)
38. Nomaking: 2066 (China)
39. Presching: 2068 (North Korea)
40. Kantan: 2070 (Russia, China)
41. Hue: 2072 (Siberia)
42. Sircalwe: 2074 (Russia)
43. Arkana: 2076 (East Siberia)
44. Mousee: 2078 (New Lemuria)
45. Donjakey: 2080 (New Lemuria)
46. Grein: 2082 (New Zealand)
47. Clayje: 2084 (Australia)
48. Angelica: 2086 (Australia)
49. Sheahah: 2088 (Australia)
50. Fron: 2090 (Australia)
51. Cresta: 2092 (Antarctica)

Shalahah Southern Door &
Adjutant Point Hierarchs

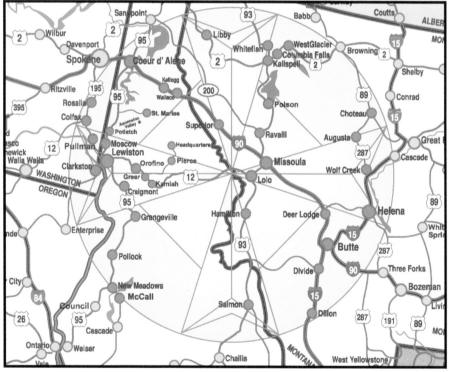

Golden City of Shalahah
I AM America Maps of the
Golden City of Shalahah.

Shalahah Southern (Red) Door

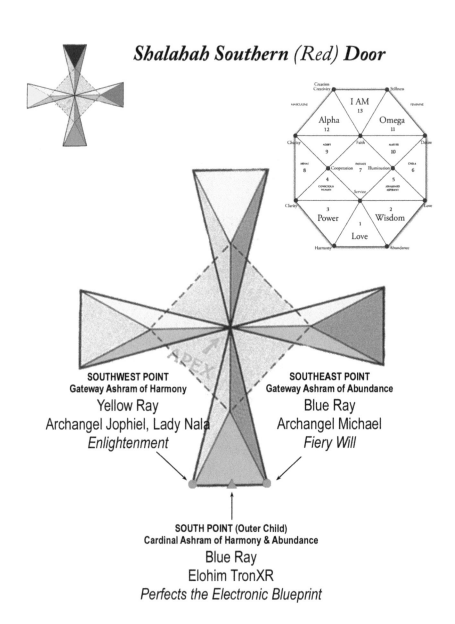

Golden City of Shalahah
Diagram of the Hierarchs of Shalahah's
Southern Door.

Adjutant Point Hierarchs

SHALAHAH GATEWAY TO HARMONY ASHRAM
Lady Master Nala

The current Hierarch of *Shalahah's Gateway to Harmony Ashram*. Lady Nala, *right*, serves the Yellow Ray and is a steadfast student of Lady Nada, and represents her Spiritual Lineage. Lady Nala serves alongside Archangel Jophiel at the Shalahah Harmony Point. The name "Nala" means *successful*. Lady Nala is an Ascended Master, and her Divine Counterpart is TronXR.

SHALAHAH SOUTH CARDINAL ASHRAM
Elohim TronXR

The Hierarch of *Shalahah's Cardinal Harmony and Abundance Ashram* is TronXR, *right*, who assists humanity to perfect the electronic blueprint of the human aura in preparation for the Ascension. "XR" means *excellence* in Latin. He serves on the Blue Ray, and his Divine Counterpart is Lady Nala of the Yellow Ray.

SHALAHAH GATEWAY TO ABUNDANCE ASHRAM
Archangel Michael

Archangel Michael is the current Hierarch of *Shalahah's Gateway to Abundance Ashram*. Archangel Michael's focus at this sublime Ashram represents the fiery Will of God and the Blue Ray. Archangel Michael, *right*, also serves as the Hierarch of Stienta, the Golden City of Iceland.

Spirit of the Night
John Atkinson Grimshaw, 1879. The Golden City of Malton's purpose is to
assist the Elemental and Deva Kingdom in their Ascension Process.

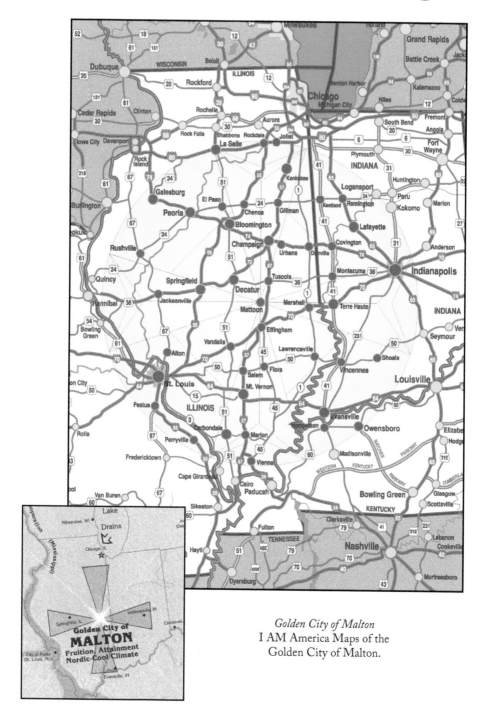

Golden City of Malton
I AM America Maps of the
Golden City of Malton.

Symbology of the I AM America Teachings through Malton's Southern (Red) Door

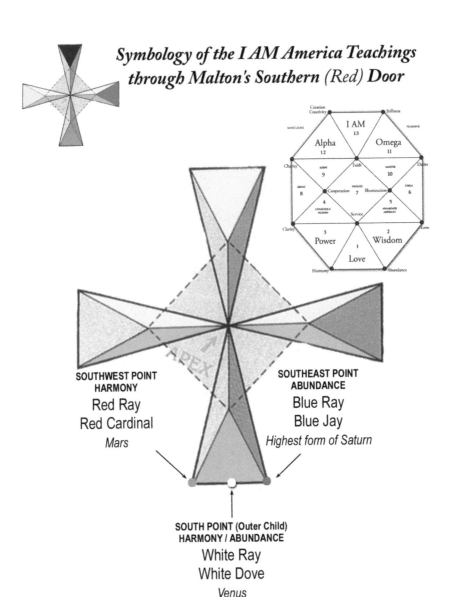

SOUTHWEST POINT
HARMONY
Red Ray
Red Cardinal
Mars

SOUTHEAST POINT
ABUNDANCE
Blue Ray
Blue Jay
Highest form of Saturn

SOUTH POINT (Outer Child)
HARMONY / ABUNDANCE
White Ray
White Dove
Venus

Symbology of Malton's Southern Adjutant Points
Golden City of Malton, Adjutant Points, and
Symbology of the I AM America Teachings.

Master Kuthumi shares the symbology for the I AM America Teachings as:

Red Cardinal or the Red Ray: The Red Ray is a Ray of devotion and determination—this is the energy of Mars in its higher, evolved state. This aspect of the Red Ray promotes Mastery over the kundalini and energy systems, producing energy healers and yogis. When the Red Ray is utilized at this level, it is often referred to as the *Spiritual Warrior.* The Red Cardinal is linked to Christianity and represents the vital faith that is necessary to realize the birth of Christ Consciousness. From an indigenous viewpoint, all birds are seen as messengers, and the Red Cardinal is an omen of good luck in relationships and healing.

Blue Jay or Blue Ray: The higher aspects of Saturn are reflected in the Blue Ray through detachment, earnestness, personal sovereignty, altruism, fidelity, loyalty to Guru, and selfless love of humanity. However, because Saturn is a taskmaster there will also be duty, selflessness, hard work, discipline, determination, and endurance. These characteristics of Saturn prepare the soul for the spiritual evolution found in Oneness, Oneship, and entrance into the ONE. The Blue Jay represents unyielding energy and vitality, truth, and freedom. Shamans claim that seeing a Blue Jay will protect you alongside readying your energy to adapt to new situations, taking risks, and making new discoveries. This is the vital power that moves the Aspirant into the Chela.

White Dove or White Ray: The White Ray represents Venus, a planet of refinement, grace, cooperation, purity, harmony, love, and compassion. Sanat Kumara, the Venusian regent and founder of Shamballa, was alleged to imitate the sublime architecture of Venus throughout the City of White's sanctuaries and buildings. The philosophical underpinning and spiritual practices of Shamballa originate from the venerated libraries and spiritual temples of Venus. Undoubtedly, the Shamballa Lineage and the I AM America Teachings are Venusian. The White Dove is a harbinger of both brotherhood and peace, and in the Christian tradition the White Dove represents the abiding presence of the Holy Spirit. The Ascended Master Saint Germain requested that the symbol of the dove be placed on the I AM America Maps to represent, "the end of one age and the beginning of a new one." White Doves are associated with Bodhisattvas and Prophets alike, and characterize the purity and devotion that aids the chela's critical spiritual evolution and passage to the initiate. The White Dove denotes the Ascension and signifies the uplifting presence of the Golden Cities.

Appendix C

Ascension Valley & the Presence of Glacium

Glacium is a naturally occurring monatomic mineral, present in Ascension Valley (Shalahah), and in similar energetic geophysical models for the New Times. The Ascended Masters claim that these dimensional shifting locations are present in every Golden City. A monatomic element is a single atom that does not bind to another and is usually derived from rare earth elements, i.e., gold, platinum, rhodium, iridium, titanium, silver, and copper. Since monatomic atoms have a ceramic property, they are also superconductive. Recent research has proven that monatomic substances exist throughout the Earth and in nature.[1]

Superconductivity creates a non-polarized energy field—best known as a Meissner Field. In fact, our own human aura is a type of Meissner Field. The appropriate use of glacium and other monatomic substances can expand and further develop your Meissner Field. According to researcher David Hudson, "You light up the room when you walk in . . . the gifts that go with this are: perfect telepathy, you can know good and evil when it is in a room with you, you can also project your thoughts into someone else's mind. You can levitate; you can walk on water because it's flowing so much light within you that you don't attract gravity. And when you understand that when you exclude all external magnetic fields, when you exclude gravity, you are no longer of this space-time. You have become a Fifth Dimensional being."[2]

Saint Germain has identified several locations of naturally occurring monatomic minerals—glacium. This form of monatomic element is perfectly safe and calibrates to your current state of spiritual development and evolution. Glacium has a powdery white appearance, and is often found in quartz deposits. It can also disperse and activate through the tornadic movement of water. Streams located near natural glacium deposits are filled with an effervescent life-giving energy and can produce healing at many levels. Glacium assists the Ascension Process and interacts with the human aura.

---

1. "David Hudson Discovered Monatomic Gold Ormus." Monatomic Orme, 26 July 2016, monatomic-orme.com/david-hudson/.

2. "What Are Monatomics (Monatomic Elements)?" Science of Wholeness Is Your Highest Fulfillment, scienceofwholeness.com/what-are-monatomics-monatomic-elements/.

Krishna, Spring in Kulu
Nicolas Roerich, 1930.

Appendix D
The Difference Between Spiritual Retreats & the Golden Cities

There is a great difference between an Ascended Master Retreat and a Golden City. An Ascended Master Retreat comes under the guiding sponsorship of the Maha Chohan, the Lord of the Seven Rays. The Maha Chohan oversees both Etheric Temples and Spiritual Retreats of specific Ascended Masters. These are the ethereal homes of the Masters, and where the Master radiates energies to Earth for the benefit of humanity. Spiritual Retreats and Temples often contain the Ascended Masters' focused school of light that radiates their individualized Ray Force. It is said that Ascended Master Retreats contain the records of past civilizations and previous Golden Ages. Many chelas study in these magnificent schools of light in between lifetimes to properly prepare for specific incarnations with special missions for the Great White Brotherhood.

Golden Cities fall under the auspice of the venerated Shamballa Lineage and are overseen by the Lord of the Transition, Sananda. In fact, Golden Cities are one of the four categories ascribed to Shamballa through the Planetary Hierarchy. (For more information see: *Appendix T, Spiritual Hierarchy.*)

A Golden City Sanctuary is not dissimilar to the singular, ethereal retreats and temples of the Ascended Masters. Golden Cities, however, contain numerous Sanctuaries of Light. A Golden City is an interconnected multi-dimensional network of ethereal ashrams, temples, and retreats, replete with minor and major lei-lines, power points, small and large sub-vortices, powerful landforms and mountain ranges, rivers and lakes, canyons and valleys, streams and meadows, fields and forests that unite energies with our Mother Earth—Babajeran—and the Spiritual Hierarchy. Remember, Shamballa is the notion of living in spiritually perfected community. Each Golden City is fashioned as a replica of the Fifth Dimensional City of White and steps-down the unique Shamballa energies. And each Golden City Ashram, Temple, and Retreat is stewarded by a certain Master Teacher, Elohim, Angel, or Archangel of Light.

Currently, many new Ascended Masters and Beings of Light are making themselves known and available for spiritual teaching and healing in Golden Cities. Because of this, Golden Cities are desired locations for spiritual pilgrimage. Golden City Spiritual Journeys accelerate an individual's Ascension Process and amplify one's spiritual techniques and practices.

Tiger's Nest Monastery
Tiger's Nest Monastery located in Paro Bhutan.

Golden Cities function multi-dimensionally and radiate and imbue evolutionary energies that assist and lead mankind into the Golden Age. They promote everyday human spiritual development into the Divine HU-man and onward to Ascension. In essence, Golden Cities are a Divine Intervention for this time—the Golden Age of Kali Yuga, to assist humanity's Global Ascension.

The Spiritual Ashrams of Golden Cities fall into four categories: Gateway, Cardinal, Heavenly, and Convergence. Each doorway contains seven primary Adjutant Points, and each point has their own distinct energy, guiding Hierarch, and Color Ray of Focus.

Located at the Peak Points of the intercardinal directions, lay the four heavenly *Temples of Perfection*. These Temples are interdimensional, and entrance is for those who have developed, "the eyes to see, the ears to hear." There are five *Golden City Star Retreats* per Golden City. Four of the Golden City Retreats are located at the cardinal, directional radius of the Golden City Star—twenty miles. The final and most powerful point of a Golden City is its Star. The following list breaks down the thirty-three Golden City Sanctuaries of Light:

- Golden City Gateway Ashrams: Eight per Golden City
- Golden City Cardinal Ashrams: Four per Golden City
- Golden City Heavenly Ashrams: Four per Golden City
- Golden City Convergence Ashrams: Eight per Golden City
- Golden City Temples of Perfection: Four per Golden City
- Golden City Star Retreats: Five per Golden City

Golden City Gateway Ashrams are focused at each Adjutant Point/ Evolutionary Point. (For more information on Evolutionary Points see: *Golden City Series, Book Three, Divine Destiny*.) The eight Gateway Ashrams are:

1. Gateway to Harmony Ashram
2. Gateway to Abundance Ashram
3. Gateway to Love Ashram
4. Gateway to Desire Ashram
5. Gateway to Clarity Ashram
6. Gateway to Charity Ashram
7. Gateway to Stillness Ashram
8. Gateway to Creation/Creativity Ashram

John's Vision of the Golden Cities
A depiction of John's vision of the *New Jerusalem*, described in the Holy Bible's Book of Revelations.

Golden City Cardinal Ashrams are focused at the Outer Marriage-Child Points, also known as *Peak Points*. (For more information see: *Golden City Series, Book Four, Sacred Energies*.) These four Ashrams unite the energies of two Evolutionary Points per Golden City Doorway and are located on the cardinal directions of each Golden City.

1. The Cardinal Ashram of Harmony and Abundance
2. The Cardinal Ashram of Love and Desire
3. The Cardinal Ashram of Clarity and Charity
4. The Cardinal Ashram of Stillness and Creation/Creativity

Remember, Gateway Ashrams and Cardinal Ashrams can often be identified through physical anomalies and distinct energetic characteristics. Adjutant Points can flux, with a five to ten mile circumference; however, they often physically affix to dynamic landform and bodies of water.

Golden City Heavenly Ashrams are Fourth Dimensional. These Adjutant Points and their inherent Ashrams of Light assist the Deva and Elemental Kingdoms. Their presence and life force are remarkably robust. Since these points shift our human consciousness into Fourth Dimension, we often experience Time Compaction or Dimensional Rifting while visiting these points. These are extraordinary locations for meditation, astral travel, and lucid dreaming. Golden City Heavenly Ashrams have concentrated energies that can align human energy fields to receive contact through the super-

City's Blessing
A depiction of a Golden Temple by *Hao Han Yeong.*

senses. Golden City Heavenly Ashrams are located at the Inner Marriage-Child Points. They are:

1. Heavenly Service Ashram
2. Heavenly Illumination Ashram
3. Heavenly Cooperation Ashram
4. Heavenly Faith Ashram

Golden City Convergence Ashrams are similar in energy to the Cardinal Ashrams as they unite Evolutionary Point energies. There are two per doorway:

1. Convergence Ashram of Service and Cooperation
2. Convergence Ashram of Service and Illumination
3. Convergence Ashram of Illumination and Service
4. Convergence Ashram of Illumination and Faith
5. Convergence Ashram of Cooperation and Service
6. Convergence Ashram of Cooperation and Faith
7. Convergence Ashram of Faith and Cooperation
8. Convergence Ashram of Faith and Illumination

What is the subtle difference between an Ashram of Service and Cooperation and an Ashram of Cooperation and Service? The difference is the location—the directional location of the Golden City Doorway. The first Ashram is located in a Southern Door; the latter is located in a Western Door. (*See following illustrations.*) A Southern Door is known as the Red Door of Healing; a Western Door is known as the Yellow Door of Knowledge. (To refresh your understanding of the four directional doorways of a Golden City see: *Golden City Series, Book One, Points of Perception.*)

Located between each Golden City Convergence Ashram is yet another set of intercardinal power points. These are the physical locations of ethereal temples that prepare the soul to enter into the five Star Retreats. These locations are known as the four **Golden City Temples of Perfection**:

Genesis II
Multi-dimensional temple by *John Stephens.*

1. Temple of Service and Cooperation
2. Temple of Cooperation and Faith
3. Temple of Faith and Illumination
4. Temple of Illumination and Service

The Five Golden City Star Retreats comprise the final set of magnificent Golden City Sanctuaries. They work directly with the primary Ray Force of the Golden City. These Golden City Retreats function mainly at the Fifth Dimensional level and are extremely evolved in their energy and vibration. Unless you are attuned to their frequency, they may be difficult to detect physically—best to identify in dream, psychic, or trance states. The outer four Retreats are located at approximately twenty miles, in the four cardinal directions from the center of the Golden City Star. They are:

1. Southern Star Retreat
2. Eastern Star Retreat
3. Western Star Retreat
4. Northern Star Retreat

Song of Shambhala
The magical city located in Tibet (Asia), depicted by *Nicholas Roerich, 1943.*

The final, fifth Golden City Sanctuary is the **Golden City Star** that functions at every level of spiritual energy, with Third, Fourth, and Fifth Dimensional frequencies. The Star coalesces and refines the energies of all of the doorways and is perhaps one of the best locations to seek spiritual refuge, retreat for reinvigorating vacations and weekends, and to perform ceremony and recite decree in groups.

In total, there are thirty-three Sanctuaries of Light dispersed throughout every Golden City. The first twelve Ashrams oversee the outer mysteries (the Gateway and Cardinal Ashrams), and the second twelve administer initiations into the inner mysteries (the Heavenly and Convergence Ashrams). The four Temples of Perfection ready the soul on its path of Innate Divinity and Perfection, preparing it for the liberating energies of the Star. The five Golden City Star Retreats assist the divine HU-man in their Ascension Process, with the fifth and final retreat—the Star—the most powerful. *Illustrations follow.*

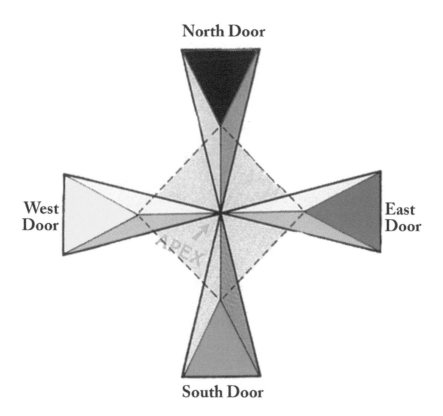

Doors (gateways) of the Golden Cities:
The four doors of the Golden Cities signify the four directions, and each represents certain attributes and characteristics. They also represent four spiritual pathways or spiritual initiations.

The Black Door
Direction: North
Esoteric Planet: Earth, Saturn, Mercury
Qualities:
1. Discipline and Labor
2. Physical Abundance
3. Worldly Benefits
4. Transmutation and Forgiveness
Attributes: The Northern Doors represent discipline and hard work. Spiritually, they denote self-control achieved through transmutation and forgiveness. Some say the Northern Doors manifest abundant consciousness and gratified wishes. The prophecies of the New Times foretell bountiful and prolific crops; this doorway is best for commercial and business endeavors.

The Blue Door
Direction: East
Esoteric Planet: Moon
Qualities:
1. Purification and Sacrifice
2. Alchemy
3. Often referred to as, "the Elixir of Life"
4. Friends, Family, Helpful Acquaintances
Attributes: According to the Master Teachers, time spent in contemplation at this doorway can resolve relationship and family problems. Prophecies of the New Times say the Eastern Doors of Golden City Vortices are perfect locations for communities, group activities, residential homes, and schools for children.

The Red Door
Direction: South
Esoteric Planet: Mars, Jupiter
Qualities:
1. "The Healing of the Nations"
2. Enlightened Love
3. Nonjudgment
4. Faith and Courage
Attributes: The energies of the Southern Door induce physical, emotional, and spiritual regenerations; and miracle healings are commonplace. That's why this doorway is a great place for hospitals, clinics, retreats, and spas.

The Yellow Door
Direction: West
Esoteric Planet: Sun
Qualities:
1. Wisdom
2. "The Philosopher's Stone"
3. Adeptship and Conclusion
Attributes: The Western Door terminates the four pathways and acts as a portal to the "Star of Knowledge." Here, Golden City inhabitants will find universities and schools of higher, spiritual learning. The Master Teachers say the energies of this doorway create the hub of civic activity: Golden City government, including its administrative structure and capitol will reside here.

The Star
Direction: Center
Esoteric Planet: Venus
Qualities:
1. Self-Knowledge
2. Empowerment
3. Ascension

Attributes: The "Star" also known as the "Star of Self-Knowledge" punctuates the center of every Golden City. This area, the most powerful of the Vortex, produces self-knowledge and self-empowerment. The energies of the four doorways coalesce here—that's why it's identified as the absence of color, white. Its power reaches beyond the boundaries of the Golden City. Forty miles in diameter, a Star's healing qualities can extend as far as sixty miles. Here, spiritual growth in the New Times happens: the Star's energies encourage self-renunciation, meditation, and spiritual liberation. During the Time of Change, the purity and beneficence of a Star's power will attract the Ascended Masters, who will then manifest in physical form. And the city's inhabitants will flock here to absorb spiritual teaching, miracle healings, and Ascensions.

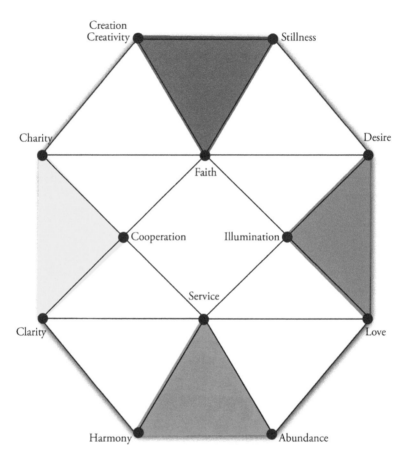

The Eight-sided Cell of Perfection
with the Four Vortex Doorways and the Twelve Jurisdictions
The Eight-sided Cell of Perfection as a Golden City Vortex identifies
the Adjutant Points as the Twelve Jurisdictions.

Golden City
Gateway Ashrams

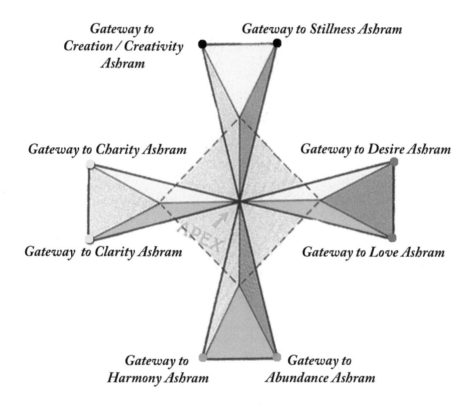

Gateway to
Creation / Creativity
Ashram

Gateway to Stillness Ashram

Gateway to Charity Ashram

Gateway to Desire Ashram

Gateway to Clarity Ashram

Gateway to Love Ashram

Gateway to
Harmony Ashram

Gateway to
Abundance Ashram

The Eight Golden City Gateway Ashrams
There are eight Golden City Gateway Ashrams;
each is located at a Vortex Adjutant Point.

Golden City
Cardinal Ashrams

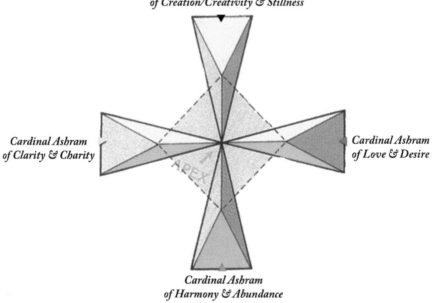

Cardinal Ashram
of Creation/Creativity & Stillness

Cardinal Ashram
of Clarity & Charity

Cardinal Ashram
of Love & Desire

Cardinal Ashram
of Harmony & Abundance

The Four Golden City Cardinal Ashrams
There are four Golden City Cardinal Ashrams;
each is located at a Vortex Adjutant Point.

Golden City
Heavenly Ashrams

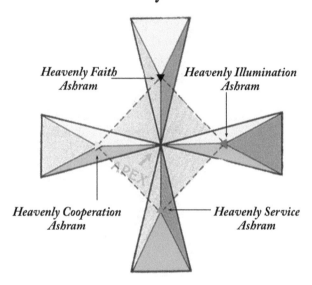

The Four Golden City Heavenly Ashrams
There are four Golden City Heavenly Ashrams;
each is located at a Fourth Dimensional Vortex
Adjutant Point.

Golden Cites & the Masters of Shamballa

Golden City
Convergence Ashrams

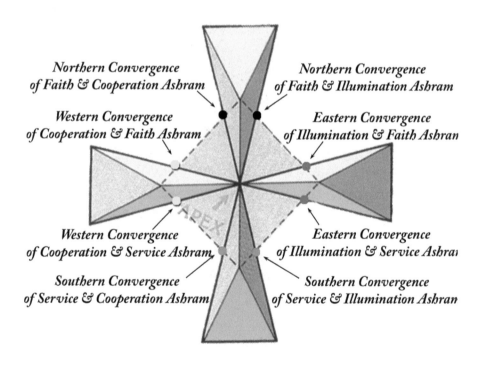

Northern Convergence
of Faith & Cooperation Ashram

Northern Convergence
of Faith & Illumination Ashram

Western Convergence
of Cooperation & Faith Ashram

Eastern Convergence
of Illumination & Faith Ashran

Western Convergence
of Cooperation & Service Ashram

Eastern Convergence
of Illumination & Service Ashraı

Southern Convergence
of Service & Cooperation Ashram

Southern Convergence
of Service & Illumination Ashran

The Eight Golden City Ashrams
The eight Convergence Ashrams unite the energies
of Evolutionary Points and their ambient energies.

Golden City Temples of Perfection

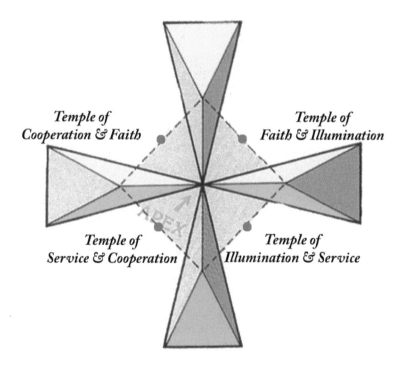

The Four Temples of Perfection
The four Temples of Perfection are present in
each Golden City.

Golden City
Star Retreats

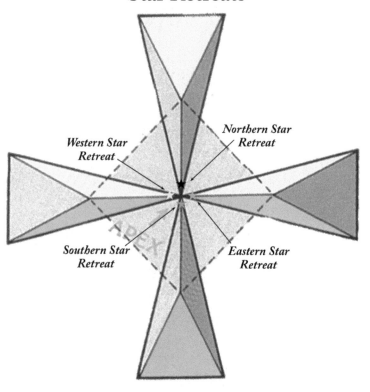

The Four Golden City Star Retreats
There are four Golden City Star Retreats; each is located twenty
miles from the center of the Golden City Star.

Golden City Star

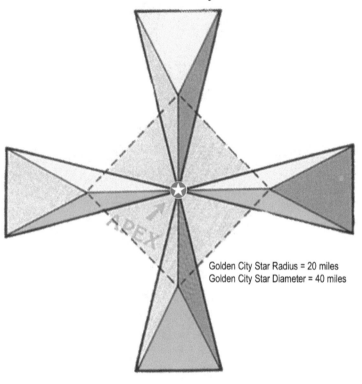

Golden City Star Radius = 20 miles
Golden City Star Diameter = 40 miles

The Golden City Star
The Golden City Star is the most powerful location in a
Golden City Vortex.

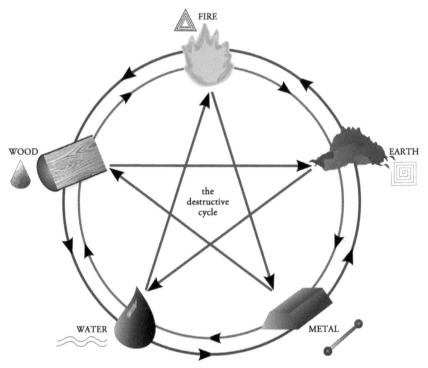

FIRE

WOOD

EARTH

the
destructive
cycle

WATER

METAL

Outer Ring: Nourishing Cycle
Inner Ring: Creative Cycle

The Cycle of the Elements

The Twenty-year Cycles of the Elements

According to the Chinese calendar, time is not linear but moves in cycles. Perhaps the most important cycle revered in China is the sexagenary cycle, which comprises sixty years. This cycle is used in the Chinese esoteric arts, including astrology and feng-shui. One sexagenary cycle—sixty years—is known as an *Era*. Three Eras, a total of one hundred eighty years, comprises the *Nine Cycles*. The Nine Cycles are divided into nine twenty-year portions. Energy ascends and decreases according to the energetic patterns that are connected to each sixty-year Era and to each twenty-year cycle. Below is a chart of the Nine Cycles (*chiu-hun*), the Three Eras (*san-yüan*), and each

Era	Cycle	Starting Year	Element
Upper Era	first cycle	1864	Water
	second cycle	1884	Earth
	third cycle	1904	Wood
Middle Era	fourth cycle	1924	Wood
	fifth cycle	1944	Earth
	sixth cycle	1964	Metal
Lower Era	seventh cycle	1984	Metal
	eighth cycle	2004	Earth
	ninth cycle	2024	Fire
Upper Era	first cycle	2044	Water
	second cycle	2064	Earth
	third cycle	2084	Wood
Middle Era	fourth cycle	2104	Wood
	fifth cycle	2124	Earth
	sixth cycle	2164	Metal
Lower Era	seventh cycle	2184	Metal
	eighth cycle	2204	Earth
	ninth cycle	2224	Fire

twenty-year cycle. According to Eva Wong, "Small changes occur between cycles, and large changes occur between each era."[1]

The Ascended Masters also utilize and often refer to the twenty-year cycle periods and their relationship to the elements. They teach that the Hierarchs of the Golden City Ashrams change Ray Forces every twenty years, according to the Cycle of the Elements. This creates adjustment in the Golden Cities to serve the needs of newer, evolving Ascended Beings, and to calibrate energies as Earth moves into the increasing Galactic Light of the Golden Age. While the Ashrams calibrate energies for each Golden City as the frequencies on Earth evolve and change, the primary Ray Force of each Golden City and its Star stays the same. This is also true for the Four Temples of Perfection and the Star Retreats.

Adjutant Point	Ray Force Can Change	Ray Force Remains the Same
Gateway Ashram	Yes	No, it can change.
Cardinal Ashram	Yes	No, it can change.
Heavenly Ashram	Yes	No, it can change.
Convergence Ashram	Yes	No, it can change.
Temple of Perfection	No	Remains the same.
Golden City Star Retreat	No	Remains the same.
Golden City Star	No	Remains the same.

1. Wong, Eva. Feng-Shui: the Ancient Wisdom of Harmonious Living for Modern Times. Shambhala, 1996.

The Hierarchs & Ray Forces of Gobean's Adjutant Points

The Hierarchs and Ray Forces of Gobean's Adjutant Points
The Golden City of Gobean (Southwest, United States),
and the Hierarchs and Ray Forces of its Adjutant Points.
Golden City Hierarchs and their Ray Forces are pursuant
to change in 2024, at the end of the Eighth Cycle and the
beginning of the Ninth Cycle.

Adjutant Point Hierarchs

GOBEAN GATEWAY TO HARMONY ASHRAM
Akhenaton

The Master Teacher of Serapis Bey is associated with truth, unity, and the Path of Beauty as the spiritual concepts to enter into Oneness. Akhenaton is the present steward of the *Gateway to Harmony Ashram of Gobean* that serves the White Ray.

GOBEAN GATEWAY TO ABUNDANCE ASHRAM
Nefertiti

As a goddess of devotion, equality, beauty, and fertility, Nefertiti teaches the Oneship through the principle of "two or more." She serves the White Ray at the *Gateway to Abundance Ashram,* located in the Southern Door of Gobean.

GOBEAN GATEWAY TO CLARITY ASHRAM
Aloah

The Lady Master of Peace, Aloah overcomes prophecies of calamities and natural disasters through her stalwart focus on peace. She also helps humanity to overcome addictions and distracting illusions through cultivating humility and dedication to truth, unity, and the ONE. In her Earthly embodiment as Hulda the Prophetess of Israel, she assisted her people through her unwavering devotion to God. Aloah serves both the Blue Ray of Truth and the Yellow Ray of Wisdom at the *Gateway to Clarity Ashram* in Gobean's Western Door.

Gobean Gateway to Charity Ashram
Eliah

The Master of Prayer advocates a return to purity through righteous action and spiritual discipline. Eliah directs his Mastery of Light to shine upon deception, fraud, and trickery. Master Eliah's God Obedience radiates both love and wisdom, reflected in devotional service to both the Yellow and Pink Rays. Master Eliah serves in the *Gateway to Charity Ashram* of Gobean's Western Door.

Gobean West Cardinal Point
Sein

This tranquil and serene Elohim of the Aquamarine and Gold Rays oversees and stewards the *Cardinal Ashram of Clarity and Charity*, located in Gobean's Western Door. Sein means, "Inner vision."

Gobean Gateway to Creation/Creativity Ashram
Mahatma Ishmar

This Master of the Ruby Ray comes from the spiritual lineage of Archangel Uriel. Mahatma Ishmar is an adept of chaos and energies to help restore righteous action and devotion to the Creator. Mahatma Ishmar serves in the *Gateway to Creation/Creativity Ashram*, located in the Northern Door of Gobean.

GOBEAN GATEWAY TO STILLNESS ASHRAM
Lady Master DeNaire

This Lady Master of the Violet Ray is said to have experienced many lifetimes in the DAHL Universe then subsequently spent many years training and receiving instruction in the libraries of Venus before her departure to the *Gateway to Stillness Ashram*, in the Northern Door of Gobean. Lady Master DeNaire is a fierce protector of the New Children and is associated with the Divine Co-creation process.

GOBEAN NORTH CARDINAL ASHRAM
Elohim Veenon

Veenon rules the harsh winds of the North through directing the Wind Elementals with the strength of his love. It is claimed that he received his greatest insights on the spiritual nature of love when he fell in love with a young maiden, and for the first time ever he experienced obsession. He lost his spiritual power and the ability to lead and direct the wind. The Elohim Veenon was able to achieve balance and regain his strength through the practice of both non-interference and detachment. Veenon serves the Violet Ray at the *Cardinal Ashram of Stillness and Creation/Creativity* in the Northern Door of Gobean.

GOBEAN GATEWAY TO LOVE ASHRAM
Angel Cresta

The Angel Cresta is affiliated with the Divine Light of Crystals and their innate Mastery over the Seven Rays of Light and Sound. She serves the White Ray of Beauty at the *Gateway Ashram of Love* located in the Eastern Door of Gobean.

GOBEAN HEAVENLY ILLUMINATION ASHRAM
Elohim Arien

Beloved Arien's mission for humanity is to assist all to possess and Master their Divine Inner Light through the cultivation of spiritual focus. Arien oversees the *Quickening*, a swift and rapid process of Spiritual Awakening. Beloved Arien serves the Gold Ray at the *Heavenly Illumination Ashram*, located in Gobean's Eastern Door.

Helena Blavatsky with her teachers.
Madame H.P. Blavatsky, *center*, pictured with her Master Teachers. Blavatsky
is the founder of the Theosophical Society. Her teachers, pictured from left are:
Master Kuthumi, Master El Morya, and Master Saint Germain. The origins of
this image are unknown.

Master Kuthumi

In the late nineteenth century, Ascended Master Kuthumi—also known as Koot Hoomi or K. H.—collaborated with Helena Blavatsky and El Morya to introduce humanity to the spiritual teachings of theosophy. And like Master M., K. H. is dedicated to advancing the spiritual fitness of mankind to a higher consciousness. Thus, Kuthumi approached his interaction with humans in the same manner as his mahatma contemporary: he veiled his identity behind the Indian dignitaries of the time, in this case, Thakar Singh Sandhawalia, leader of the Singh Sabha movement. Founded in the early 1870s, this Indian independence campaign emerged as a grassroots effort to maintain the purity of Sikhism, otherwise eroded by Christian Missionaries. Sandhanwalia, Ranbir Singh—one of El Morya's aliases—and H. P. B. joined forces to spread theosophy throughout India.

Kuthumi and El Morya shared a close relationship through the ages. Both trained by the Ascended Master Maha Chohan, the spiritual duo, as two of the wise men, paid homage to the baby Jesus: K. H. as Balthazar and Master M. as Melchior. Kuthumi also shows up as Sir Percival at the round table of King Arthur (aka El Morya). But his incarnation history isn't limited to associations with his spiritual Brother. Kuthumi's past lifetimes include the Greek philosopher Pythagoras; Thutmose III, the warrior pharaoh of the eighteenth dynasty; Shah Jahan, the emperor of India and builder of the Taj Mahal; and founder of the Franciscans, Saint Francis of Assisi.

Highly educated and extremely private, Kuthumi, a Cambridge University alumni, spent 200 years in seclusion in the Himalayan Mountains before ascending in 1889. He is a gentle Master affiliated with the Golden City Malton, and the Gold and Ruby Rays of ministration and service to humanity. In one of his earliest letters to A. P. Sinnett, Kuthumi calls the holy Golden Temple of the Sikhs his home, although he's seldom there, preferring the solitude of Tibet.[3]

Author Alice Bailey, who continued to work with the Masters after Blavatsky's death in 1891, writes about a visit from K. H.: "Master Koot Hoomi, [is] a Master who is very close to the Christ." In 1895, Kuthumi told the fifteen-year-old Bailey that she would travel the world "doing your Master's work all the time" and that "I would have to give up being such an unpleasant little girl and must try and get some measure of self-control. My future usefulness to him and to the world was dependent upon how I handled myself and the changes I could manage to make."[1]

A.D.K. Luk writes of Kuthumi: "He was such a lover of nature that he would watch a certain phase for hours, or would stay a whole day with a flower to see it open into full bloom, and perhaps watch it close again at night. He was one of the few who represented the heart of the Nature Kingdom. He was able to read through the Elemental Kingdom and accelerate his consciousness to a point where he was of assistance in that realm. Birds and animals were drawn to him to be in his radiance which was about him; drawn by his constant attention and adoration to his Source."[2]

1. Bailey, Alice A., *Unfinished Autobiography* (New York: Lucis Publishing Company), page 36.

2. Luk, A.D.K., *Law of Life, Book II* (Pueblo, CO: ADK Luk Publications), page 275.

Lady Master Nada

Lady Nada is the Ascended Goddess of Justice and Peace who is associated with Mastery of speech (vibration), communication, interpretation, and the sacred word. Nada is also known as a divine advocate of Universal Law, and she is often symbolized by the scales of blind justice.

Esoteric researchers document Lady Nada's historical narrative of the last days of Atlantis, including the archetypal building of an Ark by Noah, a Master Guru to many ancient Atlanteans. As a member of his mystery school, she escaped the demise of the fabled continent of iconic marbled temples and geomantically engineered streets to an established retreat of the Archangels. Bands of ships sailed to the higher grounds of North and South America, Europe, and the Himalayas. Upon arrival at an inland sanctuary, she was personally tutored by the Archeia Charity. This sanctuary was located near present-day Saint Louis, Missouri, located in the protected and sacred lands of Ameru. Today, this is the location of the Crystal-Pink Flame Retreat, located in the Southwest sector of the Golden City of Malton. This is perhaps one reason for Lady Nada's spiritual and physical connection to this wondrous Vortex of Deva and Elemental activity.

The youngest of a large Atlantean refugee family, Nada was an extraordinarily gifted child. At Archeia Charity's sublime temple, she focused upon meditation and the expansion of the Unfed Flame within her Eight-sided Cell of Perfection. After she achieved her Ascension, she commented about her final lifetime, "I saw the victory of each of my brothers and sisters, the fullness of my joy was in a heart of love expanded . . . but I took my leave into the higher octaves, thoroughly understanding the meaning of self-mastery and the pink flame."[1]

Lady Nada is primarily known for her service on the Pink Ray, however she is presently associated with the Yellow Ray of Wisdom, and the Ruby and Gold Rays of Ministration, Brotherhood, and Service. She lovingly serves with Master Kuthumi to assist the Deva and Elemental Kingdoms in the Golden City of Malton (Illinois and Indiana, USA) and the Golden City of Denasha (Scotland).

Lady Nada is the tender, yet steadfast hierarch of the Scottish highland's Denasha; and Master Kuthumi is the much beloved hierarch of Malton—a Golden City filled with fields, forests, lakes, and benevolent nature spirits.

---

1. Prophet, *The Masters and Their Retreats* (Corwin Springs, MT: Summit University Press), pages 274-275.

Mohammed the Prophet
Nicolas Roerich, 1925.

Appendix I
The Three Standards

The Use of the Violet Flame, Tube of White Light, and the Protection of Archangel Michael

1. Call forth the Violet Consuming Fire: "In that Mighty Christ I AM, I call forth Saint Germain's Violet Transmuting Flame of mercy, transmutation, and forgiveness. Alchemize my lower energy bodies into the perfection of the Christ! Almighty I AM! (3x)" Then proceed with any Violet Flame decree. (Use seven times.) Suggestions are: "Violet Flame I AM, God I AM Violet Flame," or "I AM a Being of Violet Fire, I AM the Purity God desires!"

2. Call upon the Tube of Light: "Beloved Mighty I AM Presence, surround me now with the Tube of White Light, ever-sustained, ever-maintained, throughout this day and onward into night! Almighty I AM! (3x)"

3. Invoke Archangel Michael's Blue Flame: "Beloved Archangel Michael, surround me now with the Blue Flame of Protection! Protect my Violet Flame in its action and activity, protect my Mighty Tube of Light, giving me multiple layers of protection! Almighty I AM! (3x)"

Complete this spiritual practice with thanks and gratitude: "I love you, I love you, I love you! I bless you, I bless you, I bless you! And I thank you, I thank you, I thank you! Almighty I AM! (3x)

Close with Almighty I AM that I AM (9x) and OM HUE (9x). (This properly seals the decree and affirmation.)

It is suggested that for those who have not completely eliminated animal products from their diets to use the above sequence. For chelas and students who have eliminated animal products and adhere to a vegan diet, the sequence is as follows: first, use of the Tube of White Light; second, call upon Saint Germain's transmuting Violet Flame; third, invoke Archangel Michael's Blue Flame. Since this is a practice associated with purification and spiritual hygiene, the difference for carnivores and vegetarians is the cleansing through the Sacred Fire. Using the Sacred Fire removes the fear substance ingested through animal products from the physical body and light bodies, transmutes karmas, and prepares the auric field for the Tube of White Light. When the Three Standards is used by vegans, it is claimed the result of the Sacred Fire is intensified, as the Violet Flame can focus its entire energy upon the transmutation of karmas.

Lineage of Gurus
Confucius, Lao-tzu, and Buddhist Arhat. Hanging scroll, ink and color on paper.
Painting is located in the Palace Museum, Beijing. Ming dynasty.[1]

1. Confucius Lao-tzu and Buddhist Arhat by Ding Yunpeng.jpg." Wikimedia Commons. 30 May 2008. Web. 08 Mar. 2011. <http://commons.wikimedia.org/wiki/File:Confucius_Lao-tzu_and_Buddhist_Arhat_by_Ding_Yunpeng.jpg>.

Appendix J
The Lineage of Gurus

The importance of the lineage of the Gurus who sponsor a specific spiritual practice cannot be overstated. This detailed history is, in essence, the ancestry of the technique and represents the seasoned Masters who have perfected its every nuance, innate potency, and effectiveness. Moreover, when using a meditation, decree or mantra suggested by a Master Teacher you are psychically tugging on its ancestral root and the sum total of energy of those who previously taught and Mastered the method. This is why it is often recommended when applying specific decrees and prayers to call upon a certain lineage of teachers or Masters. Doing so invokes their spiritual presence and timely assistance.

Throughout the I AM America Teachings, Saint Germain and others have shared insights on the lineage of not only spiritual practices, but the lineage of Christ Consciousness, Shamballa, specific Golden Cities, and many hierarchal offices. Examples of these remarkable pedigrees of renowned Gurus, Masters, founders of world religions, and spiritual practices follow:

Lineage of the Violet Flame:
Saint Germain → Kuan Yin → the Elohim Arcturus and Diana

Lineage of the Christ Consciousness:
Kuthumi, El Morya, Saint Germain → Sananda → Lord Maitreya → Lord Meru → Quetzalcoatl, Lord Apollo

Lineage of the Gold Ray:
Kuthumi → Lord Lanto → Helios, Vesta, and Lord Apollo → Alpha and Omega → Elohae and Eloha

Lineage of the Twelve Jurisdictions:
Saint Germain → Sananda → Lady Master Venus, Sanat Kumara as the Cosmic Christ (Kartikkeya, Kumar, Skanda, Guha) → Lord Apollo

Golden City Lineage:
Remaining 49 Golden Cities → Golden City of Gobean → Golden City of Gobi → Shamballa → City of the Kumaras (Venus)

Golden City Hierarch Lineage:
El Morya → Lord Meru → Lord Maitreya → Sanat Kumara → Lords of Venus

Shamballa Creation Lineage:
Serapis Bey → Lord Gautama, Lord Maitreya, the Lords of the Flame →
Sanat Kumara → the Three Kumaras → Lords of Venus

Golden City of Gobean Lineage:
El Morya → Serapis Bey → Akhenaton → Quetzalcoatl

The Shamballa Hierarchs
   Lord of the World:
   Gautama Buddha → Sanat Kumara → Sri Maga
   World Buddha:
   Lord Maitreya → Lord Lanto → Gautama Buddha
   World Teacher:
   Saint Germain → Lord Sananda, Kuthumi → Lord Maitreya
   Lord of the Golden Cities:
   Saint Germain → Lord Sananda → Sanat Kumara, Lord Apollo

Saint Germain's Lineage of Gurus:
Sananda → Lady Portia, Lord Maitreya → Kuan Yin → Lord Apollo, Sanat
Kumara

El Morya's Lineage of Gurus:
Lord Maitreya → Ahura Mazda → Maha Cohan → Akhenaton → Hercules

Master Kuthumi's Lineage of Gurus:
Lord Sananda → Lady Nada → Lord Maitreya

Mother Mary's Lineage of Gurus:
Lord Sananda → Hermes Trismegistus

Lineage of the Galactic Suns:
Osiris and Isis, Apollo and Diana, Krishna and Sophia, Helios and Vesta
(Earth's Sun), Hercules and Amazonia, Aureole and Aurea, Dawn and Luz →
Alpha and Omega → Elohae and Eloha

Lineage for the Seventh Manu (the New Children):
Goddess Yemanya (the Second Sister) and Pachamama (the Third Sister) →
Goddess Meru (the first Sister) → Mother Mary

Lord Sananda

During his paradigm-altering incarnation more than 2,000 years ago, Lord Sananda, also known as Sananda Kumara, embodied the Christ Consciousness, as Jesus, son of God. Some esoteric scholars say he's one of the four sons of Brahma—Sanaka, Sanatana, Sanat-Kumara, and Sanandana—his namesake. According to Vedic lore, the foursome possess eternally liberated souls and live in Tapaloka, the dimension of the great sages. Before manifesting in physical form, Jesus belonged to the Angelic Kingdom. His name was Micah— the Great Angel of Unity. Micah is the son of Archangel Michael who led the Israelites out of Egypt.[1]

Sananda Kumara revealed his identity to the mystic Sister Thedra. Her Master first contacted her in the early 1960s and instructed her to move to Peru, specifically, to a hidden monastery in the Andes mountains. There, undergoing an intense spiritual training, she kept in constant contact with Sananda, and he shared with her prophecies of the coming Earth Changes. After leaving the abbey, Sister Thedra moved to Mt. Shasta, California where she founded the Association of Sananda and Sanat Kumara. She died in 1992.

Sananda posed for a photograph on June 1, 1961 in Chichen Itza, Yucatan. He told Sister Thedra that though the image is valid, he is not limited by form of any kind; therefore, he may take on any appearance necessary. (*See Freedom Star, Prophecies that Heal Earth*).

---

1. Papastavro, Tellis S., *The Gnosis and the Law* (Tucson, AZ: Group Avatar), page 358.

Ascension of the Virgin
Sixteenth century painting by Michael Sittow.
This painting depicts Mother Mary's Ascension. Note the Crescent Moon,
symbology for the separation of Heaven and Earth.

Appendix L
The Light Bodies of Ascension

First Light Body: The *Electronic Blueprint* holds the electrical impulse in the light body; therefore, it is similar to the *Auric Blueprint*. It is charged with the energy of the Seven Major Chakras, the energy grids, meridians, and nadis. It resembles a grid, and is blue in color. This layer of the Human Aura contains a distinctive pulse that is synchronized with the individual's heartbeat, and lies within several inches of the physical body.

Second Light Body: The *Emotional Field* holds our instincts, feelings, and emotions. This light body is normally a vibrant pink in color. It is associated with the magnetism of the physical body. This light body is most affected by sound, especially mantras and decrees. Because varied emotions can change the characteristics of this light body, the light body can fluctuate in color. Extreme anger or violence can turn the light body dark red, while spiritual feelings of devotion can alter it to a visible light pink with hues of green. This light body is observed four to six inches from the physical body.

Third Light Body: The *Mental Body* carries our distinct thoughts, ideas, and perceptions. This energy field, to some degree, is associated with intelligence and our capability to process and implement information. This light body is associated with the color yellow, although some individuals display mental bodies that are vibrant gold. It is located six inches to one foot from the physical body.

First Three Light Bodies: The first three light bodies represent Action (electronic blueprint), Feeling (emotion) and Thought (mental). These three primary colors also represent the Unfed Flame of Power, Love, and Wisdom, respectively. The first three light bodies of the Human Aura endure throughout the Earthly incarnation, and dissipate with the death of the physical body.

Fourth Light Body: The fourth light body of the human is the *Astral Body*. This is the energy body that we use when we dream and travel at night, via different meditation techniques. It is varied in color, but often displays a rainbow of pastel colors: blues, pinks, greens, and purples. It is located a foot, to a foot and a half, from the physical body. Advanced souls often display a larger Astral Body of luminous white light, with iridescent pastels. This light body, along with the next three higher light bodies, survives the death of the physical body, and then resides in the Astral Plane for further spiritual development to prepare for the next incarnation.

Fifth Light Body: This body of energy is known as the *Auric Template*, and is similar to the Electronic Template. However, this field of vital energy gives form according to individual states of consciousness. It radiates approximately one and a half to two feet from the physical body. It is the energy layer from where a seasoned energy practitioner can detect and treat disease. The color of this energy body can vary depending on the individual strength of Ray Forces.

Sixth Light Body: This energy body carries the individual's aspirations and beliefs. Many refer to this energy body as the *Celestial Body*, but it is also known as the *Spiritual Emotional Body*. This body is often connected to feelings of bliss, unconditional love, and interconnectedness. It can be reached through meditation. This layer extends two to nearly three feet from the physical body. It is colored with opalescent pastels. Some energy practitioners report a gold-silver light shining throughout this energy body. Master Teachers, Spirit Guides, and Spiritual Teachers often enter this energy field to communicate with an individual, or to revive and heal the physical body. The Sixth and Seventh Light Bodies hold varying levels of the Akashic Records.

Seventh Light Body: The *Causal Body* is the last of the human energy bodies. It is an egg-shape ovoid that holds all of the lower energy bodies in place with extremely strong threads of light that form a golden grid. This energy body is also known as the *Spiritual Mental Body*, and contains the *Golden Thread Axis*, also known as the *Tube of Light* that connects one to the I AM Presence. Energy practitioners allege that this energy body holds the Akashic records that are keys to past-life memory. This energy body extends approximately three feet around the body but can be larger, depending on the spiritual evolution of the individual.

As human spiritual evolution advances, we begin to develop new energy bodies of light, sound, and experience. The Spiritual Teachers mention that the HU-man, the developed God Man, can acquire eight new distinct energy bodies beyond the initial, primary Seven Light Bodies. The Fifteenth Energy Body propels the soul out of duality, free from both physical and astral restraint.

An Ascended Master contains and influences twenty-two light bodies. Apparently, Light Bodies Eight through Ten have the ability to contend with varying light spectrums beyond Third Dimension and can manage space-time, including time contraction, time dilation, and time compaction.

But more importantly, the development of the HU-man Energy system implements the ever-important Ascension Process. The following information shares descriptions of the HU-man Energy Bodies Eight, Nine, and Ten.

Eighth Light Body: Known as the *Buddha Body* or the *Field of Awakening*, this energy body is initially three to four feet from the human body. It begins by developing two visible grid-like spheres of light that form in the front and in the back of the Human Aura. The front sphere is located three to four feet in front of and between the Heart and Solar Plexus Chakras. The back sphere is located in front of and between the Will-to-Love and Solar Will Chakras. These spheres activate an ovoid of light that surrounds the entire human body; an energy field associated with harmonizing and perfecting the Ascension Process. This is the first step toward Mastery. Once developed and sustained, this energy body grants physical longevity and is associated with immortality. It is known as the first level of Co-creation, and is developed through control of the diet and disciplined breath techniques. Once this light body reaches full development, the spheres dissipate and dissolve into a refined energy field, resembling a metallic armor. The mature Eighth Light Body then contracts and condenses, to reside within several inches of the physical body where it emits a silver-blue sheen.

Ninth Light Body: This body of light is known as *The Divine Blueprint*, as it represents the innate perfection of the divine HU-man. It is an energy field that is developed through uniting dual forces, and requires an in-depth purification of thought. In fact, this energy field causes the soul to face and Master those negative, dark, forces that the Spiritual Teachers refer to as a type of *mental purgatory*. This energy body processes extreme fears and transmutes them. The transmutation completely restructures beliefs, and purifies energies held in the lower mental bodies accumulated throughout all lifetimes. This produces an alchemizing, divine, HU-man Mental Body that develops approximately thirty-six feet from the human body.

This energy field first appears as nine independent triangular-gridded spheres. Apparently, the nine glowing spheres grow in circumference and, inevitably, morph into one glowing energy body. As the Ninth Light Body develops, it is extremely responsive to telepathy and group thought, and progresses to act and influence collective thought and consciousness. In its early to mid-stages of development, this energy body emits a high frequency violet light that evolves into the alchemic Violet Flame. The Spiritual Teachers claim that the decree, "I AM the Presence of Collective Thought," is its energetic mantra. The refined energies of the mature Divine Blueprint inevitably contract and concentrate in a similar manner to the Eighth Light

Body. As it draws its auric field closer to the physical body; within two to four inches, it radiates gold and then a bluish-silver light that reflects the strength of its protective shield.

Tenth Light Body: This is the final level of three protective HU-man light bodies, which is formed through the purification of desires, and is known as the *Diamond Mind*. Because this energy body gathers thought as light, it is a substantive and sizeable light body. The Spiritual Teachers often refer to the three protective HU-man energy bodies as the *Triple Gems*, and together they are strong enough to pierce human illusion. Combined with the four higher primal energy bodies—the Fourth Light Body to the Seventh Light Body—the total sum of these energy bodies produces the alchemic number seven. In this septagonal order, the Diamond Mind helps to produce the *Lighted Stance* and the inevitable attainment of the *Seamless Garment*.

The Lighted Stance is a state of conscious perfection—a precursor to Ascension. The soul's ability to manifest the Seamless Garment bestows the Master with the ability to travel and experience the Astral and Physical planes without spiritual corruption or physical disintegration. This mature energy body compacts itself to reside approximately six inches from the physical body, and is alleged to have the strength and brilliance of "ten-thousand diamonds." This energy body also exhibits complete Mastery over thought, feeling, and action—the first three primal human Energy Bodies, and can dissolve or manifest their physical presence at will; or, it can take form for whatever cause, circumstance, or "task at hand," without any limitation.

Saint Germain, the Holy Brother

The Lord of the Seventh Ray and the Master of the Violet Flame, Saint Germain, *pictured right,*[1] lived numerous noteworthy lifetimes, dating back thousands of years, before incarnating as the Comte de Saint Germainduring Renaissance Europe. He lived as the Englishman Sir Francis Bacon, the sixteenth-century philosopher, essayist, and Utopian who greatly influenced the philosophy of inductive science. His most profound and well-known work on the restoration of humanity, the *Instauratio Magna* (Great Restoration), defined him as an icon of the Elizabethan era. Research also shows his co-authoring of many Shakespearean sonnets.

According to Esoteric historians, Queen Elizabeth I of England—The Virgin Queen—was his biological mother. Before Bacon's birth, the queen married Earl of Leicester, quieting ideas of illegitimacy. Elizabeth's lady in waiting, Lady Ann Bacon, wife of the Lord High Chancellor of England, adopted him following the stillbirth of her baby. Bacon was, therefore, the true heir to the crown and England's rightful king.[2] But his cousin James I of Scotland succeeded the throne. Sir Bacon described this turn of events in his book, Novum Organo, published in 1620: "It is an immense ocean that surrounds the island of Truth." And Saint Germain often reminds us to this day "there are no mistakes, ever, ever, ever."

Bacon's philosophies also helped define the principles of Free Masonry and democracy. As an adept leader of the Rosicrucians (a secret society of that time), he set out to reveal the obsolescence and oppression of European monarchies.

---

1. Saint Germain, *The Secret Teachings of All Ages*, Diamond Jubilee Edition (Los Angeles: Philosophical Research Society, Inc.), Manly Hall.

2. Marie Bauer Hall, *Foundations Unearthed*, originally issued as Francis Bacon's Great Virginia Vault, Fourth Edition (Los Angeles: Veritas Press), page 9.

Francis Bacon
by John Vanderbank, (1731)
Francis Bacon coined the term "New Age" in the seventeenth century. The English philosopher is
said to be the last human incarnation of the Ascended Master Saint Germain.

Eventually, Bacon's destiny morphed. He shed his physical form and sought
the greatest gift of all: immortality. And that's what placed him in the most
extraordinary circumstances throughout history. Even his death (or lack of)
evokes controversy. Some say Bacon faked his demise in 1626—the coffin contained the carcass of a dog. (*Francis Bacon, pictured above.*)[3]

3. Vanderbank, John. "File:Francis Bacon, Viscount St Alban from NPG (2).jpg." Wikimedia Commons. 1 Apr. 2009. Web. 07
Feb. 2011. <http://commons.wikimedia.org/wiki/File:Francis_Bacon,_Viscount_St_Alban_from_NPG_(2).jpg>. Portrait of Francis
Bacon, Viscount St Alban, by John Vanderbank, 1731, after a portrait by an unknown artist (circa 1618). National Portrait Gallery,
London: NPG 520

According to the author, ADK Luk, Saint Germain ascended on May 1, 1684 in Transylvania at the Rakoczy mansion. He was 123 years old. Some say Saint Germain spent the lost years—from 1626 to 1684—in Tibet. During this time he took (or may have been given) the name *Kajaeshra*. Interpreted as *God's helper of life and wisdom*, it was possibly a secret name and rarely used. Kaja has several interpretations: in Greek it means pure; Balinese, toward the mountain; early Latin (Estonian), echo; Hopi, wise child; Polish, of the Gods; and Hebrew, life. The second part of the name—Eshra (Ezra)—translates into help or aid.

Indeed, Bacon's work would impact centuries to follow. During his time in Tibet, tucked away in silent monasteries, Germain designed a society that eventually created a United Brotherhood of the Earth: Solomon's Temple of the Future. It's a metaphor used to describe the raising of consciousness as the greater work of democracy. Author Marie Bauer Hall studied the life of Francis Bacon. In her book, Foundations Unearthed, she described the legendary edifice: "This great temple was to be supported by the four mighty pillars of history, science, philosophy, and religion, which were to bear the lofty dome of Universal Fellowship and Peace."[4]

But Germain embraced an even deeper passion: the people and nation of America, christening it New Atlantis. He envisioned this land—present-day United States, Canada, Mexico, and South America—as part of the United Democracies of Europe and the People of the World. America, this growing society, held his hope for a future guided by a Democratic Brotherhood.

The Comte de Saint Germain emerged years later in the courts of pre-revolutionary France—his appearance, intelligence, and worldliness baffled members of the Court of Versailles. This gentleman carried the essence of eternal youth: he was a skilled artist and musician; he spoke fluent German, English, French, Italian, Portuguese, Spanish, Greek, Latin, Sanskrit, Arabic, and Chinese; and he was a proficient chemist. Meanwhile, literary, philosophic, and political aristocracy of the time sought his company. French philosophers Jean-Jacque Rousseau and Voltaire; the Italian adventurer Giacomo Casanova; and the Earl of Chatham and statesman Sir Robert Walpole of Britain were among his friends.

In courts throughout Europe, he dazzled royalty with his Mastery of Alchemy, removing flaws from gems and turning lead into Gold. And the extent of Germain's ken reached well into the theosophical realm. A Guru of yogic and tantric disciplines, he possessed highly developed telepathic and psychic abilities. This preternatural knowledge led to the development of a cartographic Prophecy—the Map of Changes. This uncanny blueprint, now in the hands

---

4. Marie Bauer Hall, *Foundations Unearthed*, originally issued as Francis Bacon's Great Virginia Vault, Fourth Edition (Los Angeles: Veritas Press), page 13.

of the scion of Russian aristocracy, detailed an imminent restructuring of the political and social boundaries of Europe.[5]

But few grasped Germain's true purpose during this time of historic critical mass: not even the king and queen of France could comprehend his tragic forewarnings. The Great White Brotherhood—a fellowship of enlightened luminaries—sent the astute diplomat Saint Germain to orchestrate the development of the United States of Europe. Not only a harbinger of European diplomacy, he made his presence in America during the germinal days of this country. Esoteric scholars say he urged the signing of the Declaration of Independence in a moment of collective fear—a fear of treason and ultimately death. Urging the forefathers to proceed, a shadowed figure in the back of the room shouted: Sign that document!

To this day, the ironclad identity of this person remains a mystery, though some mystics believe it was Saint Germain. Nevertheless, his avid support spurred the flurry of signatures, sealing the fate of America—and the beginning of Sir Francis Bacon's democratic experiment.

The Comte de Saint Germain never could shape a congealed Europe, but he did form a lasting and profound relationship with America. Germain's present-day participation in U.S. politics reaches the Oval Office. Some theosophical mystics say Germain visits the president of the United States the day after the leader's inauguration; others suggest he's the fabled patriot Uncle Sam.

Saint Germain identifies with the qualities of Brotherhood and freedom. He is the sponsor of humanity and serves as a conduit of Violet Light—a force some claim is powerful enough to propel one into Ascension.

5. K. Paul Johnson, *The Masters Revealed: Madame Blavatsky and the Myth of the Great White Lodge* (Suny Series in Western Esoteric Traditions) (Albany, NY: State University of New York Press), page 19.

Malton Southern (Red) Door

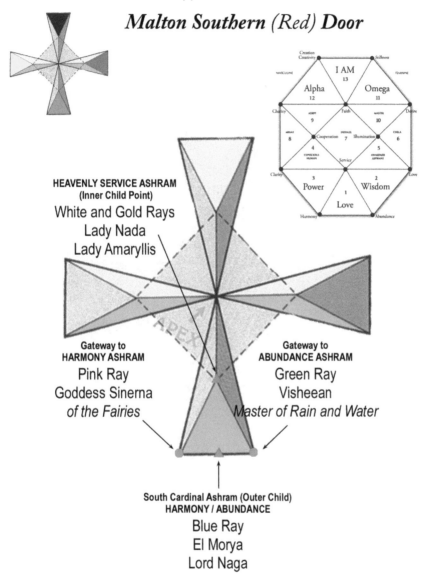

HEAVENLY SERVICE ASHRAM
(Inner Child Point)
White and Gold Rays
Lady Nada
Lady Amaryllis

Gateway to
HARMONY ASHRAM
Pink Ray
Goddess Sinerna
of the Fairies

Gateway to
ABUNDANCE ASHRAM
Green Ray
Visheean
Master of Rain and Water

South Cardinal Ashram (Outer Child)
HARMONY / ABUNDANCE
Blue Ray
El Morya
Lord Naga

The Hierarchs and Ray Forces of Malton's Adjutant Points
The Golden City of Malton (Illinois and Indiana,
United States), and the Hierarchs and Ray Forces
of its Adjutant Points.

The Golden Forest
An autumn scene in Master Kuthumi's beloved Golden
Forest. Photograph taken near the Malton Harmony
Point, Ferne Clyffe State Park, Illinois, USA.

Adjutant Point Hierarchs

MALTON GATEWAY TO HARMONY ASHRAM
Goddess Sinerna

Goddess Sinerna, *right*, of the Pink Ray is an Ascended Being of the Fairy Kingdom. She assists humanity to sense and appreciate harmony, an essential attribute of the feminine. She is the current Hierarch of the *Gateway to Harmony Ashram* located in Malton.

MALTON SOUTH CARDINAL ASHRAM
Lord Naga

Lord Naga is currently training with El Morya and will oversee the *Cardinal Ashram of Harmony and Abundance,* located in Malton. Lord Naga, *right*, serves the many chimera souls created during the Lemurian epoch, who now seek their Ascension. Both El Morya and Lord Naga serve this Adjutant Point with initiations of the Blue Flame.

MALTON SOUTH ABUNDANCE ASHRAM
Visheeah

Visheeah, *right*, is an Ascended Master of the Water Element and serves the Green Ray. He is the Hierarch of *Malton's Gateway to Abundance Ashram*, and can be called upon in times of drought to create plentiful rain.

MALTON HEAVENLY SERVICE ASHRAM
Lady Amaryllis

Lady Amaryllis, under the guiding tutelage of Lady Master Nada, will become the steward and Hierarch of the *Heavenly Service Ashram of Malton*. Since Lady Amaryllis is an Ascended Being who serves the Plant Kingdom, this Spiritual Sanctuary will focus upon and support the research and the development of medicinal aspects of plants and their innate ability to enable and enhance the Ascension Process for all Kingdoms of Creation. Lady Amaryllis has the ability to shrink her form to nearly twelve inches tall, known in Hindusim as the supernatural power of *Anima*. The Heavenly Service Ashram of Malton is affiliated with the White Ray of Beauty. Lady Amaryllis also serves on the Ruby and Gold Ray as Hierarch of the Golden City of Kreshe, located in Africa.

Appendix O
Master El Morya

El Morya incarnated from a long line of historical notables, including the fabled King Arthur of England; the Renaissance scholar Sir Thomas Moore, author of Utopia; the patron saint of Ireland, Saint Patrick; and a Rajput prince. El Morya is even linked to the Hebrew patriarch Abraham. But in spite of his illustrious lifetimes, El Morya is best known as Melchior, one of the Magi who followed the Star of Bethlehem to the Christ infant.

El Morya first revealed himself to the founder of the Theosophical Society Helena Petrovna Blavatasky—also known as Madame Blavatsky or H. P. B.—during her childhood in London; that mid-nineteenth century meeting forged a lifelong connection with her Master and other members of the Spiritual Hierarchy. Some esoteric scholars recount different, more dramatic scenarios of their initial introduction. Blavatsky herself claimed El Morya rescued her from a suicide attempt on Waterloo Bridge.[1] The gracious Master dissuaded her from plunging into the waters of the Thames River. Others say the two met in Hyde Park or on a London street. According to Blavatsky, El Morya appeared under a secret political cover as the Sikh prince Maharaja Ranbir Singh of Kashmir, who served as a physically incarnated prototype of Master M. Singh and died in 1885.

Metaphysical scholars credit Blavatsky's work as the impetus for present-day theosophical philosophy and the conception of the Great White Brotherhood. Devoted disciples learned of the Hindu teacher from Blavatsky's childhood visions, and later on in a series of correspondences known as the Mahatma Letters, which contained spiritual guidelines for humanity. El Morya's presence in H. P. B.'s life enriched her spiritual knowledge, and she shared this transformation in a prolific body of texts and writings, namely Isis Unveiled and The Secret Doctrine. During a visit with Madame Blavatsky, A.P. Sinnett, an English newspaper editor, found the first of these letters among the branches of a tree. Over the years, the true meaning and authorship of the Mahatma Letters, reportedly co-authored by fellow Mahatma Kuthumi, have spurned controversy; some say Blavatsky herself forged the messages.[2]

Master M. is associated with the Blue Ray of power, faith, and good will; the Golden City of Gobean; and the planet Mercury. A strict disciplinarian, El Morya dedicates his work to the development of the will. He assists many

---

1. Papastavro, Tellis S., *The Gnosis and the Law* (Tucson, AZ: Group Avatar), page 53.

2. Johnson, K. Paul, *The Masters Revealed: Madame Blavatsky and the Myth of the Great White Lodge* (Suny Series in Western Esoteric Traditions) (Albany, NY: State University of New York Press), page 41.

The Star of Bethlehem
Edward Burne-Jones, 1885. Melchior, one of El Morya's lifetimes,
presents a gift to the Christ child.

disciples in discovering personal truths, exploring self-development, and honing the practice of the esoteric discipline. El Morya passes this wisdom to his numerous chelas and students. The Maha Chohan—El Morya's Guru, Lord of the Seven Rays and the Steward of Earth and its evolutions—educated him during his Earthly incarnations in India, Egypt, and Tibet. Declining the Ascension a number of times, it is said that El Morya finally accepted this divine passage in 1888, ascending with his beloved pet dog and horse. (Esoteric symbols of friendship and healing.)

The Right-hand Path

Ameru and the Right-hand Path

The historical provenance of America (Ameruca)—the Land of the Plumed Serpent—is the lost history of Mu, Lemuria, and Atlantis. The Plumed Serpent metaphorically represents the developed Chakra System of the Divine God-man, the Ascended Masters' HU-man. The plume of light atop the head is the developed Crown Chakra, and the serpent's coils represent the mature Kundalini system, or human energy system comprised of seven chakras. It is claimed that many Lemurians and Atlanteans had the advanced capacity to function in both the Fourth and Fifth Dimension as Spiritual Masters, Sorcerers, and Shamans where an Alchemical and spiritual battle ensued: the Left-Hand Path versus the Right-hand Path. Spiritual development at this level of consciousness endows power over the Elemental Kingdom, and the unascended Spiritual Master is often pitted between both malevolent Black Magic and constructive White Magic. (These are the prominent abilities experienced by individuals who have achieved the Tenth Pyramid of Consciousness in HU-man development. For more information, see: *Golden City Series, Book Three, Divine Destiny.*)

The Right-hand Path

The Spiritual Masters who fled Atlantis and re-established their spiritual temples and sanctuaries in the New Lands held their chelas to the sacred vows of the Right-hand Path which today is practiced in Buddhism and Christianity as Compassion, Tolerance, Unity, the Brotherhood of Man, Mercy, and Forgiveness. This holy vow is reiterated in the Ascended Masters' Awakening Prayer: "Great Light of Divine Wisdom, stream forth to my being; and through your right use let me serve mankind and the planet . . ."

Theologians of Ascended Master teachings claim Lord Meru's temple was founded in the New World to embrace the Western ideals of the Right-hand Path, and teach Ascension attained by way of Sainthood through the rigor of humane service in the Ninth Pyramid of HU-man Consciousness. Today, many evolved Arhats choose to circumvent the spiritually arduous lure of the Tenth Pyramid and the horrifying conflict once experienced in the final days of Atlantis. Only the Adept is capable of venturing into the dualistic nomenclature of the Spiritual Master. Initiates of the Tenth Pyramid must properly prepare and strengthen their resolve with intimate knowledge and experience regarding the pitfalls of necromancy and reinforce the spiritual practice of the Right-hand Path attained through the proper use of Alchemy,

Christ in Desert
Nicholas Roerich, 1933.

Transmutation, and God-Protection. The Master Jesus Christ fasts for forty days and nights in the desert and faces the temptations of Satan in the demanding spiritual tests inherent in the Tenth Pyramid of Consciousness. The soul-trying conflict is illustrated in this Christian story:

1. Jesus Christ is asked by Satan to turn stones into bread—an abomination of the Elemental Kingdom; he responds, "One does not live by bread alone . . ."
2. Satan challenges Jesus Christ to jump off a temple's rooftop; after all, since he was a Son of God, surely an Angel will catch him. Unable to misuse the Divine Power entrusted to him, Jesus Christ responds, "You shall not put the Lord, your God, to the test." Will L. Garver, metaphysical author of the Victorian Age, clarifies this spiritual precept

in the classic occult novel Brother of the Third Degree, "Remember that the Great Brotherhood requires no tests except those which are mental and moral in nature."[1]

3. During this period, all of the Kingdoms of Creation are revealed to Jesus Christ: the Mineral Kingdom; the Vegetable Kingdom; the Elemental Kingdom; the Animal Kingdom; the Creative Hierarchy (the Human Kingdom); and the majestic Kingdoms of the Elohim and Archangels. Again, Jesus Christ is asked by Satan to assert his complete dominion, power, and authority over their realms; yet, Jesus Christ responds: "The Lord, your God, shall you worship and him alone shall you serve," affirming the spiritual principles of Unity, Cooperation, and the Sanctity of Life through the Right-hand Path.

According to the esoteric teacher Dion Fortune, there are distinct differences between the practices of the Right-hand and Left-hand Path, referred to in her works as either *White Magic* or *Black Magic*. The evolutionary enlightenment of the Arhat relies on the rich complexities of Mysticsm, and its religions of service and adoration, the power and beauty of Pantheism, and the hidden arts of astrology, divination, trance, human psychology, ceremony, decree, and the lineage of Gurus. The hidden arts are cultivated through dedication, purification, discipline, instruction, and service, which reach their culmination through the spiritual initiations of clarity, cooperation, charity, and faith—Mastery.

The devolutionary path of Black Magic relies on the confusion created through the use of drugs, sex magic, blood sacrifice, and pacts.[2]

---

1. Will L. Garver, *Brother of the Third Degree* (Garber Communications, 1989, Blauvelt, NY), page 183.

2. Dion Fortune, *The Training and Work of an Initiate*, (Weiser Books, 2000, San Francisco, CA). page 126.

Angel with the Flaming Sword
Franz Stuck, 1889.

Appendix Q
The Candle Meditation

The Candle Meditation by El Morya is one of the first steps to experience the Divine Light within and calm the mind. Use a long tapered candle, not a jarred glass candle. For this exercise a white candle is preferred, but any color should work. Light the candle and establish a constant, stable flame.

First, sit comfortably; you may use a chair for back support if needed. Look and concentrate on the candle and give attention to the different layers of the light of the flame. You will notice these layers: the outer glow; the yellow-white layer of fire; the center of the wick; and the central inner glow, which sometimes contains a blue or violet hue at the base of the flame. Focus on the overall glow of the candle until you identify the layers of light. Breathe evenly and gently as you concentrate on the light.

As you observe the Flame of Light, continue your rhythmic breath as the light begins to expand and absorb the space between you and the flame. Continue this breathing until you have established a large ovoid of light, including the candle and yourself.

Remain focused in the circle of light and you will begin to notice you are in the flame; the light is even, and it flows with your breath. You may notice a pulse in the energy field you share with the flame. At this state you are ONE with the light.

Individuals who practice the Candle Meditation have reported feeling calm and peace, even in extremely stressful conditions. Sometimes this is accompanied by a high-pitch ring. El Morya asserts the application of the Candle Meditation imparts experience with the consciousness of the ONE and develops human consciousness into the HU-man. The Candle Meditation can be performed individually or in groups.

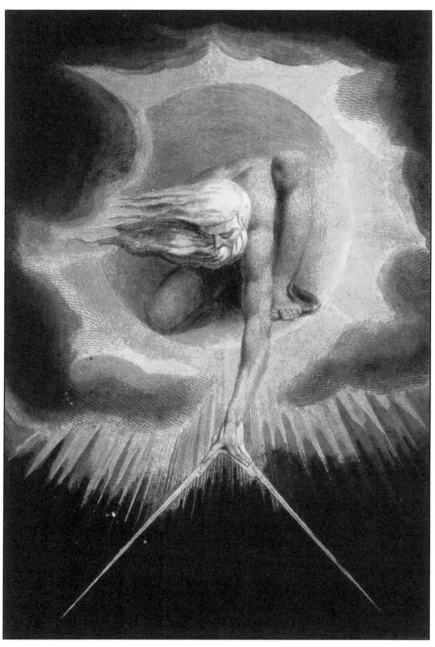

The Ancient of Days
by William Blake (1757—1827)
Sanat Kumara, portrayed by the visionary artist William Blake as *The Ancient of Days*, holds his
spiritual compass as if to engineer the spiritual city Shamballa. This portrait is housed in the British
Museum, London, and is claimed to be Blake's final painting, commissioned by Frederick Tatham.

Appendix R
Shamballa & Sanat Kumara

Shamballa, which means to *make sacred*, is the Earth's first Golden City. The notion of Shamballa represents peace, happiness, and tranquility. It's a place of spiritual cleanliness and divine dominion; it's the ethereal home and sanctuary of Sanat Kumara.

To understand Shamballa's metaphysical antiquity is to grasp its complex timeline. According to modern occult literature, this mystic metropolis existed more than 60,000 years ago. Other sources suggest that Sanat Kumara's legion of volunteers descended to Earth millions of years ago to build and inhabit the first incarnation of Shamballa. Over its long and calamitous history, the White City experienced a series of cataclysmic Earth Changes that destroyed it three times during sensitive alignments with the Galactic Light of the Great Central Sun. This cosmic susceptibility occurs when the progression of yugas (periods of Vedic timekeeping) move from one age of light to another. Sanat Kumara's followers rebuilt Shamballa twice; the third time the White City ascended beyond the physical realm where it now exists in etheric perpetuity. This is the thirty-sixth Golden City Vortex of Gobi, known today as the City of Balance. It is located in China over the Qilian Shan Mountains next to the Gobi Desert.

This City of White served a specific purpose: to save the Earth and humanity from certain annihilation. Stories like this in the Bible abound. Man's faith falters; his connection with God dims; and moral, physical, and spiritual depravity prevail—as was the state of the Earth before the Time of Shamballa. In a theosophical sense, universal principles demand a certain level of spiritual enlightenment for an entity to exist. The Earth and its inhabitants, however, consistently fell short; so a cosmic council of divine luminaries, including Sanat Kumara, voted to destroy the unfit planet.

But the compassionate Venusian Lord wouldn't allow Earth to fall into oblivion. Instead, he offered his light to balance the planet's metaphysical darkness and disharmony. As word spread of the Master's plans, devotees—144,000 of them—volunteered to accompany their Guru on his karmic Mission. One hundred of Sanat Kumara's stalwarts arrived on Earth 900 years beforehand to proliferate light; propagate the Flame of Consciousness; and prepare for the coming of Shamballa.

But, Sanat Kumara's volunteers paid a heavy spiritual price: karma. No longer would their Venusian souls enjoy the fruits of constant consciousness. Instead, as terrestrial bodies bound to the wheel of embodiment, they would follow the Laws of Earth—death, birth, and the passing of forgotten lifetimes—as their incarnating light energy lifted the consciousness of Earth.

Esoteric teachings say fellow Venusian Serapis Bey served as Sanat Kumara's first volunteer. With an affinity for architecture, this Master Teacher—along with the Seraphic Hosts he served with on the planets of Mercury, Aquaria, and Uranus—offered to oversee the creation of Shamballa.[1] Serapis Bey, the exalted being of light, performed one of the greatest sacrifices in Ascended Master legend by descending—as the light of heavens dimmed—into a physical body. On Earth, with his legions of seraphim, Serapis Bey oversaw the building of the White City for nine centuries. His sacrifice awarded him the honor of the Divine Architect of Shamballa.

This legend is analogous to the Hindu deity Tvashtri, later known as Vishvakarma, the celestial architect credited with the designing of the Universe and its contents.[2] Vishvakarma represents the power of regeneration and longevity. Serapis Bey later incarnated as Phidias, the great designer of the Parthenon, the classical sculptor of the Statue of Zeus, and the architect of the Temple of the Goddess Athena.

The builders of Shamballa modeled it after the opulent Venusian City of the Kumaras. On a white island in the sapphire-colored Gobi Sea (present-day Gobi Desert), workers erected the Elysian metropolis of light and consciousness. An ornate bridge of marble and Gold connected the White Island to the mainland. They adorned the city with hundreds of white, dome-and-spire-capped temples—that's where Shamballa earned its moniker, the City of White. Against this whitewashed backdrop, the luminous Temples of the Seven Rays and their corresponding hues—blue, pink, yellow, pearl-white, green, ruby, and violet—stood prominently along a landscaped avenue. At its terminus rose the Temple of the Lord of the World, Sanat Kumara's annular, Golden-domed sanctuary. Here, the Ascended Master; three other Venusian Kumaras (lords); and thirty high priests, also known as Lords of the Flame, held conscious light for Earth to sustain her place in the solar system. During his time in Shamballa, Sanat Kumara provided more than a spiritual safe harbor for the Earth's denizens. He also formed the Great White Brotherhood—the fellowship of the Ascended Masters.

Thus, Shamballa defined itself as the earthly seat of selflessness. Divine beings, including the unascended, flocked there to volunteer their efforts and services. To elevate their consciousness, and prepare them for upcoming lifetimes and undertakings, Sanat Kumara magnetized their energies with his Divine Love. Others seeking the Master's Heart Flame trained as messengers at Shamballa's numerous temples. Many of these servants became initiates of the Great White Brotherhood.

---

1. Tellis Papastavro, *The Gnosis and the Law* (Tucson, AZ: Group Avatar), page 28.

2. Hart Defouw and Robert Svoboda, *Light on Life: An Introduction to the Astrology of India* (London: Penguin Books Limited), page 232.

During Shamballa's physical existence on Earth, ascended and unascended members of the Great White Brotherhood returned annually for sanctuary, retreat, rejuvenation, and instruction for the upcoming year. After the third destruction of the city, and Shamballa's subsequent Ascension to the Fifth Dimension, ascended beings continued this tradition. But, without their aid, earthbound souls could no longer enter the City of White. To gain access, ascended members escorted the unascended to the etheric temples of the City of White by accelerating their light bodies during meditation and dreamtime.

For now, Shamballa will continue to exist in the ether, but Sanat Kumara prophesies its return:

"[It] shall remain there until it is lowered again, permanently, into the physical appearance world as the Golden Age proceeds and mankind, individually and collectively prove themselves worthy to sustain it for all eternity. It will be My Gift to the evolution that I have loved, and will remain a part of the Star of Freedom, long after I have returned to my home ..."[3]

Mythical Names for Shamballa from other cultures:

Hindu: Aryavarsha

Buddhist: Shambhala, a hidden community of perfect and semi-perfect beings.

Chinese: Hsi Tien, Western paradise of Hsi Wang Mu, the Royal Mother of the West.

Greek: Hyperborea

Russian: Belovodye and Janaidar

Jewish and Christian: Garden of Eden

Celtic: Avalon

Esoteric: Shangri-La; Agartha; Land of the Living; Forbidden Land; Land of White Waters; Land of Radiant Spirits; Land of Living Fire; Land of Living Gods; Land of Wonders.[4]

Sanat Kumara

Sanat Kumara, the venerated leader of the Ascended Masters, is best known as the founder of Shamballa, the first Golden City on Earth. He is also known in the teachings of the Great White Brotherhood as the Lord of the World and is regarded as a savior and eminent spiritual teacher. Sanat Kumara is revered in many of the world religions as the familiar Ancient of Days in Judeo-Christianity, Kartikkeya in Hinduism, the Persian deity Ahura Mazda

---

3. Tellis Papastavro, *The Gnosis and the Law* (Tucson, AZ: Group Avatar), page 103.

4. Mary Sutherland, In Search of Shambhala, http//www.living in the lightms.com (2003).

Ahura Mazda Investiture
Ahura Mazda (right) with Ardeshir I (left) in this archaeological relief at Naqh-e-Rustan (Iran).
This rock carving is from the birth of the Sassanian Empire (224—651). Ahura Mazda, a Persian
Deity and God of Zoroastrianism, is one of Sanat Kumara's noteworthy incarnations.

in Zoroastrianism (*pictured above*),[5] and as Moses' challenging teacher and the
Sufi initiator of Divine Mysteries Al Khdir. C. W. Leadbeater and Alice Bailey
referred to Sanat Kumara as the Youth of Sixteen Summers—a paradox to his
Ancient of Days identity—and the One Initiator, as the Master of spiritual cer-
emonies of initiation. According to esoteric historians, Sanat Kumara was one
of the few Ascended Masters who revealed his four-fold identity as the Cosmic
Christ: first as Kartikkeya, the Hindu commander of God's Army; second, as
Kumar (Kumara), the holy youth; third, as Skanda, son of Shiva; and fourth, as
Guha—a Sanskrit term for the secret place in the heart, as he lives in the cave
of all hearts.[6]

Sanat Kumara's Vedic and Buddhist Connection

The leader of the Spiritual Masters of the World appears historically in
Vedic religious texts as a rishi who was one of the four sons of Brahma, the
Creator. The four sons are born as liberated souls, and in early life take vows
of celibacy. Since they are young, unmarried males, this becomes their eternal

---

5, Ginolerhino, *Naqshi Rustam Investiture d'Ardashir,*Wikimedia Commons (2002).

6. Wikipedia, *Sanat Kumara,* http://en.wikipedia.org/wiki/Sanat_Kumara, (2011).

The Four Kumaras
The four youthful, immortal Brothers are depicted in this Indian print.

appearance, and the four sons are naturally attracted to devotional service to humanity, *pictued above*.[7] The four sons, or Kumaras, are known as: Sanaka Kumara; Sanandana Kumara (Sananda); Sanatana Kumara; and Sanat Kumara. In Sanskrit the name Sanat Kumara means eternal youth. Vedic scholars claim that the four sons are actually one incarnation manifesting on different planes of spiritual and physical reality. [8]

Santana Kumara	Supra Cosmic Plane
Sanaka Kumara	Solar Plane
Sanandana Kumara	Earth Plane
Sanat Kumara	Earth Planet

7. Four Kumar Blogspot.com, *Four Kumar Sanaka, Sanandana, Sanatana and Sanat Kumara*, 2019.

8. Wikipedia, *Sanat Kumara*, http://en.wikipedia.org/wiki/Sanat_Kumara, (2011).

Sanat Kumara's affiliation with the Earth is often referred to by esoteric researchers as the station or office of Planetary Logos—a soul whose evolutionary journey leads them to oversee entire planets. Dr. Joshua Stone describes this cosmic position: "The job of the Planetary Logos is to set up a framework on the physical level for all evolving life forms which allows them all to evolve and grow. The Planetary Logos could be symbolically likened to a mountain and the paths on the mountain which the life forms travel to evolve. The Planetary Logos is also at the top of the mountain so he can guide all life forms toward the top."[9] Perhaps this understanding alone gives explanation for Sanat Kumara's abiding presence in Shamballa, known in ancient India as the true spiritual center of Earth, akin to Earth's Sahasrara—Crown Chakra.

The Vedic epic of ancient India, the Mahabharata, states that Sanat Kumara is reborn as the son of Lord Krishna, Pradyumna. Pradyumna was an incarnation of the God of Love—Kama—and met a Karmic death at Dwaraka, one of the seven sacred cities of ancient India. With this final Earthly Karma completed, Pradyumna resumes his cosmic identity as Sanat Kumara and secures his rightful seat as the Planetary Lord of Shamballa.

Buddhist lore defines Shambhala (Shamballa) as the place of happiness, tranquility, and peace; and where the records of the Kalachakra Tantra—advanced spiritual practices, spiritual philosophies, and meditation techniques—are claimed to be safeguarded. The teachings of Vajrayana Buddhism declare the King of Shambhala as King of the World, and this royal lineage descends from the Kalki Kings who maintain the integrity of the Kalachakra teachings. Early Tibetans claim Shambhala's location to be North of Lake Manasarovar, the highest fresh-water lake in the world, and nearby Mount Kailash, which derives its name from the phrase the precious one and is considered a sacred mountain of religious significance to the Bon, Buddhism, Hinduism, and Jainism. This area is considered the hydrographic center of the Himalaya, and its melted snows are the source for the Brahmaputra River, the Indus River, and Karnali River—an important tributary of the Ganges River. It is thought that all of the Earth's dragon currents—energy lei-lines—intersect at Mount Kailash.[10]

Evolution and Training of a Planetary Logos
Sanat Kumara's evolution is said to have occurred primarily on an Earth-like planet located in the Milky Way Galaxy. It is claimed that after sixty-nine lifetimes, he achieved the Ascension. After a brief study of the Music of the Spheres, he elected the path of Planetary Logos. This training was arduous and

---

9. Joshua Stone, *The Complete Ascension Manual: How to Achieve Ascension in This Lifetime*, (Light Technology Publishing, 1994, Sedona, AZ), pages 178–9.

10. Wikipedia, *Sanat Kumara*, http://en.wikipedia.org/wiki/Sanat_Kumara, (2011).

Golden Cites & the Masters of Shamballa

spiritually challenging and the Master divided his consciousness into 900,000 fragments with each portion strewn to a different planet of the galaxy. From there he wove each individual piece back into the ONE through unconditional love and equanimity. After this great test of Mastery, Sanat Kumara was required to take on a physical body to continue his training on the Planet Venus, where he encountered the cosmic being Adonis who became his Guru. It is claimed that Sanat Kumara was educated in the beautiful Fourth Dimensional temples of Venus for 2,000 years. During his epoch tenure on Venus, Sanat Kumara was assigned to work with the Venusian Planetary Logos. As the Master grew in experience and knowledge of planetary infrastructure and patterns, he evolved his spiritual Mastery to embrace Unity Consciousness, integration, balance, and the power of choice. These important spiritual precepts ultimately groomed the young Lord for his chief assignment: Earth.[11]

Some esoteric texts claim Shamballa existed more than 60,000 years ago, while others claim Sanat Kumara was sent to Earth to build the restorative Golden City more than 18,000,000 years ago. This complex timeline may be explained by the cosmic susceptibility to the progression of the Yugas (periods of Vedic timekeeping) and their correlation with cataclysmic Earth Changes. The provenance of Shamballa states that the wondrous City of Light was destroyed and rebuilt three times. The first Golden City on Earth, however, was in all of its various stages of planning, construction, destruction, modification, and transformation, under the stewardship of Sanat Kumara. His assignment was simple but relatively complex: raise the consciousness of humanity. Should he fail in his mission, Earth would likely be destroyed. The compassionate Venusian Lord offered his light to balance the planet's metaphysical darkness and disharmony.[12] (For more information read: *Points of Perception, Shamballa.*)

Prior to Sanat Kumara's descent to Earth, he was given a well-deserved vacation of fifty years. Upon his return, he was given a party where it was announced that Sanat Kumara would be accompanied by the Venusian volunteers Lord Gautama and Lord Maitreya. Along with the angelic Serapis Bey, these two Lords would play invaluable roles in humanity's spiritual history and development.[13,14]

---

11. Joshua Stone, *The Complete Ascension Manual: How to Achieve Ascension in This Lifetime*, (Light Technology Publishing, 1994, Sedona, AZ), page 179.

12. Lori Toye, *Points of Perception: Prophecies and Teachings of Saint Germain*, (I AM America Seventh Ray Publishing, 2008, Payson, AZ), page 248.

13. Joshua Stone, *The Complete Ascension Manual: How to Achieve Ascension in This Lifetime*, (Light Technology Publishing, 1994, Sedona, AZ), page 181.

14. Lori Toye, *Points of Perception: Prophecies and Teachings of Saint Germain*, (I AM America Seventh Ray Publishing, 2008, Payson, AZ), pages 248–9.

Sanat Kumara
The Venusian Leader of Shamballa.

As Sanat Kumara, *pictured left,*[15] entered Earth, his three Brothers—the immortal Kumaras—held their focused energies to assist the heavenly incarnation. Today this is known as the Astrological Spiritual Trinity transmitted to the Earth through Jupiter, the Sun, and Mars. And to this day, energies of the Galactic Center triangulate to the Earth through these planets. While Sanat Kumara's incarnation took effect immediately, another 1,000 years was needed to properly seat the celestial powers and link the supreme consciousness to Earth. During this 1,000-year period, occult historians claim the Earth's atmosphere was filled with electrical storms.

Sanat Kumara and his stalwart volunteers patiently calibrated the Earth's energy fields and established their spiritual headquarters located near the Himalayan Mountains, near the present-day Gobi Desert.[16]

Sanat Kumara: Shamballa and the Great White Brotherhood

H. P. Blavatsky first coined the phrase "Lords of the Flame," to describe Sanat Kumara's association with humanity's Divine Evolution. Yet it was the theosophists Leadbeater and Annie Besant who claimed Sanat Kumara deployed thirty Lords of the Flame to accompany him on his spiritual mission to Earth. Classic Ascended Master teachings concur with this legendary story, however Sanat Kumara's group numbered 144,000 Venusian volunteers—pledged to enlighten Earth at a time of collective spiritual darkness.

One hundred of Sanat Kumara's volunteers arrived on Earth 900 years beforehand to proliferate light, propagate the Flame of Consciousness, and

15. See *Illustrations Endnotes.*

16. Joshua Stone, *The Complete Ascension Manual, How to Achieve Ascension in This Lifetime,* (Light Technology Publishing, 1994, Sedona, AZ), page 182.

prepare for the coming of the Golden City of Shamballa. Esoteric teachings say fellow Venusian Serapis Bey served as Sanat Kumara's first volunteer. With an affinity for architecture, this Master Teacher—along with the Seraphic Hosts he served with on the planets of Mercury, Aquaria, and Uranus—offered to oversee the creation of Shamballa. Serapis Bey, the exalted being of light, performed one of the greatest sacrifices in Ascended Master legend by descending into a physical body. On Earth, with his legions of seraphim, Serapis Bey oversaw the building of Shamballa—the City of White—for nine centuries. His sacrifice awarded him the honor of the Divine Architect of Shamballa.

The builders of Shamballa modeled it after the opulent Venusian City of the Kumaras. On a white island in the sapphire-colored Gobi Sea (present-day Gobi Desert), workers erected the Elysian metropolis of light and consciousness. An ornate bridge of marble and gold connected the White Island to the mainland. They adorned the city with hundreds of white, dome-and-spire-capped temples—that's where Shamballa earned its moniker, the City of White. Against this whitewashed backdrop, the luminous Temples of the Seven Rays and their corresponding hues—blue, pink, yellow, pearl-white, green, ruby, and violet—stood prominently along a landscaped avenue. At its terminus rose the Temple of the Lord of the World, Sanat Kumara's annular, golden-domed sanctuary. Here, the Ascended Master; three other Venusian Kumaras (lords); and thirty high priests, also known as Lords of the Flame, held conscious light for Earth to sustain her place in the solar system. During his time in Shamballa, Sanat Kumara provided more than a spiritual safe harbor for Earth's denizens. He also formed the Great White Brotherhood—the fellowship of the Ascended Masters.

Sanat Kumara's Return to Venus

Before Sanat Kumara's appointment as Lord of the World, Sri Magra held the office in Earth's spiritual-political hierarchy. After millions of years of service to Earth, Sanat Kumara was granted his freedom on January 1, 1956 and the noble Lord returned to his beloved Venus and his Divine Consort, Lady Master Venus. His three beloved Venusian volunteers—Lord Gautama, Lord Maitreya, and Serapis Bey—had successfully developed and advanced their sacred mission.

Serapis Bey became renowned as the World Architect and was also revered as the Hindu deity Vishvakarma.

Lord Maitreya became the leader of the Great White Brotherhood as a representation of the Cosmic Christ. He is the magnificent Guru of Jesus, Kuthumi, El Morya, Saint Germain, and many other Masters, saints, and spiritual teachers. Through the process of overshadowing, this avatar "enfolded Jesus in

His Cosmic Consciousness through Jesus' form." [17] The overshadowing process is described by Joshua Stone, PhD, in *The Complete Ascension Manual:*

> "Overshadowing was a process of melding his consciousness from the spiritual world into the physical body and consciousness of Jesus. In a sense, they shared the same physical body during the last three years of Jesus' life. Most people do not realize this. Many of the miracles and sayings attributed to Jesus were really those of Lord Maitreya who holds the position in the Spiritual Government as the Christ. Jesus so perfectly embodied the Christ Consciousness that it enabled the Lord Maitreya, who is the Planetary Christ, to meld his consciousness with that of Jesus." [18]

Using the same technique initiated by Lord Maitreya as the World Teacher, Sanat Kumara overshadowed and accelerated the Earth's spiritual development through Venusian Lord Gautama's earthly embodiment as Prince Siddhartha Gautama, an Indian prince (563–483 BC). Through Sanat Kumara's careful guidance, their consciousness melded as ONE, and Lord Gautama became the Enlightened One and qualified as Earth's first Buddha. According to A.D.K. Luk in the Law of Life, the activity and service of a Buddha is, "to step-down the high spiritual vibrations and radiate them to nourish, expand, and sustain the light in all beings during their development on the planet. He is to radiate God's love to a planet and its evolutions; to draw and hold the spiritual nourishment around a planet for all evolving lifestreams on that planet both while in and out of embodiment, sustaining them spiritually and developing their inner God natures especially the emotional bodies. He guards and sustains the flame of the least developed soul, so that it will not go out. A Buddha's work is through radiation, by radiating." [19]

Buddha's radiation of the indwelling spiritual consciousness of humanity paved the pathway for the development of humanity's conscious mind and the Christ activity, or Christ Consciousness in self-realization. Lord Buddha also assumed Sanat Kumara's vacant position at Shamballa as present-day Lord of the World, an honor bestowed from the now seasoned Planetary Logos: Sanat Kumara—mentor, Guru, and friend.

---

17. Joshua Stone, *The Complete Ascension Manual: How to Achieve Ascension in This Lifetime*, (Light Technology Publishing, 1994, Sedona, AZ), page 138.

18. Ibid.

19. A..D .K. Luk, *Law of Life*, (A.D.K. Luk Publications, 1989, Pueblo, CO), Book II, page 310.

The Spiritual Contributions of Sanat Kumara

The spiritual role played by Sanat Kumara in Earth's history and humanity's spiritual enrichment is truly invaluable and, without question, almost impossible to measure. There are, however, several significant and remarkable accomplishments worth noting.

Sanat Kumara spearheaded the mission to graft the sublime Unfed Flame—a Flame of Divinity and spiritual consciousness—to the carnal human heart. The Unfed Flame urges humanity to evolve beyond its present state of spiritual consciousness through Co-creative thought, feeling, and action and the Divine Tenets of Love, Wisdom, and Power. This empowers humans to achieve a higher sense of consciousness, thereby assuring humanity a type of spiritual immortality. With an etheric silver cord, Sanat Kumara connected the Unfed Flame to every life stream incarnation on Earth. This ensured the development and growth of spiritual consciousness among individuals.

During the 1,000-year period while Earth energies were purified to receive the spiritual presence and teachings of Sanat Kumara, the esteemed Lord performed yearly sacred fire ceremonies to clear Earth's etheric atmosphere of darkness. These ceremonies assisted the spiritually awakened to maintain contact with their I AM Presence. It is claimed that many attended these rites, and each attendee would take home a piece of the sacred wood used for the fire—likely sandalwood—to keep throughout the year. These ceremonies forged an indelible bond between Sanat Kumara and those he once served. A. D. K. Luk writes, "Sanat Kumara came ages ago to give assistance to the Earth when it would have been dissolved otherwise. He offered of his own free will to supply the light required to sustain her and keep her place in the system until enough of mankind could be raised to a point where they could carry the responsibility of emitting sufficient light . . . Now when people first come in contact with his name they usually feel a sense of happiness come over them. This is because of his connection with their lifestreams through radiation during the past."[20]

The sacred City of Shamballa is said to be both "a location and a state of consciousness."[21] Sanat Kumara's service to advancing spiritual students is never static and always unfolding; and along with various counsel meetings among the Spiritual Hierarchy, Sanat Kumara's purpose at Shamballa is to continue the initiatory process of students and chelas and to provide a haven for those who have successfully passed the fifth initiation. The seven levels of human evolution and their initiatory processes are:

> The spiritually un-awakened, yet conscious human.
>
> The Aspirant—a newly awakened, ambitious student.

20. A. D. K. Luk, *Law of Life*, (A. D. K. Luk Publications, 1989, Pueblo, CO), Book II, page 306.

21. Joshua Stone, *The Complete Ascension Manual: How to Achieve Ascension in This Lifetime*, (Light Technology Publishing, 1994, Sedona, AZ), page 185.

The Chela—the disciple who has entered a formal student relationship with a guru or teacher.

The Initiate—personal experience by degree, test, and trial that is encountered morally and mentally.

The Arhat—one who has overcome antagonistic craving, including the entire range of passions and desires—mental, emotional, and physical.

The Adept—one who has attained Mastery in the art and science of living; a Mahatma.

The Master—"human beings further progressed on the evolutionary pathway than the general run of humanity from which are drawn the saviors of humanity and the founders of the world-religions."

(*See diagram of the Eight-sided Cell of Perfection, depicting stages of spiritual evolution through the Twelve Jurisdictions.*)

"These great human beings (also known by the Sanskrit term Mahatma 'great self') are the representatives in our day of a Brotherhood of immemorial antiquity running back into the very dawn of historic time, and for ages beyond it. It is a self perpetuating Brotherhood formed of individuals who, however much they may differ among themselves in evolution, have all attained mahatma-ship, and whose lofty purposes comprise among other things the constant aiding in the regeneration of humanity, its spiritual and intellectual as well as psychic guidance, and in general the working of the best spiritual, intellectual, psychic, and moral good to mankind. From time to time members from their ranks, or their disciples, enter the outside world publicly in order to inspire mankind with their teachings."[22]

In metaphysical terms, Sanat Kumara may be seen as a mastermind of Earth's spiritual evolutionary process. A mastermind contains organized effort—a true measure of everlasting power. Sanat Kumara had the ability to hold the focus of the Elemental and Fourth Dimensional energies to create Shamballa on Earth and then actively engage the help of literally thousands of Lords, Masters, sages, saints, angels, Elohim, and adepts throughout our galaxy. Esoteric scholars claim that the entire spectrum of the Seven Rays are indeed embodied in Sanat Kumara and distributed through the synthesizing radiance of the Lord of the World.

Sanat Kumara Today

Presently the ethereal City of Shamballa is open to all who have acquired the eyes to see, and the ears to hear from December 17th to January 17th on an

---

22. *Encyclopedic Theosophical Glossary*, http://www.theosociety.org/pasadena/etglos/etg-hp.htm, (2011).

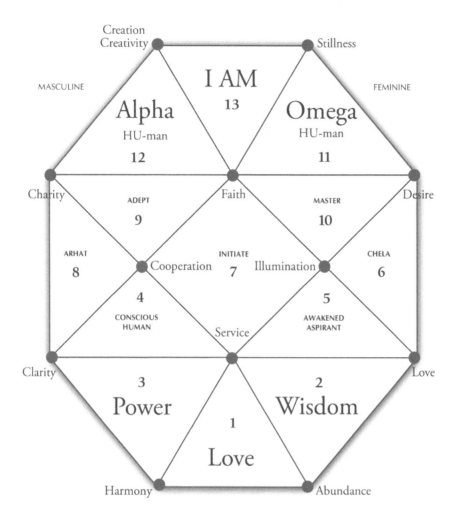

The Thirteen Pyramids and Twelve Evolution Points of the Eight-Sided Cell of Perfection
The Thirteen Initiatory Pyramids (stages) of the growth of the HU-man and their states of consciousness depicted in the geometry of the Eight-Sided Cell of Perfection. Also shown are the Twelve Evolution Points (Twelve Jurisdictions).

Golden Cites & the Masters of Shamballa

Apollo
by Briton Rivière (1840—1920)
Apollo often accompanies Sanat Kumara and is considered one of the Ancestral Teachers of Ascended Master Teaching. It is claimed that Apollo is the Master of Music, and is depicted with his lyre, whose stringed vibrations calm the Animal Kingdom. Briton Rivière was a British illustrator, famous for his realistic paintings of animals.

annual basis. During this time, Sanat Kumara returns to Shamballa and gives guidance to the Brotherhoods and Sisterhoods of Light for their yearly plan for humanity's spiritual growth and progress. Sanat Kumara's visit is accompanied by the Celebration of the Four Elements: a twenty-eight day festivity centered on devotional sacraments dedicated to the elements of earth, air, water, and fire in conjunction with thanksgiving, gratitude, love, friendship, intention, and unity. (For more information see: *Points of Perception*, and *The Celebration of the Four Elements*.)

Sanat Kumara is the Guru of four of the Twelve Jurisdictions—spiritual precepts on Co-creation designed to guide human consciousness into the New Times. As he gave this important wisdom, his ethereal presence was often accompanied by the Golden Radiance of the second Galactic Sun: Apollo.

The Eight Pathways of Ascension

Form of Ascension: Rapture.
Ray Force: Blue Ray.
Provenance: Egyptian Mystery Schools; Christianity.
Techniques: Devotion through belief systems.

Form of Ascension: Spiritual Liberation, "As above, so below."
Ray Force: Pink Ray.
Provenance: Indigenous.
Techniques: Oneness, Oneship, and the ONE through unifying the individual light fields with Mother Earth.

Form of Ascension: Enlightenment.
Ray Force: Yellow Ray.
Provenance: Buddhist; Contemporary.
Techniques: Purification of the Mental Body through spiritual practice.

Form of Ascension: Neutral Point.
Ray Force: White Ray.
Provenance: Contemporary.
Techniques: Balancing the light fields through the principle of love. This influences the Mental Body and the reincarnation process is no longer required.

Form of Ascension: Liberation from the body; dropping the body.
Ray Force: Green Ray.
Provenance: Vedic.
Techniques: Yogic techniques create harmony through healing, and the consciousness moves from the physical body to the Astral Plane, and onward.

Form of Ascension: Ceremonial worship and the Group Mind.
Ray Force: Ruby Ray.
Provenance: Late Lemurian culture; Atlantis.
Techniques: The power of the Group Mind lifts the participant's consciousness into the Astral Plane (Heaven).

Form of Ascension: Sacred Fire.
Ray Force: Violet Ray.
Provenance: Saint Germain.
Techniques: The Alchemy of the Violet Flame activates throughout the human kundalini system and dissolves karma. The karmic need for a physical body dissipates. Consciousness moves to the Astral Plane, then onward to the Causal Plane.

Form of Ascension: Golden City.
Ray Force: Gold Ray in tandem with the Yellow Ray during the Golden Age of Kali Yuga.
Provenance: Shamballa, Sanat Kumara, and Sananda.
Techniques: Refinement of the Mental Body through spiritual practice from all of the Seven Rays of Light and Sound, use of Group Mind, and Spiritual Pilgrimage. Ascension is obtained after physical or astral entrance into a Golden City Ashram, Temple, or Retreat.

The Spiritual Hierarchy

The term *Spiritual Hierarchy* often refers to the Great White Brotherhood and Sisterhood, however, this term also connotes the spiritual-social structure that exists within the organization, their members, and their various states of evolution. This includes the different offices and activities that serve the Cosmic, Solar, and Planetary Hierarchies. The following outline summarizes the Hierarchy's spiritual infrastructure:

1. **Cosmic Hierarchy, the Great Central Sun**
   a. The Silent Watcher: Galactic Architect
   b. Cosmic Beings
   c. The Galactic Suns
   d. Galactic Council
   e. Galactic Rays of Light and Sound
2. **Solar Hierarchy, our Solar Sun**
   a. Solar Rays of Light and Sound
      i. Elohim: Magnetize the Planetary Unfed Flame at the center of Earth
      ii. Archangels: Arch the Rays of Light and Sound to Earth
   b. Solar Manu: oversees the incarnation processes on various planets within this Solar System
   c. Planetary Silent Watcher: Architect of this Solar System
   d. The Cosmic I AM Presence: origination of the I AM Presence in the Creative Hierarchy
3. **Planetary Hierarchy**
   a. Karmic Board
   b. Manu: Protects the current race of humanity
   c. Axis of the Earth: Polaris (North) and Magnus (South)
   d. Earth's Elohim
      i. The Four Elements
      ii. Devas
      iii. Animal and Nature Kingdoms
   e. Earth's Archangels
      i. Seraphim
      ii. Cherubim
      iii. Angels

  f. Shamballa: Rules and balances the magnetism of Earth; keeper of the Rod of Power
    i. Lord of the World
      1. Great White Brotherhood
      2. Lords of Karma
      3. The Right-hand Path
    ii. World Teacher
      1. Spiritual Knowledge and World Religions
      2. Ascension Teachings
      3. The ONE
      4. Christ Consciousness
    iii. The Buddha
      1. World Buddha
      2. Kings of Shambahla: the Earth Protectors
    iv. The Golden Cities: overseen by Lord of the Transition Jesus the Christ, also known as Lord Sananda
      1. Adjutant Point Ashrams
      2. The Temples of Perfection
      3. Star Retreats
      4. The Star
  g. Lord of the Rays—Maha Chohan
    i. Seven Rays of Light and Sound
    ii. Seven Chohans of the Seven Rays
      1. Etheric Temples
      2. Spiritual Retreats
    iii. The New Ray Forces for the Golden Age
      1. Gold Ray
      2. Aquamarine Ray
  h. Heart of the Dove—Babaji
4. **Creative Hierarchy** (Human)
  a. The Ascended Master: the God-free being
  b. The I AM Presence: descends from the Cosmic I AM Presence as the Electronic Body
    i. Causal Body (Solar Angel)
      1. Abstract Mind
      2. Concrete Mind
    ii. Astral Body
      1. Christ-self
      2. Guardian Angel, Spirit Guides, and Spirit Teachers

c. The HU-man: the integrated and spiritually evolved human
    i. Master
    ii. Adept
    iii. Arhat
    iv. Initiate
        1. Bodhisattva
        2. Prophet
    v. Chela (disciple)
    vi. Aspirant (student)
d. The Human
    i. Unfed Flame: the spark of divinity
    ii. Eight-Sided Cell of Perfection: the atom of God-perfection
    iii. Flame of Consciousness: the Intellectual Consciousness separates the Human from the Third Hierarchy
    iv. Higher Self: the Holy Spirit
    v. Lower Self: the animal nature

Esoteric historians claim the Spiritual Hierarchy embodies religious principles from Christianity, Hinduism, Buddhism, Neo-Theosophy, and Ascended Master Teachings. However, to correctly understand the provenance of the Spiritual Hierarchy, it is essential to embrace its unique and concurrent Creation Story. The Ascended Masters' chronicle of the mythological formation of our galaxy, our Solar System, and the Earth offers significant insight and knowledge regarding the Spiritual Hierarchy.

According to the Ascended Master legend, the Silent Watcher embraces the Great Central Sun—the Galactic Center. This Cosmic Being is also known as the Galactic Architect who designed the galaxy along with its many Solar Systems. The Galactic Silent Watcher works in tandem with various Solar Silent Watchers who assist in the design of the individual Solar Systems within the galaxy. Scientists theorize that our Sun is one of 200 billion stars in the Milky Way, and so far, astronomers have discovered approximately seventy Solar Systems in our galaxy.[1] The Solar Systems of our galaxy are overseen by the Galactic Silent Watcher and the Galactic Council—comparable to a Galactic United Nations—which comprises many Ascended Cosmic Beings from a variety of solar and star systems, including: the Sirius System, the Pleiades Cluster, the Arcturus System, the Constellation of Centaurus, the Constellation of Pegasus, the Constellation of Hercules, the Constellation of Volans, the Constellation of

---

1. "How Many Solar Systems are in Our Galaxy?," http://nasa.gov, (2011).

Days of Creation,
the First Day
Edward Burne-Jones,
1870-1876

Aquila, the Orion System, and representatives from the neighboring DAL or DAHL Universe. At the time of this writing, scientific research discovered that the Earth may in fact originate from another galaxy: the Sagittarius Dwarf Universe.

Researchers surveying the sky with infrared light at the University of Massachusetts mapped a New Star Map, through the use of a supercomputer to sort out a half-billion stars. Through the study of star debris and by pinpointing the exact location of our Solar System—at the crossroads where two galaxies join—they discovered that the Milky Way Galaxy is absorbing smaller galaxies. The Sagittarius Dwarf Universe was discovered by a British team of astronomers in 1994, and in 2003 the Massachusetts team altered their angle of telescopic view to find the Earth in perfect alignment with the smaller galaxy, or what was left of it. Researcher Martin Weinberg believes this process is two-billion years in the making: "After slow, continuous gnawing by the Milky Way, Sagittarius has been whittled down to the point that it cannot hold itself together much longer . . . we are seeing Sagittarius at the very end of its life as an intact system." Metaphysicians theorize the discovery of the new galaxy may be the basis for the ending of the Mayan Calendar, because the Pleiades Star Cluster—which the calendar is based upon—is no longer a reliable point for celestial navigation as the Earth and its Solar System veer into a new direction.[2]

The Solar Hierarchy encompasses the Elohim and the Archangels. The Elohim (magnetism) are known as the Universal Builders and with the Archangels (radiation)—the Master conductors of the Rays—jointly formed a Creation Grid. At a central juncture of the grid the center of the Earth was created through the appearance of the Unfed Flame. To this day, the Unfed Flame is claimed to exist in the center of the Earth, and forms the cohesive power for the electrons and atoms of the Four Elements of the Earth.[3] Through the direction of the Rays, the Elohim managed the Four Elements (Virgo, Neptune, Aries, and Helios), the Gods of Mountains and Seas, and Amaryllis—the Goddess of Spring. The Devas created mountains, rivers, valleys, prairies, and lakes.

2. "Scientists Now Know: We're Not from Here!," http://viewzone2.com/milkywayx.html, (2011).

3. A. D. K. Luk, *Law of Life*, (A. D. K. Luk Publications, 1989, Pueblo, CO), Book II, page 206.

It is claimed that the Ascended Beings Virgo and Pelleur oversaw the creation of the earth element to hold water, and from this substance the human form was ultimately created.[4] The Solar Manu—a Cosmic Being—holds the creative authority to sponsor a generation of incoming lifestreams (approximately 2,000 to 5,000 years). The office of Manu oversees humanity's spiritual evolutionary process throughout various epochs by protecting the current, incoming race. Two Manus protect incarnating souls; the Solar Manu protects the generations of souls incarnating throughout our Solar System, and the Planetary Manu protects souls incarnating on Earth. In the New Times it is prophesied that Mother Mary occupies the Earthly post as guardian of the Seventh Manu—highly-evolved souls currently incarnating on Earth.

It is said that the gravity of the Earth is held through a mystical Rod of Power, a symbol of the office of Lord of the World that is kept securely in the Golden City of Shamballa. The mysterious wand is said to be constructed of orichalcum—the ancient metal of Atlantis—and encrusted with diamonds on either end.[5]

The history of Shamballa involves another important position in the Earth's Spiritual Hierarchy, the leader of the Great White Brotherhood: the World Teacher. Various Ascended Master teachings assert Jesus the Christ was the former resident of this appointment, and Lord Maitreya was the current World Teacher. The Golden Cities stream through the hierarchal radiance of Shamballa, and their importance for the planet and evolving humanity during the New Times has equal significance to the Earthly hierarchal offices of the World Teacher and the Buddha.

On Earth, the office of the Lord of the Seven Rays is claimed to be held by the Maha Chohan, who oversees the Chohans (Lords) of the activity of the Seven Rays on Earth. The Lord of the Seven Rays is likely the archetypal Mithra. The Lords of the Seven Rays oversee vital Temples and Spiritual Retreats located in both etheric and physical locations on Earth. These spiritual sanctuaries provide a focus for the activity of the Rays of Light and Sound on Earth and shepherd humanity's continued spiritual education and evolution through the Rays. The Maha Chohan—which means the Major Lord—is said to be surrounded by the white light of all the Rays. The Maha Chohan instructs:

"... the day of Our return into the consciousness of the mankind of Earth looms closer because the door has been opened by Faith and held back by the arms of Love, and the pathway of consciously dedicated energy passing out of your bodies and molded into form is wit-

---

4. Ibid., page 207.

5. Wikipedia, *Orichalcum*, http://en.wikipedia.org/wiki/Orichalcum, (2011).

ness before the great Cosmic Tribunal that the mankind of Earth do wish to walk and talk with a free Hierarchy, the Angels, the Devas, and the Gods once more. We come in answer to an invitation from your hearts—we have waited many centuries for such an invitation and Our gratitude to the lifestreams who are able to accept the logic within Our words and counsel cannot be measured by any human concept, but it can be felt, I am sure, by those of you who are now sensitive enough to note the radiation of Our individual Presences."[6]

Ascended Master creation myths place the origination of the human soul from the heart of the Sun God-Goddess who constructs at the end of a Ray the Three-Fold (Unfed) Flame. This generates a Divine Presence, or a God-Flame; a Co-creator with the Source, the Cosmic I AM Presence. According to esoteric historians, some God-Flames choose to remain in the eternal embrace of the loving aura of the parental Sun; those who choose to progress further project their spiritual essence into two Rays—Twin Rays. The Twin Rays develop a new light substance: an electrical light field which separates the Rays into two distinct individuals. The I AM—the individualized presence of God—dwells within the newly formed soul, and the electrical field of light is known as the I AM Presence.[7]

The Presence of the I AM on Earth forms the nexus of evolution in the Creative, or Human Hierarchy. The Electronic Body of light is formed of both the Causal and Astral Bodies. The Causal Body is known primarily as a mental plane, and many Ascended Masters reside in the higher levels of the Causal Plane during their service to humanity and Earth. In Theosophical texts, the Causal body is known as the Karanopadhi, and its lower manifestation is as-sociated with the causes bringing about re-embodiment on the Earth Plane; however, the Causal Plane is also associated with the Buddhi (Sanskrit for intellect) and the enlightenment of pure consciousness through discrimination between material and spiritual reality.[8] It is also the location of both the abstract and rational mind. The Astral Body or Astral Plane has various levels of evolu-tion and is the heavenly abode where the soul resides after the disintegration of the physical body. Within the Astral Plane lie our individual desires and salva-tion from their incessant demands—the Christ. This plane of emotional energy becomes the proverbial heaven or hell.

The Ascended Master who is free from incarnating on Earth directs the Unfed Flame within the heart and builds a new etheric body focused through the immortal spiritual fire and light. Hence, the unascended are directed by

---

6. Tellis Papastavro, *The Gnosis and the Law,* (Group Avatar, 1972, Tucson, AZ), page 119.

7. A. D. K. Luk, *Law of Life,* (A. D. K. Luk Publications, 1989, Pueblo, CO), Book II, page 208.

8. *Encyclopedic Theosophical Glossary,* http://www.theosociety.org/pasadena/etglos/etg-hp.htm, (2011).

the emotional desires of the Astral Body, symbolized by the earthly element of water. The Ascended Master has dissipated encumbering desires into a living flame; human desire is composed of etheric wandering. The human body is flesh; the Ascended Master is a body of spiritual fire—light. The luminous body of spiritual fire is developed through the use of the Unfed Flame in the physical plane.[9]

Elohim focus their etheric Flame of Consciousness into the pineal gland of the human. This creates the Intellectual Consciousness. An outgrowth of the individual consciousness as thought, feeling, and action is the development of Mass Consciousness. Mass Consciousness is often measured by two methods: Collective Consciousness, the total consciousness of all forms of life currently present on Earth; and the Group Mind. Societal and cultural beliefs are the creators of the Group Mind's collection of thoughts, feelings, and actions.

The Cosmic I AM Presence of the Solar Hierarchy projects into the Creative Hierarchy through the human heart, and radiates into the Unfed Flame; this is surrounded by the Eight-Sided Cell of Perfection. Human growth evolves through basic psychological and physical needs through ongoing spiritual interaction with the Guardian Angel, Spirit Guides, and Spirit Teachers. According to Theosophical thought, a spirit is incorporeal intelligence and can exist in almost limitless ranges of hierarchical classes: highest, intermediate, and lower.[10] Naturally, these interactions evolve the Lower Self, the animal nature within man, and awaken the Higher Self, as a direct and personal experience of our true nature.[11]Interaction with the Higher Self is also known as the Holy Spirit, a component of the I AM Presence. [Editor's Note: Some esoteric scholars claim that animals are evolved Elemental Beings of the Third Kingdom.]

The Awakened Human evolves to embrace the higher qualities of the Astral Body through the Christ-self (friendship, love, compassion), and the advanced characteristics of the Causal Body through the Solar Angel (leadership, confidence, respect, achievement). The I AM Presence instigates the human need for morality, ethics, Co-creation, and problem solving.

9. A.D.K. Luk, *Law of Life*, (A. D. K. Luk Publications, 1989, Pueblo, CO), Book II, page 214.

10. *Encyclopedic Theosophical Glossary*, http://www.theosociety.org/pasadena/etglos/etg-hp.htm, (2011).

11. "Discovering Your Higher Self," http://www.thevoiceforlove.com/higher-self.html, (2011).

Caritas, Madonna and Child
By Stanislaw Wypsiański, 1905.
National Museum,
Warsaw, Poland.

The Seventh Manu, the Swaddling Cloth of South America, & Mother Mary

The Master Teachers describe the Seventh Manu as a large group of souls that incarnate for over 1,500 years on Earth (1981 AD to 3650 AD). The purpose of the Seventh Manu soul-group is to raise the overall vibration of Earth through their spiritually evolved understanding of Freedom and Peace. Their attributes include:

1. Many of the souls incarnating as the wave of souls known as the Seventh Manu have not incarnated on Earth for thousands of years; and some were last present on Earth during the time of Atlantis.

2. Some souls of the Seventh Manu have a natural talent and propensity toward the technological sciences, which inevitably assists the Earth and its evolutionary process.

3. Previous incarnations on diverse planets and different solar systems are common among Seventh Manu souls. According to Saint Germain, the system of evolving souls does not consider physical proximities restricted only to Earth. The soul is "timeless" and is not bound by the Third Dimensional aspects of time and space. When viewed through this understanding, the veil separating physical and spiritual realities is a thin line of demarcation, and the soul's consciousness often evolves between galaxies and star-systems literally thousands of light-years away.

4. The New Children are prophesied as spiritual Masters who will incarnate on Earth at a critical juncture of humanity's evolutionary process to help the masses transmute difficult karmas and lead many into the liberation, or Ascension Process.

5. Children of the Seventh Manu are also known as the *Indigo Children*. Seventh Manu refers to the Seventh Alchemic Ray— the Violet Ray. The scientific wavelength of the color Indigo is between Blue and Violet; however, many consider Indigo analogous to Purple.

6. Since Seventh Manu souls carry a higher vibration and less karmic burden than the average Earth soul, they are prophesied to lead humanity into the *Age of Transportation*. During this Earth epoch, spiritual technology will embrace the ancient practice of bi-location and the spiritual ideals of timelessness.

7. The Spiritual Technology of the children of the Seventh Manu is prophesied to develop and is derived from varied experiences gleaned from their incarnations in different galaxies. This exposes the Earth to new ideas, processes, and perceptions that evolve our current sciences and reshape much of our current technology.
8. The influence of the New Manu children will shape human consciousness for several thousand years. As these souls are wise beyond their years, they will be seen as the new elders of Earth. The New Children will lead a renaissance in reformation of our societies, cultures, religions, and scientific knowledge.
9. While this group of souls is highly evolved, Saint Germain explains that they, too, have their own unique karmas and "Time of Testing," to be played out upon the Earth Plane and Planet.

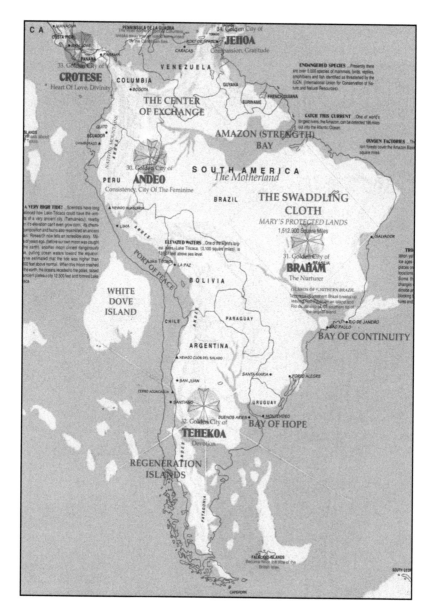

The Swaddling Cloth

An area of over a million square miles located in Brazil, South America. According to the Ascended Masters, this area is the primary prophesied physical location for the incarnation of the children of the Seventh Manu. The Swaddling Cloth is protected by the Ascended Master Mother Mary. *See above map.*

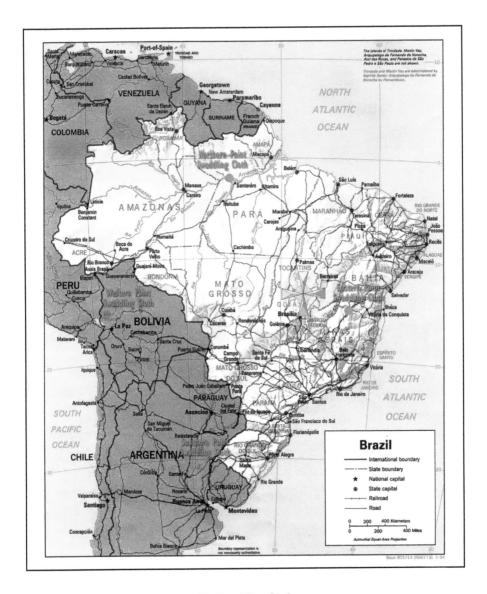

The Swaddling Cloth
The Golden City Braham is located in Brazil,
and the Swaddling Cloth. The Four Red Points
of the Swaddling Cloth delineate the protected
lands of Mother Mary, dedicated to the New
Children.

Mother Mary, the Western Goddess and Archetype of the Feminine

The Ascended Master and Western Goddess of the Feminine Archetype was an initiate of the ethereal Temples of Nature before her incarnation as Mary, Mother of Jesus Christ. It is claimed that as a child Mary was raised in the mystical traditions of the Essenes, and throughout her lifetime as Mother Mary, she was constantly overshadowed by the Angelic Kingdom. Some Ascended Master texts claim Mary was once a member of the heavenly realm.

Mary's lifetime as the mother of Jesus Christ was planned in-between lifetimes on Earth, "Her embodiment as Mother of Jesus was in the Divine Plan long before she entered the physical realm. She went through a severe initiation at inner levels to test her strength some time before taking embodiment."[5] Throughout her life as the Master's mother, Mary was attuned to the spiritual planes which gave her strength and insight to fulfill her role as the Mother of Jesus. And, no doubt, Mary or Maryam, as she is known in Aramaic, lived in perilous times. The Biblical story in the Book of Matthew accounts the Holy Family's flight to Egypt to avoid King Herod's Massacre of the Innocents. It is claimed that Mother Mary made a vow to assist anyone who had lost their life as a Christian martyr to obtain the Ascension in a future life.[6] Mary the Mother of Jesus became an archetype of the Cosmic Mother for all of humanity.

As an archetype of the Feminine, Mary is also a form of Isis, the Virgin of the World of Hermetic Teaching. The name Isis draws its meaning from Hebrew and Greek sources, which means wisdom or to serve.[7] However, the myth of the Virgin Goddess is contained in the ancient language of Scandinavia as Isa; and is similarly portrayed as the Eleusian Goddess Ceres and Queen Moo of the Mayans. Manly Hall writes, "She was known as the Goddess with ten-thousand appellations and was meta-morphosed by Christianity into the Virgin Mary, for Isis, although she gave birth to all living things—chief among them the Sun—still remained a virgin, according to legendary accounts." As the eldest daughter of Kronus the Ancient Titan, and the wife and sister to Osiris, Isis was the student of the great Master Hermes Trismegistus. Through this affiliation it is claimed the laws for humanity were developed, including an alphabet for written language, astronomy, and the science of seamanship. Isis helped humanity to overcome paternal tyranny through instructing men to love women and children to love and respect their elders through the philosophic teachings of beauty as truth, and the intrinsic value of justice. The teachings of Isis are not for the irreverent. The discipline of emotion and the acquisition of wisdom are required in order to access and understand the evolutionary energies of the Feminine.

The Immaculate Conception of the Venerable Ones, by Murillo (1678)
Murillo, Bartolomé Esteban. The Immaculate Conception of the Venerable Ones. 1678.
Oil on canvas. A depiction of Mother Mary with new souls.

Ancient initiates were advised to keep silent their venerated knowledge of the spiritual truths underlying the vulgar and profane.[1]

In Christianity Mary is known as the Virgin Mother of Jesus; however, Catholics and Protestants differ regarding their worship of the Mother of the Son of God. In Islam, the Virgin Mary is esteemed as the mother to the Prophet Issa.[2] Jesus' birth was prophesied by the Archangel Gabriel in a visit to Mary during her betrothal to Joseph, and the Archangel declared, "She was to be the mother of the promised Messiah by conceiving him through the Holy Spirit."[3] The New Testament places Mary at Nazareth in Galilee, the daughter of Joachim and Anne. Apocryphal legend claims Mary's birth was also a miracle—her mother was barren. To many Roman Catholics, Mary was the perfect vessel to carry the Christ, and was "filled with grace from the very moment of her conception in her mother's womb and the stain of original sin."[4] This spiritual precept is known as the Immaculate Conception of Mary.

Contemporary interpretations of the Immaculate Concept state this spiritual practice is the Alchemy of holding the image of perfection through the use of prayer, meditation, and visualization. Thought-forms of "Beauty, poise, and grace on behalf of others," is claimed to create Divine Energies of purity and protection.[5] David C. Lewis writes regarding the spiritual exercise of holding the Immaculate Concept for ourselves:

> "Ultimately we must first hold the immaculate concept for ourselves by attuning to our own Higher Self and maintaining a vigil of Oneness through presence and awareness of our own Divine Nature. Once we have learned to live in this unified field of stillness and beingness and maintain our spiritual poise, especially during challenging times and situations, we can more easily practice the science of the immaculate concept on behalf of others."[6]

According to the Ascended Masters Mother Mary holds the Immaculate Concept for the incoming generations of the Seventh Manu through the energies of the Swaddling Cloth, located in Brazil, South America. In the I AM America teachings, Mother Mary often

1. Manly P. Hall, *The Secret Teachings of All Ages: An Encyclopedic Outline of Masonic, Hermetic, Qabbalistic and Rosicrucian Symbolical Philosophy*, (Philosophical Research Society, Inc., 1988, Los Angeles, CA), page 45.

2. Wikipedia, *Mary (Mother of Jesus)*, http://en.wikipedia.org/wiki/Mary_(mother_of_jesus), (2009).

3. Ibid.

4. Ibid.

5. David C. Lewis, "The Immaculate Concept: Creating Alchemical Change," http://www.theheartscenter.org, (2009).

6. Ibid.

merges her energies with Kuan Yin, the Feminine Bodhisattva of Mercy and Compassion, and together they channel the energies of the Divine Mother to Earth. Divine Mother is an archetype of Feminine Unity and the ONE. Beloved Mary is known to appear at times of physical or emotional crisis, often to convey the healing power of wholeness and unconditional love. Mother Mary's Temple of the Sacred Heart, located in the Fifth Dimension, prepares souls for re-embodiment.[7] She is the Ascended Master sponsor of the Golden City of Marnero, located in Mexico. Marnero means the ocean of candles; its quality is Virtue; and this Golden City is affiliated with the Green Ray.

---

7. A.D.K Luk, *Law of Life*, Book II, (ADK Luk Publications, 1989, Pueblo, CO), page 347.

The Four Pillars: Schools of Shamballa

According to Saint Germain, there are four distinct schools that stream through the lineage of Shamballa, the glorious *City of White*, built by the Venusian leader Sanat Kumara, who modeled many of the majestic buildings and temples after the luminous cities of Venus.

Lord of the World: The original and primary Venusian teachings as they were established on Earth by Sanat Kumara. Sanat Kumara was assisted by three Venusian Lords and thirty high priests, known as the *Lords of the Flame*. The soul-expanding knowledge of the Seven Rays of Light and Sound was first established in these teachings, alongside the creation of the Great White Brotherhood, the Lords of Karma, and the Karmic Board. The symbol for this school is the mystical Rod of Power, a metaphysical object that is said to keep the Earth's poles in balance. It is constructed of orichalcum, the ancient metal of Atlantis, and is encrusted with jewels and diamonds.

World Teacher: This school was organized to structure religious and philosophical teaching for the fifth root race—the Aryan, which is the dominant Manu since the destruction of Atlantis. The teachings of this Second Pillar of Shamballa embrace the ancient and contemporary spiritual knowledge of the world including Mithraism, Vedic scriptures, Taoism, the Buddha, Judaism, and Christianity. The office of the World Teacher oversees humanity's cultivation of the (Quetzelcoatl) Christ Consciousness. It is claimed that their disciplines are based on the history of a total of 14,000 years, with a span of 2,000 years given to each of the Seven Rays of Light and Sound. These ethereal halls of wisdom educate the Gurus of the Masters, Angels, pandits, monks, priests, ministers, rabbis, missionaries, and anyone associated with, "spreading the Word of God," that leads the soul to Ascension.[1] Various Ascended Masters have served as the head of this important branch of Shamballa: Lord Maitreya, Master Kuthumi, and Jesus the Christ (Lord Sananda).

---

1. Tellis Papastavro, *The Gnosis and the Law* (Tucson, AZ: Group Avatar), page 122.

The Buddha: The sublime Kingdom of Heaven is stepped-down into the atmosphere of the Earth through the Third Pillar and this School of Shamballa. The Buddha is the overseer of the Buddhist faith through many forms of Buddhism. Its roots lie in the royal lineage of the Tibetan Shamballa Kingdom, often spelled: *Shambhala*. This is the path of Venusian harmony of the mind—enlightenment. These spiritual techniques include traditional meditation, feng shui, calligraphy, poetry, and contemplative flower arrangement and dance. This school also includes a dharmic lineage of Shambhala Kings, who are the protectors of the Earth through their philosophy of courage, wisdom, and compassion.[2] The great Gautama Buddha oversees the office of "World Buddha."

The Golden Cities: Overseen by Lord Sananda of the Transition, the Golden Cities are Sanat Kumara's and Lord Apollo's divine intervention for humanity during the Golden Age of Kali Yuga. The Golden Cities are replete with thirty-three Third, Fourth, and Fifth Dimensional ashrams, temples, and retreats. These sanctuaries amplify and potentiate spiritual practice and focused techniques that lead the ordinary human onward to HU-man development and to the inevitable liberation and soul-freeing Ascension. The Golden Cities also serve Earth's weather and climate, humanity's social and cultural evolution, and worldwide economic and political environments through calibrating and refining the Seven Rays of Light and Sound that emanate and radiate from the Galactic Center. This also involves the Eighth Ray that is destined to spiritually advance and progress humanity during the ten-thousand year Golden Age—the Gold and Aquamarine Ray. The symbol for the Golden Cities is Five Stars, which represents *Divine Man* and the first Five Golden Cities of the United States, accompanied by the White Dove of Peace.

---

2. "Sakyon Mipham." Shambhala, 2019, shamhala.or/teachers/sakyong-mipham

The Number of Adjutant Points

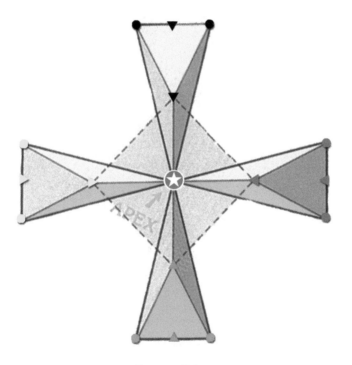

The Seventeen Primary Adjutant Points of a Golden City

Seventeen Points
The seventeen primary Adjutant Points of a
Golden City include the Star.

Thirty-three
Golden City Points

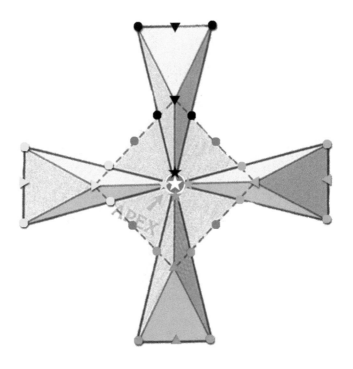

Thirty-three Points
The thirty-three points of a Golden City include
Ashrams, Temples, Star Retreats, and the Star.

The Heart of the Dove

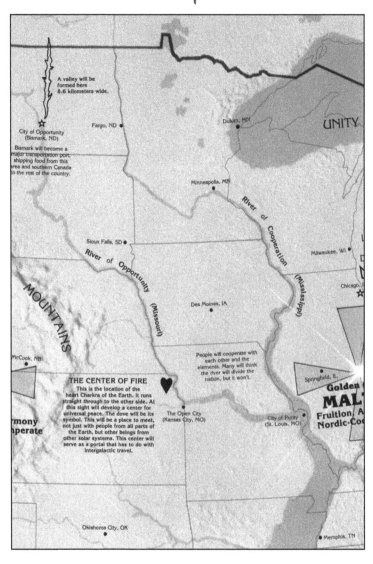

Heart of the Dove

Also known as the *Center of Fire*, this energy anomaly is prophesied to exist Northwest of Kansas City, Missouri. (The center of this portal is near Atchison, Kansas.) It is here that Master Teachings claim an umbilicus connection between Earth, the Galactic Center, and the Galactic Suns exists, creating time anomalies and the potential for time travel in the New Times. The Heart of the Dove is also prophesied to become a spiritual center for learning and self-actualizing the Christ Consciousness. This portal of purity and sanctity radiates restorative, rejuvenating energies that assist Ascension, and it is stewarded by the great Avatar Babaji.

Aries View from the Wheat Fields
Vincent van Gogh, 1888.

Golden Ray Diet

The Golden Ray diet is a supplemental regime that you can add to your everyday meals to increase the Gold Ray throughout your energy system. It consists of fruits, vegetables, legumes, and grains whose plants, rinds, pods, or skins turn an orange or yellow color upon maturation. The plant must grow above the ground, no root vegetables. The plant absorbs the Gold Ray from our Sun. Here are a few suggestions:

Fruits:
Orange
Lemon
Banana
Grapefruit
Tangerine
Peach
Gold Kiwi
Yellow Dragonfruit
Yellow Raspberry
Mango
Pineapple
Yellow Apple
Yellow Fig
Yellow Pear
Nectarine
Persimmon
Papaya

Vegetables:
Sweet Yellow Pepper
Yellow Squash
Pumpkin
Yellow Cauliflower
Yellow Wax Bean

Nuts:
Cashew
Almonds (ripe)

Beans and Grains:
Garbanzo Bean
Yellow Lentil
Yellow Split Pea
Quinoa
Wheat
Barley
Oats

The Milky Way Galaxy Center
The NASA/ESA Hubble Space Telescope, the Spitzer Space Telescope and the Chandra X-ray Observatory have collaborated to produce an unprecedented image of the central region of our Milky Way galaxy. In this image, observations using infrared light and X-ray light see through the obscuring dust and reveal the intense activity near the galactic core. Note that the centre of the galaxy is located within the bright white region to the right of and just below the middle of the image. The entire image width covers about one-half a degree, about the same angular width as the full Moon. Each telescope's contribution is presented in a different colour: Yellow represents the near-infrared observations of Hubble. They outline the energetic regions where stars are being born as well as reveal hundreds of thousands of stars. Red represents the infrared observations of Spitzer. The radiation and winds from stars create glowing dust clouds that exhibit complex structures from compact, spherical globules to long, stringy filaments. Blue and violet represent the X-ray observations of Chandra. X-rays are emitted by gas heated to millions of degrees by stellar explosions and by outflows from the supermassive black hole in the galaxy's centre. The bright blue blob on the left side is emission from a double star system containing either a neutron star or a black hole. When these views are brought together, this composite image provides one of the most detailed views ever of our galaxy's mysterious core.[1]

1. NASA, and ESA. "Plik:The Milky Way Galaxy Center (composite Image).jpg – Wikipedia, Wolna Encyklopedia." Wikimedia Foundation - Secure Portal. 12 Mar. 2010. Web. 29 Oct. 2011. <https://secure.wikimedia.org/wikipedia/pl/wiki/Plik:The_Milky_Way_galaxy_center_(composite_image).jpg>.

Lineage of the Seven Galactic Suns

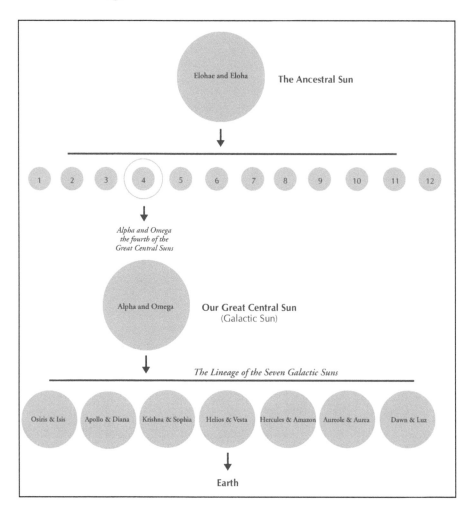

The Ancestral Sun — Elohae and Eloha

Alpha and Omega the fourth of the Great Central Suns

Our Great Central Sun (Galactic Sun) — Alpha and Omega

The Lineage of the Seven Galactic Suns

Osiris & Isis · Apollo & Diana · Krishna & Sophia · Helios & Vesta · Hercules & Amazon · Aureole & Aurea · Dawn & Luz

Earth

The Lineage of the Seven Galactic Suns

According to Ascended Master teachings, our solar Sun is one of seven evolved Suns from the lineage of Twelve Ancestral Suns. Alpha and Omega—our current Great Central Sun—is overseen by a larger ancestral Sun, known in Ascended Master myth as the Mighty Elohae-Eloha. It is claimed that of the twelve Great Central Suns, Alpha and Omega is the fourth, and from their lineage, seven smaller solar Suns evolve: the Seven Galactic Suns. Currently, Helios and Vesta serve as Earth's solar Sun. It is claimed that each of the Seven Galactic Suns emit spiritual light which guards, protects, and evolves incarnating souls in these solar systems.[1]

---

1. Tellis Papastavro, *The Gnosis and the Law*, (Group Avatar, 1972, Tucson, AZ), page 31.

Pearl of Searching
Nicolas Roerich, 1924.

Illustrations Endnotes

"Archangel Chamuel." *YouTube Channel, Bram Ardianto: How to Recognize Archangel Chamuel*, 31 Oct. 2016, www.youtube.com/watch?v=4yvEwWTJHvI.

Archangel Jophiel. i.pinimg.com/736x/76/7b/f1/767b f147b881e4022e5e69427b5875c3--angels-beauty-heavenly-angels.jpg. Accessed 7 July 2018.

"Archangel Jophiel." *Archangels Jophiel and Christine*, 2019, www.pinterest.com/pin/526147168946144884/.

"Archangel Michael." *Https://Mysticcircle.wordpress. com/Tag/Archangel-Michael/*, 8 July 2018.

Ardianto, Bram. "Archangel Gabriel." *How to Recognize Archangel Gabriel*, YouTube, 31 Oct. 2016, www.youtube.com/watch?v=7RKUBQZSGKk.

Ascension Now, anow.org/. Accessed 7 July 2018.

"Astrea, Goddess of Purity." *Prayers/Angels of Pure Love*, pure-love.org/prayers-and-angels/. Accessed 8 July 2018.

Beautiful Fairy. 2019, everyhdwallpapers.blogspot. com/2015/09/beautiful-fairy-angel-wallpaper.html.

Beckler, Melanie. "Archangel Christiel." *The Archangels*, 15 Dec. 2016, www.ask-angels.com/archangels/.

Bergersen, Thomas. "Ocean Princess." *Cape Tranquility*, YouTube, 21 June 2011, www.youtube.com/watch?v=gbEob28Dxag.

Boulet, Susan Seddon. "Shaman." *Susan Seddon Boulet Visionary*, 2019, www.tuttartpitturasculturapoesiamusica.com/2013/01/Susan-Seddon-Boulet.html.

Boulet, Susan Seddon. *Turning Point Gallery*, www.turningpointgallery.com/saint_germain.htm. Accessed 7 July 2018.

"Cassiopea, Elohim of the Yellow Ray." *The Power of Prayer, Appeal to the Elohims*, holisticocromocaio.blogspot.com/2013/10/o-poder-da-oracao-apelos-aos-elohins.html. Accessed 8 July 2018.

"Claire, Elohim of Purity." *I AM That I AM YouTube Channel*, www.youtube.com/watch?v=XqojGswJlnw. Accessed 6 Jan. 2018.

"Donna Grace." *The Archeia*, 2019, earthangel555. blogspot.com/2011/05/archeia.html.

"El Morya." *Summit Lighthouse*, 2019, summitlighthouse.org/el-morya.

"Elohim Arcturus and Diana." *Metaphysical School of Maitreya*, metafisicacdelu.blogspot. com/2012_12_15_archive.html. Accessed 8 July 2018.

Elohim Hercules. librosmetafisica.com/elohim-hercules-lamina-imagen/. Accessed 8 July 2018.

"Elohim of Peace." *Beloved Elohim of Peace*, 2019, lightgrid.ning.com/group/6goldenrubyrayaauriel/forum/topics/beloved-elohim-of-peace-on-her-1.

Faget, Caroline. *Message De l'Ange Haziel.* www.carolinefaget.fr/message-de-lange-haziel/.

Fox, Jon C. "Hilarion." *The Hilarion Page*, hilarion. com/. Accessed 7 July 2018.

George, Marius Michael. "Astrea." *Marius Fine Art Studio*, www.mariusfineart.com/Astrea_info. html. Accessed 8 July 2018.

"Goddess of Wisdom Yum Chenmo, a Form of Minerva." *Okar Research*, balkhandshambhala. blogspot.com/2015/06/yum-chenmo-shenlha-okar.html. Accessed 8 July 2018.

"Godfre and Saint Germain." *Saint Germain Foundation*, www.saintgermainfoundation. org/SGF_08_TheOrigTeachings.html. Accessed 8 July 2018.

Great White Brotherhood. 2019, www.meetup.com/The-Miami-Metaphysical-Study-Group/events/126134722/?value=The+Great+White+Brotherhood+-The+Great+Spirtual+Hierarchy+Of+Ascended+Master.

Hall, Manly P. *Manly P. Hall, The Phoenix: An Illustrated Overview of Occultism and Philosophy,* . Philosophical Research Society, 1983.

Hao Han, Yeong. "City's Blessings." *Https://Www. artstation.com/Artwork/J2YeD*, 2019.

Holy Prophet Elijah. 2019, www.iconsandechoes. com/2013/12/holy-prophet-elijah.html.

"Huldah." *A Closer Look at the Prophet Huldah,* 2019, amaichuldahprophetess.wordpress. com/2013/10/20/a-closer-look-at-the-prophet-huldah/.

John's Vision. 2019, nwspiritism.com/your-destiny/the-apocalypse-according-to-spiritism/.

Johnson, Howard David. "Archangel Uriel." *Angel Art,* 2014, howarddavidjohnson.com/Angel-art. htm.

King Akhenaton. 2019, www.egypttoursportal.com/ king-Akhenaton/.

Korsolm, Celeste. "Soltec." *Art Gallery Portraits by Celeste,* www.artsedona.net/albums/album_ image/3958827/7245023.htm. Accessed 7 July 2018.

"Kuan Yin." *Kuan Yin, the Way of the Bodhisattva,* mykuanyin.blogspot.com/p/kuan-yin-quotes. html. Accessed 7 July 2018.

"Lady Lotus." *Art, Angels, and Ascended Masters,* 2019, www.pinterest.ca/pin/246290673348701187/.

"Lady Master Reya, the Goddess Parvati." *Ganesha, the Supreme Lord,* 8 July 2018, thesecretsoflordganesha.wordpress. com/2012/09/10/wallpapers-of-lord-ganesha/goddess-parvati/.

Lady Nada. padmadiva.wordpress.com/2014/10/17/ ascended-heart-by-lady-nada/. Accessed 8 July 2018.

Lightning Warrior. 2019, img00.deviantart. net/218e/i/2012/275/1/2/lightning_warrior_ by_justmick-d5gkni6.jpg.

Lindupp, Amanda. *Horned God.* 2013, www.pinterest. ca/pin/306315212134306969/.

"Lord and Goddess Meru." *My Own Universe,* noarosauniversoespiritual.blogspot. com/2015/07/conociendo-los-maestros-ascendidos-el.html. Accessed 7 July 2018.

"Lord Gautama Buddha Ji." *My God Pictures,* 2019, www.mygodpictures.com/category/lord-gautama-buddha-ji/page/10/.

"Lord Himalya." *Land of Lord Shiva,* 8 July 2018, landoflordshiva.blogspot.com/2011/07/ embodiment-of-welfare-o-lord-shiva.html.

"Lord Meru." *Metaphysical School of Maitreya,* metafisicacdelu.blogspot.com/2012/08/ lunes-dia-de-iluminacion-dioses-meru.html. Accessed 8 July 2018.

Macomber, Mary Lizzie. "Faith, Hope, and Love." Wikimedia Commons, 6 Mar. 2012.

"Maha Avatar Babaji." *Who Are the Spiritual Gurus Still Alive?,* 2019, www.quora.com/Who-are-the-spiritual-Gurus-still-alive.

Matthews, Pamela. *Angel of the Crystal Kingdom.* 2019, www.pinterest.com/ pin/380624605978685837/.

Matthews, Pamela. *Orion and Angelica.* www.grail. co.nz/shop/prints/orion-and-angelica/. Accessed 7 July 2018.

"Mother Mary." *The Rainbow Scribe,* www. therainbowscribe.com/mothermaryjune2017. htm. Accessed 7 July 2018.

Muhammed, Sultan. *The Ascent of Muhammed to Heaven.* 18 Nov. 2018, en.wikipedia.org/wiki/ File:Miraj_by_Sultan_Muhammad.jpg.

Nash, Robin. *Sun Goddess.* 2010, thewitcontinuum. wordpress.com/2010/07/06/sun-goddesses-enter-here/.

Nefertiti. 2011, rudebutgood.blogspot.com/2011/11/ nefertiti.html.

Ninhursag. 2019, historymaniacmegan. com/2015/05/26/mesopotamian-mythology-reexamined-the-gods/.

"Pachamama." *Pachamama, Astral Flowers,* chordify. net/chords/pachamama-astral-flowers-dany-matos. Accessed 7 July 2018.

"Paul the Venetian." *Paul the Venetian Prayer,* https:// monthly-slov.rf/pavel-venetsianets-molitva/. Accessed 7 July 2018.

"Peter." *Peter Fought Against Fear and Doubt,* www. jw.org/en/publications/books/true-faith/ peter-fought-fear-doubt/. Accessed 7 July 2018.

"Saint Paul the Apostle." *The Newman Connection,* www.newmanconnection.com/faith/saint/ saint-paul-the-apostle. Accessed 7 July 2018.

"Sanat Kumara." *Sanat Kumara,* 2019, shekinah-el-daoud.com/2019/01/09/sanat-kumara-shielding-and-setting-boundaries-is-more-important-than-ever-genoveva-cole/.

"SeRaya, the White Buddha." *Eat Till Tummy Full*, tummyfull.blogspot.com/2010/05/temples-visit-in-tumpat-kelantan.html. Accessed 8 July 2018.

"Shamballa." *Ancient Awakenings*, 1 May 2016, higherdensity.wordpress.com/2016/05/02/ancient-awakenings-sananda-st-germain-and-5-1-16/.

Shwartzeeis. *God of Rain*. 2019, www.deviantart.com/schwarzeeis/art/Xavier-Stormbringer-God-of-Rain-637341448.

Star Goddess. fineartamerica.com/art/goddess. Accessed 7 July 2018.

Stephens. *Genesis II*. 2019, www.imaginus.ca/Stephens_Genesis_II_Surrealism_Fantasy_Poster_p/s477a.htm.

Sunna, the Norse Goddess. 2019, www.pinterest.com/pin/251849804139123546/.

Suvorov, Valdimir. "Ascended Masters." *Ascended Masters*, 2019, i.pinimg.com/736x/3e/a6/60/3ea66089879ec718b83fc8c9081cdb1b--arch-angels-ascended-masters.jpg.

Suvorov, Valdimir. "Holy Amethyst." *Archangel Zadkiel: Inner Peace During Change*, 2019, www.pinterest.com/pin/571183165225980636/.

Suvorov, Valdimir. *Mighty Victory*. www.pinterest.com/pin/473440979554315271/. Accessed 8 July 2018.

"Svarog, Slavic Sun God." *Myths and Legends*, 2019, www.pinterest.ca/pin/479351954064004388/.

The Art of Receiving by Lady Portia. www.crystalwind.ca/awaken-the-soul/channeled-messages/the-ascended-masters/the-art-of-receiving-by-lady-portia. Accessed 7 July 2018.

The King Marduck and His Dragon. 2019, historymaniacmegan.files.wordpress.com/2015/05/the-king-marduk-and-his-dragon-maugdo-vasquez.jpg.

"Threefold Flame." *Balancing Your Threefold Flame*, www.summitlighthouse.org/balancing-your-threefold-flame/. Accessed 8 July 2018.

"Tiger's Nest." *Http://Www.byronevents.net*, 2019.

"Vista, Elohim of the Green Ray." *YouTube Channel, Servers of the New Era: Personal Prayer to the Supreme Creator*, 16 Aug. 2015, www.youtube.com/watch?v=dw1WgR35Gkg.

Walker, Connie. *Birth of the Mighty Goddess of Wind*. 2019, orig07.deviantart.net/9529/f/2012/152/3/e/birth_of_the_mighty_goddess_of_wind_by_conniewalker7919-d51w1bz.jpg.

Waters, M. "Archangel Raphael." *Is That Cool?*, 2019, isthatcoool.blogspot.com/2010/07/archangels.html.

Wind Spiritu Aparctias. 2019, legendofthecryptids.fandom.com/wiki/(Jetstream)_Wind_Spirit_Aparctias.

"Yemanya." *Flavors of Brazil*, flavorsofbrazil.blogspot.com/2012/02/february-second-festival-of-yemanja.html. Accessed 7 July 2018.

The Holy Grail Is Carried In
Arthur Rackham from "The Legends of King
Arthur and the Knights of the Round Table," by
Nelly Montigin-De Fouw, 1917.

Glossary

Adept: One who has attained Mastery in the art and science of living; a Mahatma.

Adjatal: This Golden City of the Blue and Gold Rays is overseen by Lord Himalaya and promotes Spiritual Awakening. It is located primarily in Pakistan and Tajikistan, and is a twin to the Golden City of Zaskar.

Adjutant Point Ashrams: The Spiritual Ashrams of Golden Cities fall into four categories: Gateway, Cardinal, Heavenly, and Convergence. Each Golden City contains seventeen Primary Adjutant Points. There are a total of thirty-three Adjutant Points in a Golden City, the balance comprised of additional Golden City Ashrams, Temples, and Retreats. Each point has their own distinct energy, guiding Hierarch, and Ray of Focus.

Adjutant Point(s): Power points that form where the lei-lines of the geometric Maltese cross formation of a Golden City traverse or intersect. Adjutant points support the infrastructure of a Golden City, both geometrically and spiritually, and assist and disburse the unique energies held by Babajeran, the Ascended Masters, and the Golden City's Ray Force.

Afrom: A Golden City of the White Ray that is located mainly in Hungary and Romania. Its stewards are Claire, the Elohim of Purity, along with the Goddess SeRaya, also known as the White Buddha. Afrom assists Earth's Ascension through the spiritual attribute of purity.

Akashic Records: Timeless, immortal records of all created things, especially souls and their many lifetimes.

Akhenaton: The ancient king of Egypt (1388 BC) embraced the unfolding consciousness of the ONE, which culturally replaced the polytheistic religion of his Kingdom. A pioneer of monotheistic religion, Akhenaton embraced the Christ Consciousness and some esoteric historians view him as a spiritual forerunner who led the way for the incarnation of Jesus Christ. According to the Master Teachers, Akhenaton is one of the prior lifetimes attributed to Ascended Master Serapis Bey.

Alchemy: The process of transmutation.

Aloah: An Adjutant Point Lady Master of Gobean who overcomes prophecies of calamities and Earth Changes through her focus on peace and the ONE.

Amerigo: Ascended Master Godfre serves in this Golden City, located in Spain. Amerigo facilitates the spiritual ideal of, "God in All," through its alignment to the Gold Ray.

Andeo: The thirtieth Golden City located in Peru, Columbia, and Brazil, South America. Its qualities are consistency; its Ray Force is Pink and Gold; and its Master Teachers are the Goddesses Meru and Constance. The Golden City of Andeo is also known as the City of the Feminine.

Angel Cresta: An angel of the White Ray who serves as a Hierarch to one of Gobean's Adjutant Point Ashrams. Cresta is affiliated with the White Ray of Purity and the Divine Light of crystals.

Angelica: The Golden City of Angelica is guided by the Elohim Angelica and is affiliated with the Pink Ray. It is located in Queensland, Australia, and is paired to the Golden City of Clayje.

Lord Apollo: A God of healing, truth, music, and Prophecy. This Ascended Master is a venerated scholar of the Ascended Master tradition and is considered a guru, or Master Teacher, of many contemporary Ascended Masters.

Aquamarine Ray: A Ray of human ascent, spiritual liberation, and perfection. The Aquamarine Ray is considered a new, yet revolutionary Ray Force and is associated with change and the New Times. The influence of this Ray is destined to develop the higher spiritual qualities of humanity and guide Earth's entrance into the New Times—the Golden Age. This Ray is also associated with Unity Consciousness and is said to originate from the Galactic Center: the Great Central Sun.

Archangels (Seven): The seven principal angels of creation are: Michael, the Blue Ray; Jophiel, the Yellow Ray; Chamuel, the Pink Ray; Gabriel, the White Ray; Raphael, the Green Ray; Uriel, the Ruby Ray; and Zadkiel, the Violet Ray.

Archangel Crystiel: The Archangel who protects the ongoing spiritual evolution and enlightment of humanity. Crystiel's angelic complement is the Archeia Clarity who works with the principles of precision and transparency. Crystiel's color ray is aquamarine and gold. His weapon is a heavenly laser. He serves in the Golden City of Cresta, located in Antarctica.

Arctura: The thirty-seventh Golden City is located in China. Arctura's stewards are the twin Elohim Arcturus and Diana of the Violet Ray. This Golden City is associated with freedom, precipitation, and the rhythm of universal harmony.

Arhat: The Arhat—one who has overcome antagonistic craving, including the entire range of passions and desires—mental, emotional, and physical. Because of this, the Arhat has undergone and passed arduous spiritual initiations, which make the individual a spiritual teacher and master of meditation and various spiritual techniques.

Arien, Elohim of Focus: An Adjutant Point Master of Gobean who assists spiritual seekers to discover their inner light.

Arkana: This Golden City is overseen by Archangel Gabriel of the White Ray. Located in East Siberia, Russia, this sacred Vortex radiates and transfigures the HU-man for Ascension.

Ascended Master(s): Once an ordinary human, an Ascended Master has undergone a spiritual transformation over many lifetimes. He or she has Mastered the lower planes—mental, emotional, and physical—to unite with his or her God-Self or I AM Presence. An Ascended Master is freed from the Wheel of Karma. He or she moves forward in spiritual evolution beyond this planet; however, an Ascended Master remains attentive to the spiritual well-being of humanity, inspiring and serving the Earth's spiritual growth and evolution.

Ascension: A process of Mastering thoughts, feelings, and actions that balance positive and negative karmas. It allows entry to a higher state of consciousness and frees a person from the need to reincarnate on the lower Earthly planes or lokas of experience. Ascension is the process of spiritual liberation, also known as moksha.

Ascension Valley: According to the I AM America Prophecies, Ascended Masters appear in physical form in the Golden City Vortices during and after a prophesied twenty-year period. At that time, Mass Ascensions occur in the Golden Cities, at the Golden City Star locations, and in select geophysical locations around the world, which are hosted by the complimentary energies of Mother Earth. A model of this geophysical location is Ascension Valley, located in the Shalahah Vortex. The energy of Ascension Valley prepares students to integrate their light bodies and spiritual consciousness into the Oneship, the divinity within, and further prepares the body, mind, and spirit to experience and travel into the New Dimensions.

Asonea: The Twelfth Golden City of the Americas is located in Cuba. Its qualities are alignment and regeneration; its Ray Force is Yellow; and its Master Teacher is Peter the Everlasting.

Astral Body or Plane: The subtle light body that contains our feelings, desires, and emotions. It exists as an intermediate light body between the physical body and the Causal body (Mental Body). According to the Master Teachers, we enter the Astral Plane through our Astral Body when we sleep, and many dreams and visions are experiences in this Plane of vibrant color and sensation. Through spiritual development, the Astral Body strengthens, and the luminosity of its light is often detected in the physical plane. Spiritual adepts may have the ability to consciously leave their physical bodies while traveling in their Astral Bodies. The Astral Body or Astral Plane has various levels of evolution and is the heavenly abode where the soul resides after the disintegration of the physical body. The Astral Body is also known as the Body Double, the Desire Body, and the Emotional Body.

Atlantis: An ancient civilization of Earth, whose mythological genesis was the last Puranic Dvapara Yuga—the Bronze Age of the Yugas. Its demise occurred around the year 9628 BCE. Esoteric historians suggest three phases of political and geophysical boundaries: the Toltec Nation of Atlantis (Ameru); the Turian Nation of Atlantis (the invaders of the Land of Rama); and Poseid, the Island Nation of the present-day Atlantic Ocean.

The early civilizations of Atlantis were ruled by the spiritually evolved Toltec. Their spiritual teachings, ceremonies, and temples were dedicated to the worship of the Sun. According to Theosophical thought, Atlantis' evolving humanity brought about an evolutionary epoch of the Pink Ray on the Earth, and the development of the Astral-Emotional bodies and Heart Chakra. Ascended Master provenance claims that the Els—now the Mighty Elohim of the Seven Rays—were the original Master Teachers to the spiritual seekers of Atlantis. Atlantean culture later deteriorated through the use of nuclear weapons and cruelty toward other nations, including the use of genetic engineering. The demise of Atlantis was inevitable; however, modern-day geologists, archaeologists, and occultists all disagree to its factual timing.

Ascended Master teachings affirm that Atlantis—a continent whose geophysical and political existence probably spanned well over 100,000 years—experienced several phases of traumatic Earth Change. This same belief is held by occult historians who allege that Earth repeatedly cycles through periods of massive Earth Change and cataclysmic pole shifts, which activate tectonic plates and subsequently submerge whole continents, creating vital New Lands for Earth's successors.

Awakening Prayer: Ascended Masters Saint Germain and Kuthumi offered this prayer to more than 200 people at the 1990 Global Sciences Congress in Denver, Colorado. Group and individual meditation of the Awakening Prayer encourage a heightened spiritual consciousness and Cellular Awakening.

Great Light of Divine Wisdom,
Stream forth to my being,
And through your right use
Let me serve mankind and the planet.
Love, from the Heart of God,
Radiate my being with the presence of the Christ
That I walk the path of truth.
Great Source of Creation,
Empower my being,
My Brother,
My Sister,
And my planet with perfection,
As we collectively awaken as one cell.
I call forth the Cellular Awakening.
Let wisdom, love, and power stream forth to this cell,
This cell that we all share.
Great Spark of Creation, awaken the Divine Plan of Perfection.
So we may share the ONE perfected cell,
I AM.

Babajeran: A name for the Earth Mother that means, "Grandmother rejoicing."

Babaji: The birthless, deathless Master is the Hierarch of the Heart of the Dove, located in Kansas and Missouri, (United States). He initiates chelas into restorative spiritual techniques for body, mind, and soul.

Belief(s): An opinion, conviction, or doctrine based upon insufficient grounds, or proof.

Blue Flame: The activity of the Blue Ray, based upon the activation of the individual will, manifests the qualities of truth, power, determination, and diligence in human endeavors. The Blue Flame is associated with the transformation of our individual choices, and its inherent processes align the individual will to the Divine Will through the HU-man qualities of detachment, steadiness, calm, harmony, and God-protection.

Bodhisattva: A level of spiritual development and enlightenment achieved through the constant application of compassion for all living things. This process is affiliated with the Pink Ray.

Braham: The fourteenth Golden City of the Americas is located in Brazil, South America. Its quality is nurturing; its Ray Force is Pink; and its Master Teacher is the Goddess Braham or Yemanya, progenitor of the New Manu. Braham literally means *the nurturer* and this Golden City is the second of the Three Sisters in South America.

Braun: Mighty Victory overshadows and radiates the Yellow Ray of glory and achievement in this Vortex. The fifteenth Golden City is located in Germany, Austria, and the Czech republic.

Breath Technique: The conscious, spiritual application of breath, often accompanied by visualization and meditation. Ascended Master teachings often incorporate various breathing techniques to activate and integrate Ray Forces in the Human Aura and light bodies.

Buddha: A level of spiritual development and Mastery achieved through a wholly awakened state of consciousness. The Buddha Body is affiliated with the aquirement of the Eighth Light Body, a percursor to Ascension. The realized Buddha radiates light, compassion, and spiritual wisdom and oversees the Third Shamballa School which cultivates the harmony of the mind—enlightenment.

Causal Body: The Fifth Dimensional Body of Light, which is affiliated with thought. Its name is associated with "cause," and is alleged to be the source of both the Astral and physical body. The Causal Body is also defined as the *Higher Mind* – superior to the Mental Body.

Chakra: Sanskrit for wheel. There are seven separate spinning wheels that are human bioenergy centers. They are stacked from the base of the spine to the top of the head.

Chela: Disciple

Chimera: A type of living organism that carries two distinct sets of DNA. It is alleged that many Chimeras contain both human and animal characteristics and were biologically engineered by scientists.

Christ or Christ Consciousness: The highest energy or frequency attainable on Earth. The Christ, or Christ Consciousness, is a step-down Transformer of the I AM energies, which enlightens, heals, and transforms all human conditions of degradation and death.

Clayje: This is known as the *Golden City of Many Planets* through its divine quality of Universal Oneness. Clayje is the forty-seventh Vortex and is associated with the Elohim of Divine Love – Orion, and the Pink Ray. Clayje covers the entire island of Tasmania in Australia, and is a Twin Golden City to Angelica.

Co-creation: Creating with the God-Source.

Collective Consciousness: The higher interactive structure of consciousness as two or more.

Consciousness: Awakening to one's own existence, sensations, and cognitions.

Creative Hierarchy: The Human Kingdom that includes evolving humanity through the nascent stages of spiritual development to self-determination, spiritual enlightenment, and Mastery. This Kingdom is served and overseen by the Ascended Masters.

Cresta: The fifty-first and final Golden City to be activated serves the uplifting and evolutionary Gold and Aquamarine Rays. Beloved Archangel Crystiel is the hierarch of this sublime Vortex of eternal protection, healing, and clarity for humanity, located in Antarctica on Eternity Range.

Crotese: The sixteenth Golden City of the Americas is located in the Heartland countries of Costa Rica and Panama, Central America. This Golden City's qualities are divinity and the Heart of Love; its Ray Force is Pink; and the resident Master Teacher is Paul.

Cup or Cup Ceremony: A symbol of neutrality and grace. The Ascended Masters often refer to our human body as a Cup filled with our thoughts and feelings. Cup Ceremony is a Water Ceremony that blesses Mother Earth.

Cycle of the Elements: According to Taoist understanding, the Earth undergoes a cyclic series of nine twenty-year segments. This is known as the Nine Cycles, a total of one hundred and eighty years. A further division of the one-hundred and eighty years is the Three Eras—sixty years each, comprised of upper, middle, and lower. Universal energy is said to change during each of the Three Eras, and Earth is currently in the Lower Era which started in 1984. Each era contains three cycles of twenty years each, hence the Nine Cycles. According to Taoist philosophy small changes occur between cycles; considerable changes occur between eras. Currently Earth is in the eighth cycle that began in 2004. The ninth cycle begins in 2024. The flow of universal energy significantly changes between each of the Nine Cycles, or every twenty years. The Ascended Masters often refer to the twenty-year cycles of the Earth, and their influence on culture, societies, and individuals. They prophesy a twenty-year period that is likely the Ninth Cycle, in the year 2024, or the Beginning of the Upper Era (first cycle) in 2044, when the spiritual Masters appear on Earth, in physical bodies to teach and heal the masses.

Dahl Universe: The parallel, twin universe to our universe. The Dahl Universe is spiritually and technologically advanced, and it is alleged that members from the Dahl Universe visit our Universe, known as the Dern, at timely junctures for spiritual evolution and intervention.

Decree: Statements of intent and power, similar to prayers and mantras, which are often integrated with the use of the I AM and requests to the I AM Presence.

Denasha: The Golden City of Denasha is primarily located over Scotland, and the Ascended Masters assert this Vortex holds the energies of Divine Justice for all of humanity. Denasha is also the Sister Golden City to Malton (Illinois and Indiana, USA) and both Vortices mutually distribute energies to the Nature and Elemental Kingdoms during the New Times. The Master

Teacher is Lady Nada; the Ray Force is Yellow; and Denasha's translation means, "Mountain of Zeus."

Divine Service: Service based on one or a combination of these three principles: love, wisdom, and power. These are known in Hindusim as *Karma Yoga* (action), *Jnana Yoga* (knowledge, wisdom), and *Bhakti Yoga* (love and compassion).

Divine Will: The idea of God's plan for humanity; however, from the perspective of the HU-man, the Divine Will is "choice."

Donjakey: This Golden City currently presides over the Pacific Ocean and prophesied new land that rise in the New Times—New Lemuria. The Elohim Pacifica guards and protects this Golden City of both the Gold and Aquamarine Rays.

Eabra: The seventh Golden City located in Canada in the Yukon and Northwest Territories. Its qualities are joy, balance, and equality; its Ray Force is Violet; and its Master Teacher is Portia.

Earth Changes: A prophesied Time of Change on the Earth, including geophysical, political, and social changes, alongside the opportunity for spiritual and personal transformation.

Earth Plane: The dual aspect of life on Earth.

Eighth Energy Body: Known as the Buddha Body or the Field of Awakening, this energy body is initially three to four feet from the human body. It begins by developing two visible grid-like spheres of light that form in the front and in the back of the Human Aura. The front sphere is located three to four feet in front of and between the Heart and Solar Plexus Chakras. The back sphere is located in front of and between the Will-to-Love and Solar Will Chakras. These spheres activate an ovoid of light that surrounds the entire human body; an energy field associated with harmonizing and perfecting the Ascension Process. This is the first step toward Mastery. Once developed and sustained, this energy body grants physical longevity and is associated with immortality. It is known as the first level of Co-creation, and is developed through control of the diet and disciplined breath techniques. Once this light body reaches full development, the spheres dissipate and dissolve into a refined energy field, resembling a metallic armor. The mature Eighth Light Body then contracts and condenses, to reside within several inches of the physical body where it emits a silver-blue sheen.

Eight-sided Cell of Perfection: An atomic cell located in the human heart. It is associated with all aspects of perfection, and contains and maintains a visceral connection with the Godhead.

Elemental Kingdom: A kingdom comprising an invisible, subhuman group of creatures who act as counterparts to visible nature on Earth.

Eliah: An Adjutant Point Master of Gobean dedicated to prayer, righteous action, and spiritual discipline.

El Morya: Ascended Master of the Blue Ray, associated with the development of the will.

Elohim: Creative beings of love and light that helped manifest the Divine idea of our solar system. Seven Elohim (the Seven Rays) exist on Earth. They organize and draw forward Archangels, the Four Elements, Devas, Seraphim, Cherubim, Angels, Nature Guardians, and the Elementals. In Ascended Master teaching, the Silent Watcher—the Great Mystery—gives them direction. It is also claimed the Elohim magnetize the Unfed Flame at the center of the Earth. Some esoteric historians perceive the Elohim—also referred to as the Els—as the Ancient Gods, or the Master Teachers of Lemuria and Atlantis.

Elohim Sein: An Elohim of the tranquil Aquamarine Ray who is an Adjutant Point Master of Gobean, dedicated to helping humanity to obtain inner vision.

Elohim TronXR: One of Shalahah's Adjutant Point Masters, TronXR perfects the electronic blueprint of the human aura in preparation for the Ascension.

Elohim Veenon: Adjutant Point Master of Gobean who overcame harshness through non-interference and detachment. Veenon is an Elohim of the Wind that he tames and harnesses through the strength of love.

Energy-for-energy: The transfer of energies. To understand this spiritual principle, one must remember Isaac Newton's Third Law of Motion: "for every action there is an equal and opposite reaction." However, while energies may be equal, their forms often vary. The Ascended Masters often use this phrase to remind chelas to properly compensate others to avoid karmic retribution, and repayment may take many different forms.

Evolutionary Points: Stages of spiritual development identified through specific processes that assemble and Co-create Human Consciousness. There are twelve points total, with each phase of development physically manifest and perceptible through the Eight-sided Cell of Perfection. Each of the twelve junctures of spiritual evolution regulate through one of Twelve Jurisdictions, in deliberate sequence.

Fifth Dimension: A spiritual dimension of cause, associated with thoughts, visions, and aspirations. This is the dimension of the Ascended Masters and the Archetypes of Evolution, the city of Shamballa, and the templates of all Golden Cities.

Flame of Freedom: The evolutionary process of the monad. This flame extends throughout the chakra system and develops throughout the entire kundalini system and the Golden Thread Axis.

Four Pillars: The four Master Teachers of the I AM America Spiritual Teachings: El Morya, Kuthumi, Saint Germain, and Lord Sananda. Four Pillars is also associated with the Four Schools of Shamballa.

Fourth Dimension: A dimension of vibration associated with telepathy, psychic ability, and the dream world. This is the dimension of the Elemental Kingdom and the development of the super senses.

Freedom Star World Map: The Ascended Masters' map depicts prophesied global Earth Changes and the locations of worldwide Golden City Vortices. This map's spiritual teachings are divided into three unique maps of prophesied social, cultural, and geophysical changes. The Americas Map is composed of Greenland, Canada, the United States, Mexico, Central and South America, and New Atlantis. The Greening Map is composed of India, Pakistan, Afghanistan, Russia, China, Japan, Malaysia, Australia, and New Zealand. The Map of Exchanges is composed of Iceland, Europe, the Middle East, Africa, Antarctica, and New Lemuria. The Map of the Americas, including the I AM America Map, is sponsored by Saint Germain. The Greening Map is sponsored by Kuan Yin, and the Map of Exchanges is sponsored by Lady Nada, Kuthumi, and El Morya.

Each distinctive map depicts the location of seventeen Golden Cities. Three sets of seventeen Golden Cities comprise a total of fifty-one Golden City Vortices. Fifty-one is a pentagonal number and is esoterically connected to Divine Man, Divine Intervention, perfect harmony, and the planet Venus. Gobean, the first Golden City Vortex, was activated in 1981. Cresta, the fifty-first Golden City Vortex, activates in the year 2092 AD.

Fron: Beloved Desiree of the Blue Ray guides and overshadows this Golden City located in Western Australia. This Vortex is fiftieth in the activation pattern, and assists aspirants, chelas, and developing HU-man's to spiritually focus upon their inner balance.

Galactic Light: Energy streams from the Great Central Sun, or Galactic Center, as the Seven Rays of Light and Sound to Earth. Galactic Light calibrates the level of intelligence on Earth through memory function; the ability to absorb, recognize, and respect spiritual knowledge; the length of lifespans; and our ability to access the Akashic Records. The amount of Galactic Light streaming to Earth at any given time is classically measured through the Hindu Puranic timing of the Yugas, and through a contemporary method—the Electric Cycle—advocated by the Eastern Indian guru Sri Yuteswar.

Galactic Suns: Planets which have ascended into Suns. The Galactic Suns oversee evolving races throughout several solar systems in our Galaxy, and are also known as the Lords of Galactic Consciousness. Helios and Vesta are the Galactic Suns for Earth, and assist the evolutionary process of the human to the HU-man.

Galactic Web: A large, planet-encircling grid created by the consciousness of all things on Earth—humans, animals, plants, and minerals. Magnetic Vortices, namely the Golden Cities, appear at certain intersections.

Ganakra: The seventeenth Golden City is located in Turkey and is overseen by the Elohim Vista of the Green Ray. Ganakra is known as the "All Seeing City," and is affiliated with the qualities of Divine Focus and concentration.

Gandawan: The Master Kuthumi oversees the Golden City of Gandawan, also identified as the *Infinite Garden*. This Golden City of the Ruby and Gold Rays is located in Africa.

Gobean: The first United States Golden City located in the states of Arizona and New Mexico. Its qualities are cooperation, harmony, and peace; its Ray Force is Blue; and its Master Teacher is El Morya.

Gobi: Steps-down the energies of Shamballa into the entire Golden City Network. This Golden City is located in the Gobi Desert. It is known as the City of Balance, and means *Across the Star*; its Master Teachers are Lord Meru and Archangel Uriel.

Golden Age: A peaceful time on Earth that is prophesied to occur after the Time of Change. It is also prophesied that, during this age, human life spans will increase and sacred knowledge will be revered. During this time, the societies, cultures, and the governments of Earth will reflect spiritual enlightenment through worldwide cooperation, compassion, charity, and love. Ascended Master teachings often refer to the Golden Age as the Golden-Crystal Age and the Age of Grace.

Golden Age of Kali Yuga: According to the classic Puranic timing of the Yugas, Earth is in a Kali-Yuga period that started around the year 3102 BCE the year that Krishna allegedly left the Earth. During this time period, which according to this Puranic timing lasts a total of 432,000 years—the ten-thousand year Golden Age period, also known as the Golden Age of Kali Yuga, is not in full force. Instead, it is a sub-cycle of higher light frequencies within an overall larger phase of less light energy.

Golden City Doorway: The four doorways of a Golden City. They comprise the North Door (or the Black Door); the East Door (or the Blue Door); the South Door (or the Red Door); the West Door (or the Yellow Door). The center of a Golden City is known as the "Star" and is affiliated with the color white.

Golden City Hierarch: The spiritual and administrative overseer of a Golden City Vortex. This Elohim, Archangel, or Spiritual Master directs and protects numerous lei-lines, power points, sub-Vortices, Adjutant Points, Ashrams, Temples, and Retreats throughout a Golden City. The Golden City Hierarch works in tandem with other Angels, Ascended Masters, and Elohim associated throughout their Golden City and within the Golden City Network.

Golden City Vortex: According to the prophecies, these large Vortex areas are havens of safety and spiritual growth during the Time of Change.

Golden City Star Retreat: Four spiritual retreats situated in the four cardinal directions that provide added support and protection to the Golden City Star.

Golden City Star and Retreat: The center or apex of the Golden City and location of the Golden City Hierarch's Ashram of Light.

Golden Orb: An anomaly of Group Mind, created specifically for spiritual focus, intent, and is primarily used for Ascension.

Gold(en) Ray: The Ray of Brotherhood, Cooperation, and Peace. The Gold Ray produces the qualities of perception, honesty, confidence, courage, and responsibility. It is also associated with leadership, independence, authority, ministration, and justice. The Gold Ray vibrates the energies of Divine Father on Earth. Its attributes are: warm; perceptive; honest; confident; positive; independent; courageous; enduring; vital; leadership; responsible; ministration; authority; justice. The Gold Ray is also associated with the Great Central Sun, the Solar Logos, of which our Solar Sun is a Step-down Transformer of its energies. According to the Master Teachers, the Gold Ray is the epitome of change for the New Times. The Gold Ray is the ultimate authority of Cosmic Law, and carries both our personal and worldwide Karma and Dharma (purpose). Its presence is designed to instigate responsible spiritual growth and planetary evolution as a shimmering light for humanity's aspirations and the development of the HU-man. The Gold Ray, however, is also associated with Karmic justice, and will instigate change: constructive and destructive. The extent of catastrophe or transformation is contingent on humanity's personal and collective spiritual growth and evolutionary process as we progress into the New Times.

Golden Thread Axis: Also known as the Vertical Power Current. The Golden Thread Axis physically consists of the Medullar Shushumna, a life-giving nadi comprising one-third of the human Kundalini system. Two vital currents intertwine around the Golden Thread Axis: the lunar Ida Current, and the solar Pingala Current. According to the Master Teachers, the flow of the Golden Thread Axis begins with the I AM Presence, enters the Crown Chakra, and descends through the spinal system. It descends beyond the Base Chakra and travels to the core of the Earth. Esoteric scholars often refer to the axis as the Rod of Power, and it is symbolized by two spheres connected by an elongated rod. Ascended Master students and chelas frequently draw upon the energy of the Earth through the Golden Thread Axis for healing and renewal using meditation, visualization, and breath.

Great Awakening: The time period humanity is currently experiencing marked by political and societal turmoil alongside humanity's collective Spiritual Awakening. As one moves through extreme polarity, the soul awakens to its divine and innate Co-creatorship that initiates the Ascension Process. The Great Awakening transpires concurrently with the turbulent Time of Change.

Great Central Sun: The great sun of our galaxy, around which all of the galaxy's solar systems rotate. The Great Central Sun is also known as the Galactic Center, which is the origin of the Seven Rays of Light and Sound on Earth.

Great White Brotherhood and Sisterhood: A fraternity of ascended and unascended men and women who are dedicated to the universal uplifting of humanity. Its main objective includes the preservation of the lost spirit, and the teachings of the ancient religions and philosophies of the world. Its mission is to reawaken the dormant ethical and spiritual sparks among the masses. In addition to fulfilling spiritual aims, the Great White Lodge pledges to protect mankind against the systematic assaults – which inhibit self-knowledge and personal growth – on individual and group freedoms.

Greening Map: The second Map of Earth Changes Prophecies. It contains a total of seventeen Golden City Vortices and is sponsored by Ascended Master Kuan Yin. It entails all of Asia, Japan, and Australia. New land is prophesied to appear near New Zealand, New Guinea, Hawaii, and the Easter Islands, and is referred to as "New Lemuria" by the Spiritual Teachers. The Greening Map signifies personal and transpersonal healing of the feminine. It balances Mother Earth through the awakening of Ecological Alchemy. During the Greening Map's Time of Change, Earth is healed and rejuvenated with new flora and fauna appearing throughout the planet.

Grein: Viseria, the Goddess of the Stars and Divine Compliment to Soltec serves in Grein, the Golden City of New Zealand's South Island. The Vortex radiates the energies of the Green Ray and is associated with Divine Consecration, and service to humanity's upliftment through scientific development.

Group Mind: A conscious intelligent force formed by members of distinguished cultures, societal organizations, and more prominently, by religious church members. The Group Mind is held together by rituals and customs that are typically peculiar to its members; newcomers instantly sense the energies of the atmosphere, and will either accept or reject their influence. The physics of the Group Mind are important to comprehend, as this collective intelligence is purposely formed to aid the Aspirant to raise human consciousness beyond present limitations.

Gruecha: Gruecha is Norway and Sweden's Golden City of the Blue Ray. The Elohim Hercules serves in this sacred refuge, and its qualities produce spiritual strength through the principle of truth.

Guru: A spiritual teacher who tranmits vital energies that transmute karmas and engenders a spiritual evolutionary process.

Heart Chakra: Known in Sanskrit as the Anahata. The location is in the center of the chest. Its main aspect is Love and Relationships, and includes our ability to feel compassion, forgiveness, and hold our own Divine Purpose.

Heart of the Dove: Also known as the Center of Fire, this energy anomaly is prophesied to exist Northwest of Kansas City, Missouri. It is here that Master Teachings claim an umbilicus connection between Earth and the Galactic Center exists, creating time anomalies and the potential for time travel in the New Times. The Heart of the Dove is also prophesied to become a spiritual center for learning and self-actualizing the consciousness of Quetzalcoatl—the Christ.

Helios and Vesta: The God and Goddess of our physical Sun.

Hercules: An Elohim and Master Teacher of cooperation, truth, and strength. Hercules is the venerated teacher of many Master Teachers and oversees spiritual techniques associated with time travel and Ascension. Like Apollo, Hercules is a solar being from the lineage of the Seven Galactic Suns. He oversees the fifth sun from this celestial pedigree along with his divine counterpart, Amazonia. Hercules is the Golden City Hierarch of Gruecha (Norway, Sweden), and also claims affiliation with the Golden City of Stienta, (Iceland).

Hermetic Law: Philosophical beliefs and principles based on the writings of Hermes Trismegistus, the Greek sage who is analogous to the Egyptian God Thoth.

Higher Self: The *Atma* or *Atman*. This is the true identity of the soul, which resides in the spiritual planes of consciousness. Although it is energetically connected to each individual in the physical plane, the Higher Self is free from the karmas of the Earth Plane and from identification with the material world.

Hue (Golden City): This Golden City is also known as the *City of Many Spiritual Paths*, and is aligned with the Violet Ray. This Vortex's steward is Lord Gautama and its sacred quality is earnestness. It is located in Siberia, Russia.

HU-man: The God-Man.

Human Aura: The subtle energy field of luminous light that surrounds the human body.

HU, or HUE: In Tibetan dialects, the word hue or hu means breath; however, the HU is a sacred sound and when chanted or meditated upon is said to represent the entire spectrum of the Seven Rays. Because of this, the HU powerfully invokes the presence of the Violet Flame, which is the activity of the Violet Ray and its inherent ability to transform and transmit energies to the next octave. HU is also considered an ancient name for God, and it is sung for spiritual enlightenment.

I AM: The presence of God.

I AM America: According to the I AM America Prophecies, Saint Germain claims that the people of America have a unique destiny in the New Times. AMERICA contains within it a unique anagram: IAMRACE.
  The I AM Race of people is a unique group of souls who lived in America as Atlanteans. But their destiny has evolved since those ancient times. Instead of sinking on a continent destroyed by the misuse of technology and spiritual knowledge, their active intelligence continues to develop in modern times. Their service is focused on the Brotherly love of all nations.

I AM Presence: The individualized presence of God.

I AM THAT I AM: A term from Hebrew that translates to, "I Will Be What I Will Be." "I AM" is also derived from the Sanskrit Om (pronounced: A-U-M), whose three letters signify the three aspects of God as beginning, duration, and dissolution—Brahma, Vishnu, and Shiva. The AUM syllable is known as the omkara and translates to "I AM Existence," the name for God. "Soham," is yet another mystical Sanskrit name for God, which means "It is I," or "He is I." In Vedic philosophy, it is claimed that when a child cries, "Who am I?" the universe replies, "Soham—you are the same as I AM." The I AM teachings also use the name "Soham" in place of "I AM."

Indigo Cloak: The vow or understanding of secrecy or privacy.

Initiate: The third level of the Ascension Process that relies on personal experience by degree, test, and trial that is encountered both morally and mentally.

Inner Earth: Below the Earth's Crust lie many magnificent cities and cultures of various break-away races of humans, evolved HU-mans, and extraterrestrials. The Inner Earth is filled with reservoirs, streams, rivers, lakes, and oceans. According to metaphysical researchers the Earth is honey-combed with pervasive caves and subterranean caverns measuring hundreds of miles in diameter. This viewpoint is held by the Ascended Masters and shared throughout their Earth Changes Prophecies and historical narratives.

Jeafray: The eighth Golden City located in Quebec, Labrador, and Newfoundland, Canada. Its qualities are stillness and the celebration of the Violet Flame; its Ray Force is Violet; and its Master Teachers are Archangel Zadkiel and Amethyst.

Jehoa: The seventeenth Golden City of the Americas is prophesied to exist over new lands that rise in the Time of Change. The Golden City of Jehoa is located over the Lesser Antilles Islands of: Guadeloupe, Dominica, Martinique, Saint Lucia, Barbados, and Grenada. Its qualities are compassion, acts of love, and gratitude; its Ray Force is Violet; and its Master Teacher is Kuan Yin.

Kantan: The city of regeneration, assimilation, and dedication is located in Russia and China. This Golden City Vortex is overseen by Great Divine Mother and the Archangel Raphael. Kantan is affiliated with the Green Ray.

Karma: Laws of Cause and Effect.

Klehma: The fifth United States Golden City located primarily in the states of Colorado and Kansas. Its qualities are continuity, balance, and harmony; its Ray Force is White; and its Master Teacher is Serapis Bey.

Kreshe: Overseen by the Lord of Nature and Lady Amaryllis—the Goddess of Spring. It is associated with the Ruby and Gold Rays and is located Botswana, Namibia, Angola, and Zambia. Kreshe aligns its energies to the silent star and is in perpetual service to elemental life.

Kundalini: The coiled energy located at the base of the spine, often established in the lower Base and Sacral Chakras. In Sanskrit, Kundalini literally means coiled, and Kundalini Shatki (shatki means energy) is claimed to initiate spiritual development, wisdom, knowledge, and enlightenment.

Kuthumi: An Ascended Master of the Pink, Ruby, and Gold Rays. He is a gentle and patient teacher who works closely with the Nature Kingdoms.

Lady Amaryllis: An Ascended Being of the Elemental Kingdom. Lady Amaryllis is the Golden City Hierarch of Krseshe, an African Golden City affiliated with the Ruby and Gold Rays. Lady Amaryllis is also the Hierarch of the Malton Adjutant Point of Service, where she works closely with the Plant Kingdom for humanity's Ascension. Her Master Teacher is Lady Master Nada.

Lady Master Nada: The Ascended Goddess of Justice and Peace is associated with Mastery of speech (vibration), communication, interpretation, and the sacred Word. Nada is also known as a divine advocate of Universal Law and she is often symbolized by the scales of blind justice. She is associated with the Yellow Ray of Wisdom and the Ruby and Gold Rays of Ministration, Brotherhood, and Service. Lady Nada is the hierarch of Denasha, a Golden City located in Scotland.

Laraito: Beloved Lanto and Tara share their Divine Service in this Golden City of the Yellow Ray. This sacred Vortex is located in Ethiopia and is affiliated with spiritual understanding and illumination.

Law of Attraction and Repulsion: Like charges repel; unlike charges attract.

Law of Compensation: The spiritual understanding that states whatever we give to others returns to us in direct proportion.

Law of Love: Per the Ascended Master tradition, to consciously living without fear, without inflicting fear on others. Perhaps every religion on Earth is founded on the Law of Love, per the notion of "treating others as you would like to be treated." The Fourth of the Twelve Jurisdictions instructs us that Love is the "Law of Allowing, Maintaining, and Sustainability." All of these precepts distinguish love from an emotion or feeling, and observe Love as action, will, or choice. The Ascended Masters affirm, "If you live love, you will create love." This premise is fundamental to understanding the esoteric underpinnings of the Law of Love. The Master Teachers declare that through practicing the Law of Love, one experiences acceptance, understanding, and tolerance, alongside detachment. Metaphysically, the Law of Love allows different and varied perceptions of ONE experience, situation, or circumstance to exist simultaneously. From this viewpoint, the Law of Love is the practice of tolerance.

Law of Sacrifice: The spiritual ideal that through giving selflessly, or taking a short-term loss, that a greater long-term return for others is created. It is claimed that all great civilizations are built upon this premise.

Left-hand Path: A malevolent spiritual path, based on the intentional practice of fear, mistrust, suspicion, division, and degradation of life and the Co-creative process.

Lei-line: Lines of energy that exist among geographical places, ancient monuments, megaliths, and strategic points. These energy lines contain electrical or magnetic points.

Lemuria: A continent that primarily existed in the Pacific Ocean before it was submerged by Earth Changes. It is deemed to have been the remaining culture and civilization of Mu – an expansive continent that once spanned the entire present-day Pacific Ocean. It is alleged that the lands of Lemuria, also known as Shalmali, existed in the Indian and Southern Pacific Oceans, and included the continent of Australia.

Thus, it is believed to have integrated with the Lands of Rama, and is to be considered one the earliest cultures of humanity. Sri Lanka is alleged to have been one of the empire's capital cities. Esoteric historians theorize that the tectonic Pacific Plate formed this lost continent. Asuramaya is one of the great Manus of Lemuria's Root Race.

Some esoteric writers place the destruction of Mu around the year 30,000 BCE; others place its demise millions of years ago. According to Theosophical history, the Lemurian and Atlantean epochs overlapped. The apparent discrepancy of these timelines is likely due to two different interpretations of the Cycle of the Yugas. It is claimed that the venerated Elders of Lemuria escaped the global tragedy by moving to an uninhabited plateau in central Asia. This account mirrors Ascended Master teachings and Lord Himalaya's founding of the Retreat of the Blue Lotus.

The Lemurian elders re-established their spiritual teachings and massive library as the Thirteenth School. Spiritual teachers claim that the evolutionary purpose of this ancient civilization was to develop humanity's Will (the Blue Ray of Power). Lemurian culture also venerated the Golden Disk of the Sun and practiced the Right-hand Path. It is claimed that these teachings and spiritual records became foundational teachings for the Great White Brotherhood of the mystical lands of His Wang Mu (the Abode of the Immortals) and the Kuan Yin Lineage of Gurus. Present-day Australia —once known by Egyptian gold-miners as the ancient Land of Punt—is considered the remainder of the once great continent of Mu and Lemuria, which likely existed in the time period of Dvapara-Yuga, over 800,000 years ago.

Lineage of Gurus: The venerated ancestral root of certain spiritual teachings. Kuan Yin and Lord Apollo are two of Saint Germain's spiritual teachers; therefore, they compose his Lineage of Gurus.

Light Body (Bodies): A body of subtle energy surrounding the human body. It survives death, and develops and evolves over lifetimes. Also known as the aura, the light body divides into layers of light energy. These strata are referred to as light bodies or layers of the field of the aura.

Lords of Venus: A group of Ascended Masters who came to serve humanity. They once resided on the planet Venus.

Love: "Light in action." The fourth of the Twelve Jurisdictions evolves our understanding of love as the Law of Allowing, Maintaining, and Sustainability.

Malton: The second United States Golden City located in the states of Illinois and Indiana. Its qualities are fruition and attainment; its Ray Force is Gold and Ruby; and its Master Teacher is Kuthumi.

Manu: A root race or a group of souls inhabiting a vast time period (era or epoch) on Earth.

Map of Exchanges: The Ascended Masters' Map of prophesied Earth Changes for Europe and Africa. Its seventeen Golden City Vortices focus on the self-realization of the HU-man through the exchange of heavenly energies on Earth, which usher in the Golden Age.

Marnero: The eleventh Golden City of the Americas is located in Mexico. Marnero means Virtue; its Ray Force is Green; and its Master Teacher is Mother Mary.

Master Teacher: A spiritual teacher from a specific lineage of teachers—gurus. The teacher transmits and emits the energy from that collective lineage.

Mastery: Possessing the consummate skill of command and self-realization over thought, feeling, and action.

Meissner Field: A magnetic energy field that does not contain polarity. It is produced during a transitory state of superconductivity. Ascended Master teaching associates this type of energy field with HU-man development, Unana, and Christ Consciousness.

Mental Body: A subtle light body of the Human Aura comprising thoughts.

Migratory Sequence: A Golden City spiritual pilgrimage that travels through a certain progression of Adjutant Points. The progression of each sacred site may vary, dependent on the desired spiritual result for the chela or initiate. Some sequences focus on healing processes; others focus on integration of Golden City Energies, especially certain Golden City Doorways.

Monad: From an Ascended Master viewpoint, the Monad is the spark or flame of life of spiritual consciousness and it is also the Awakened Flame that is growing, evolving, and ultimately on the path to Ascension. Because of its presence of self-awareness and purpose, the Monad represents our dynamic will and the individualized presence of the Divine Father. Ultimately, the Monad is the spark of consciousness that is self-determining, spiritually awake, and drives the growth of human consciousness. The Monad is the indivisible, whole, divine life center of an evolving soul that is immortal and contains the momentum within itself to drive consciousness to learn, grow, and perfect itself in its evolutionary journey.

Mother Mary: Ascended Goddess of the Feminine who was originally of the angelic evolution. She is associated with the Green Ray of Healing, Truth, and Science, and the Pink Ray of Love.

Mousee: Located in the Pacific Ocean, northwest of the Hawaiian Island of Kauai. It is served by the Ascended Master Kona and the Gold and

Aquamarine Rays. Mousee's attribute is "the eye of spiritual fire," and assists Earth's aquatic beings to instigate or achieve Ascension.

Mudra: A symbolic ceremonial or spiritual gesture, mostly expressed by the hands and fingers. It is often used by evolved spiritual beings and Ascended Masters to signify or emit spiritual energies.

New Shamballa: The Golden City Network and affiliated Elohim, Archangels, Angels, Cosmic Beings, and Ascended Masters focused upon humanity's Ascension and spiritual evolution during the Golden Age of Kali Yuga.

Ninth Energy Body: An energy field that is developed through uniting dual forces, and requires an in-depth purification of thought. In fact, this energy field causes the soul to face and Master those negative, dark, forces that the Spiritual Teachers refer to as a type of *mental purgatory*. This energy body processes extreme fears and transmutes them. The transmutation completely restructures beliefs, and purifies energies held in the lower mental bodies accumulated throughout all lifetimes.

Nomaking: Located in China, this Golden City of the Yellow Ray is overseen by Cassiopeia, the Elohim of Wisdom, and Minerva, the Goddess of Wisdom. This is the thirty-eighth Golden City in activation and is affiliated with the spiritual qualities of wisdom, illumination, the power of attention, and perception.

ONE: Indivisible, whole, harmonious Unity.

Oneness: A combination of two or more, which creates the whole.

Oneship: A group or group mind that is based on the notion of whole, harmonious Unity.

Overshadowing: The process whereby an Ascended Master or being of light follows and monitors a student or chela through a specific phase of spiritual development. This may also include influencing and assisting the student or chela through difficulties with spiritual insight and influencing energies.

Pashacino: The sixth Golden City is located in Alberta and British Columbia, Canada. Its quality serves as a Bridge of Brotherhood for all people; its Ray Force is Green; and its Master Teacher is Soltec.

Pearlanu: Lady Master Lotus serves in the Golden City of Pearlanu, located on Madagascar. This is the twenty-fifth Golden City, is affiliated with the Violet Ray, and the transmuting quality of forgiveness.

Pleiades: A seven-star cluster that exists in the same Orion Arm of the Milky Way Galaxy near Earth. Also known as the Seven Sisters, the Pleiades is located in the Taurus Constellation. Its seven stars are: Sterope, Merope, Electra, Maia, Taygeta, Celaeno, and Alcyone.

Polarity: A Hermetic Law that states everything is dual; everything has poles; everything has its pair of opposites; like and unlike are the same; opposites are identical in nature, but different in degree; extremes meet; all truths are but half-truths; all paradoxes may be reconciled.

Prana, Golden City: The Golden City of India is overseen by its hierarch, Archangel Chamuel. It is affiliated with the Pink Ray and serves through adoration and the continuous heart.

Presching: Archangel Jophiel of the Yellow Ray serves in this Golden City located in North Korea. It is the thirty-eighth sacred Vortex and is known as, "The City for the Angels." It is also associated with the enduring love of ordered service.

Prophecy: A spiritual teaching given simultaneously with a warning. It's designed to change, alter, lessen, or mitigate the prophesied warning. This caveat may be literal or metaphoric; the outcome of these events are contingent on the choices and the consciousness of those willing to apply the teachings.

Prophet: An inspired revealer, interpreter, or spokesman. One whose office it is to deliver a message. The prophet is an initiate, the third level of spiritual development in the Ascension Process.

Purensk: The Divine Beings of Faith, Hope, and Charity serve the Blue, Yellow, and Pink Rays of the Unfed Flame in this twenty-first Golden City. Purensk radiates the spiritual gifts of love, wisdom, and power. It is located in Russia and China.

Quetzalcoatl: The Quetzalcoatl Energies, as explained and taught by Lord Meru, are akin to the Christ energies when applied in the esoteric Western Christian tradition. This ancient spiritual teacher, however, predates

Christianity and likely has its roots in alchemic Atlantean (Toltec) teaching. Quetzalcoatl, in contemporary terms, is the Incan Christ.

Rapture: A form of spiritual liberation, based on sincerity, peace, faith, and acceptance.

Ray or Ray Force(s): A force containing a purpose, which divides its efforts into two measurable and perceptible powers, light and sound.

Right-hand Path: Spiritual teaching based on love, trust, choice, unity, cooperation, and the sanctity of life.

Sacred Fire: The Unfed Flame of Divine Consciousness within the human heart. Often the term "Sacred Fire" is used to signify the Violet Fire. This is also in refererence to the sublime flame as it activates througout the kundalini.

Saint Germain: Ascended Master of the Seventh Ray, Saint Germain is known for his work with the Violet Flame of Mercy, Transmutation, Alchemy, and Forgiveness. He is the sponsor of the Americas and the I AM America material. Many other teachers and Masters affiliated with the Great White Brotherhood help his endeavors. Saint Germain serves in the Golden City of Wahanee, a Vortex that helps humanity to spiritual apply justice, liberty, and forgiveness.

Lord Sananda: The name used by Master Jesus in his ascended state of consciousness. Sananda means joy and bliss, and his teachings focus on revealing the savior and heavenly kingdom within. Sananda is associated with Christ Consciousness and the Golden City of Shalahah.

Sanat Kumara: Sanat Kumara is a Venusian Ascended Master and the venerated leader of the Ascended Masters, best known as the founder of Shamballa, the first Golden City on Earth. He is also known in the teachings of the Great White Brotherhood as the Lord of the World, and is regarded as a savior and eminent spiritual teacher. Sanat Kumara is the guru of four of the Twelve Jurisdictions: Cooperation, Charity, Desire, and Stillness. These spiritual precepts are based on the principles of Co-creation, and are prophesied to guide human consciousness into the New Times. These four Jurisdictions reiterate the symbolic revelation of Sanat Kumara's four-fold identity as the Cosmic Christ, which assist humanity's evolutionary process into the New Times. As Kartikkeya, the commander of God's Army, Sanat Kumara teaches Cooperation to overcome the lower mind; as Kumar the holy youth, Sanat Kumara imparts Charity to conquer the darkness of disease and poverty; as Skanda, the son of Shiva and the spiritual warrior, Sanat Kumara offers Desire as the hopeful seed of God's transformation; and as Guha, the Jurisdiction Stillness restores the cave of all hearts.

Seamless Garment: The Ascended Masters wear garments without seams. This clothing is not tailored by hand but perfected through the thought and manifestation process.

Serapis Bey: An Ascended Master from Venus who works on the White Ray. He is the great disciplinarian—essential for Ascension; and works closely with all unascended humanity who remain focused for its attainment. He oversees and serves in the Golden City of Klehma, to promote cooperation and the attainment of Ascension.

Seven Rays of Light and Sound: The traditional Seven Rays of Light and Sound are: the Blue Ray of Truth; the Yellow Ray of Wisdom; the Pink Ray of Love; the White Ray of Purity; the Green Ray of Healing; the Gold and Ruby Ray of Ministration; and the Violet Ray of Transmutation.

Seventh Manu: Highly evolved lifestreams that embody on Earth between 1981 to 3650. Their goal is to anchor freedom and the qualities of the Seventh Ray to the conscious activity on this planet. They are prophesied as the generation of peace and grace for the Golden Age. South America is their forecasted home, though small groups will incarnate in other areas of the globe.

Shalahah: The fourth United States Golden City located primarily in the states of Montana and Idaho. Its qualities are abundance, prosperity, and healing; its Ray Force is Green; and its Master Teacher is Sananda.

Shamballa: Venusian volunteers, who arrived 900 years before their leader Sanat Kumara, and built the Earth's first Golden City. Known as the City of White, located in the present-day Gobi Desert, its purpose was to hold conscious light for the Earth and to sustain her evolutionary place in the solar system.

Sheahah: Located in Australia, this Golden City is the forty-ninth in activation. Its steward is the Elohim Astrea, the twin force to the Elohim of Purity – Claire. Sheahah is associated with the White Ray and its spiritual qualities are transmutation and purity. This Vortex is affiliated with the Golden City of Shalahah, located in Idaho and Montana, United States.

Shehez: The steward is Tranquility, the Elohim of Peace, and is the nineteenth Golden City. Located primarily in Iran and Afghanistan, this sacred site radiates the Ruby and Gold Ray. Its spiritual qualities are peace, serenity, and calm.

Sircalwe: The Group of Twelve, also known as an ever-changing and anonymous group of Ascended Masters of Light, serve this Golden City of the White Ray. Located in East Siberia Russia, Sircalwe is known as the *Circle of Life*.

Soltech: An Ascended Master of science and technology who is affiliated with the Green Ray. Soltec is the hierarch of Pasahcino, located primarily in Alberta, Canada.

Spiritual Hierarchy: A fellowship of Ascended Masters and their disciples. This group helps humanity function through the mental plane with meditation, decrees, and prayer. The term Spiritual Hierarchy often refers to the Great White Brotherhood and Sisterhood. However, the term also connotes the spiritual-social structure for the organization, its members, and the various states of member evolution. The hierarchy includes the different offices and activities that serve the Cosmic, Solar, Planetary, and Creative Hierarchies.

Star: The apex, or center of each Golden City.

Star Retreats: Four retreats that surround the Star of a Golden City at the four cardinal directions.

Step-down Transformer: The processes instigated through the Cellular Awakening rapidly advance human light bodies. Synchronized with an Ascended Master's will, the awakened cells of light and love evolve the skills of a Step-down Transformer to efficiently transmit and distribute currents of Ascended Master energy—referred to as an Ascended Master Current (A.M. Current). This metaphysical form of intentional inductive coupling creates an ethereal power grid that can be used for all types of healing.

Stienta: The eleventh Golden City of the Blue Ray is served by Archangel Michael and is located in Iceland. It is known as the *City of Inner Vision*.

Swaddling Cloth: An area of over one million square miles. It is located in Brazil, South America. According to the Ascended Masters, this area is the primary prophesied physical location for the incarnation of the children of the Seventh Manu. The Swaddling Cloth is protected by the Ascended Master Mother Mary.

Tehekoa: The fifteenth Golden City of the Americas is located in Argentina, South America. Its quality is devotion; its Ray Force is Pink and Violet; and its Master Teacher is Panchamama, the Third Sister of South America.

Temples of Perfection: Four heavenly, interdimensional Temples located at the Peak Points of the intercardinal directions of each Golden City Vortex.

Tenth Energy Body: The final level of three protective HU-man light bodies, which is formed through the purification of desires, and is known as the *Diamond Mind.* Because this energy body gathers thought as light, it is a substantive and sizeable light body. The Spiritual Teachers often refer to the three protective HU-man energy bodies as the *Triple Gems,* and together they are strong enough to pierce human illusion.

Thirteen Evolutionary Pyramids: Thirteen phases of spiritual growth and evolution as the soul proceeds through the Eight-sided Cell of Perfection with the Ascension Process.

Three Standards: A spiritual practice that applies the Violet Flame, the Tube of Light, and the Blue Flame of Protection.

Time of Change: The period of time currently underway. Tremendous changes in our society, cultures, and politics in tandem with individual and collective spiritual awakenings and transformations will abound. These events occur simultaneously with the possibilities of massive global warming, climactic changes, and seismic and volcanic activity—Earth Changes. The Time of Change guides the Earth to a New Time, the Golden Age.

Tube of Light: Light surges from the tributaries of the Human Energy System: Chakras, meridians, and nadis—to create a large pillar of light. Decrees, prayers, and meditation with the Tube of Light increase its force and ability to protect the individual's spiritual growth and evolution.

Twelve Jurisdictions: Twelve laws (virtues) for the New Times that guide consciousness to Co-create the Golden Age. They are: Harmony, Abundance, Clarity, Love, Service, Illumination, Cooperation, Charity, Desire, Faith, Stillness, and Creation/Creativity.

Unfed Flame: The Three-Fold Flame of Divinity that exists in the heart and becomes larger as it evolves. The three flames represent: Love (Pink), Wisdom (Yellow), and Power (Blue).

Unte: Known as the City of Grace, this Golden City is served by Donna Grace, the Archeia of the Ruby and Gold Rays. It is located Tanzania and Kenya and cultivates the spiritual principle of ministration and service to humanity.

Uverno: The Canadian Golden City of the Pink Ray. Also known as the *Song of God*, the Golden City Vortex is located primarily in Ontario, and Manitoba, Canada. This Golden City is served by Paul the Venetian, an ascended being associated with music, art, and literature.

Violet Flame: The Violet Flame is the practice of balancing karmas of the past through Transmutation, Forgiveness, and Mercy. The result is an opening of the Spiritual Heart and the development of bhakti—unconditional love and compassion. It came into existence when the Lords of Venus first transmitted the Violet Flame, also knows as Violet Fire, at the end of Lemuria to clear the Earth's etheric and psychic realms, and the lower physical atmosphere of negative forces and energies. This paved the way for the Atlanteans, who used it during religious ceremonies and as a visible marker of temples. The Violet Flame also induces Alchemy. Violet light emits the shortest wavelength and the highest frequency in the spectrum, so it induces a point of transition to the next octave of light.

Wahanee: The third United States Golden City located primarily in the states of South Carolina and Georgia. Its qualities are justice, liberty, and freedom; its Ray Force is Violet; and its Master Teacher is Saint Germain.

Yuthor: The tenth Golden City is located in Greenland. Its quality is abundance of choice; its Ray Force is Green; and its Master Teacher is Hilarion.

Zaskar: Located in Tibet, this Golden City is overseen by Lady Master Reya. Zaskar radiates the energies of the White Ray and is affiliated with the guiding spiritual principle of simplicity.

The Sower with Setting Sun
Vincent van Gogh, 1888.

Discography

This list provides the recording session date and name of the original selected recordings cited in this work that provide the basis for its original transcriptions.

Toye, Lori
In the Garden, I AM America Seventh Ray Publishing International MP3. ℗© August 22, 2018.

Every Push, Every Pull, I AM America Seventh Ray Publishing International MP3. ℗© October 13, 2018.

Acceleration, I AM America Seventh Ray Publishing International MP3. ℗© October 14, 2018.

Leveraging Consciousness, I AM America Seventh Ray Publishing International MP3. ℗© October 19, 2018.

A Great Love, I AM America Seventh Ray Publishing International MP3. ℗© October 20, 2018.

Human to HU-man, I AM America Seventh Ray Publishing International MP3. ℗© October 21, 2018.

The Golden Orb, I AM America Seventh Ray Publishing International MP3. ℗© November 1, 2018.

The Guiding Light, I AM America Seventh Ray Publishing International MP3. ℗© November 2, 2018.

Temples of Ascension, I AM America Seventh Ray Publishing International MP3. ℗© December 17, 2018.

From Shadows to Light, I AM America Seventh Ray Publishing International MP3. ℗© December 18, 2018.

One-thousand and Eighty-eight, I AM America Seventh Ray Publishing International MP3. ℗© December 19, 2018.

Tipping Point, I AM America Seventh Ray Publishing International MP3. ℗© December 20, 2018.

Activation, I AM America Seventh Ray Publishing International MP3. ℗© January 5, 2019.

Great Awakening, I AM America Seventh Ray Publishing International MP3. ℗© January 6, 2019.

The Aquamarine Ray, I AM America Seventh Ray Publishing International MP3. ℗© January 7, 2019.

Golden Age of Co-creation, I AM America Seventh Ray Publishing International MP3. ℗© June 27, 2019.

Illustrations Resources

Earth Changes Maps, Golden City Maps:
I AM America Maps
iamamerica.com

Saint Germain and Visionary Art:
Susan Seddon Boulet
susanseddonboulet.com

El Morya, Kuthumi, and Spiritual Art:
Summit Lighthouse
summitlighthouse.org

Archangel Gabriel, Astrea, and Visionary Art:
Marius Michael-George
mariusfineart.com

Prince Ragoczy (Saint Germain), Symbolic Prints and Posters:
Philosophical Research School
prs.org

Archangel Uriel and Angelic Art:
Howard David Johnson
howarddavidjohnson.com

Soltec and Visionary Art:
Celeste Korsolm
artsedona.net

Orion and Angelica, Angel of the Crystal, and Visionary Art:
Pamela Matthews Art of the Soul
grail.co.nz

Genesis II and Symbolic Art:
John Stephens
johnstephens.com

Holy Amethyst, Mighty Victory, and Ascended Master Art:
Suvorov Vladimir
artnow.ru

Ascended Masters and Sacred Images:
Saint Germain Press
saintgermainpress.com/pictures

Chimera
Gustave Moreau, 1884.

Index

Clayje, Golden City of: 219
definition: 359
Co-creation: 113
and the Eighth Energy Body: 289
Co-creative dominion: 190
definition: 359
Group Mind: 115
inner Adjutant Points: 152
Cole, Thomas
Study for the Pilgrim of the World on
His Journey: 214
Collective Consciousness: 67, 189
and cleansing: 147
and severity of changes: 41
a part of Mass Consciousness: 329
definition: 359
Sacred Fire: 77
conscious human: 317
consciousness: 52
and the HU-man: 305
Ascension: 122
definition: 359
Golden Consciousness: 184
immortality: 36
individualization: 126
leveraged during Shamballa: 157
manipulation of Collective Conscious-
ness: 190
mass: 329
"Ray Force fits your consciousness.": 124
Shamballa: 119
Cosmic Hierarchy: 323
Cosmic I AM Presence: 323
Creative Hierarchy: 324
definition: 359
the Human Hierarchy: 328
Cresta, Golden City of: 219
definition: 359
Crotese, Golden City of: 220
definition: 360
Cup or Cup Ceremony
Adjutant Points: 166
definition: 360
Cycle of the Elements: 56
definition: 360
diagram: 268

D

Dahl Universe
definition: 360
Group Mind: 183
Violet Flame: 143
darkness
is a teacher: 73
"Darkness gives contrast to light.": 80
death
and the dissipation of the First Three
Light Bodies: 287
removing the death consciousness: 36
decree
Alchemizing Fire: 161
Alignment to the Divine Will: 178
Ascension: 36, 159
Blue Flame of Protection: 100
definition: 360
Dissolve the Shadow: 173
Divine Protection: 108
Divine Service: 167
Group Mind: 183
New Shamballa Grid: 164
to empower the Ninth Light Body: 289
transcend limitation: 193
Violet Flame for Ascension: 192
White Fire of Ascension: 174
White Flame of Purity: 114
Denasha, Golden City of: 220, 279
aligns to Malton: 71
definition: 360
depression
use of Violet Flame: 104
devotion
Ascension: 140
Diamond Mind: 290, 380
diet: 34
and development of the Eighth Light
Body: 289
disasters
mitigating through the Step-down
Transformer: 131
Divine Blueprint: 289
Divine Justice
Lady Nada: 88

Divine Mother: 226, 338
Divine Service: 142
  definition: 361
Divine Will
  Blue Ray: 107
  definition: 361
  Holy Father: 142
DNA
  Collective Consciousness: 190
  Great Intervention: 169
  Violet Flame: 33
Donjakey, Golden City of: 221
  definition: 361
dropping of the body
  form of Ascension: 121
drought
  and Visheeah: 98

E

Eabra, Golden City of: 221
  definition: 361
Earth Changes
  Afghanistan: 133
  Alaska: 133
  Aleutian Islands: 132
  ameliorating: 67
  Cascadia fault line: 131
  Central America: 131
  Chile: 131
  definition: 361
  humanity changes: 129
  Los Angeles: 133
  movement of energy: 132
  Philippines: 131, 133
  San Andreas: 131
  South America: 133
  South American coastline: 131
  Turkey: 132
  United States West Coast: 131
  Volcanic Explosions: 130
  volcanoes: 189
Earth Plane and Planet
  cleansing: 147
  definition: 361

earthquake(s)
  Middle East: 132
  Shadow Governments: 130
eclipses
  lunar and solar: 41
Egypt
  remnant of Atlantis: 171
Eighth Energy Body
  and Ascension: 36, 78
  and Group Mind: 42
  anomalies: 85
  definition: 361
Eight Pathways of Ascension
  diagram: 321
Eight-sided Cell of Perfection: 80, 160,
    170, 325, 329
  and the Sacred Fire: 76
  definition: 362
  development of higher Light Bodies: 190
  diagram: 319
  Golden Orb: 96
  love: 115
  *The Thirteen Pyramids and Twelve
    Evolution Points: 319*
  Violet Flame engineering: 33
Elemental Kingdom: 69
  definition: 362
  *"One does not live by bread alone...":
    302*
Eliah: 62, 273
  definition: 362
El Morya: 107, 152, 173, 223, 276
  appendix: 305
  biography: 299
  Blue Flame Initiations: 99
  candle meditation
  definition: 362
  Kuthumi's brother: 277
  tempering the Will: 40
Elohim
  definition: 362
  of Earth: 323
Elohim Angelica: 217
Elohim Arcturus and Diana: 217
Elohim Arien: 275
Elohim Astrea: 233

Tiger's Nest Monastery: 252
time
contraction and release: 135
flow of breath: 136
opening and closing: 137
viewing events: 136
Time of Change: 193
definition: 380
polarity: 40
revelation of truth: 76
the new humanity: 52
time travel
teaching by Hercules: 135
Tranquility, Goddess of the Dawn: 234
transmutation
and the Ninth Light Body: 289, 375
Triple Gems
and the Tenth Light Body: 290, 380
TronXR: 45
Tube of Light: 281
and the human aura: 288
appendix and instruction: 281
definition: 380
Turkey
Golden City of Ganakra: 132
Twelve Jurisdictions: 198
and Sanat Kumara: 320
definition: 380
diagram: 319
lineage of: 283
Twenty-year Cycles of the Elements: 56,
269, 360
change of: 59
Twin Rays: 328
"Two shall become as ONE."
Oneship: 84

U

Unfed Flame: 325
and Sanat Kumara: 317
and the Ascended Master: 329
and the Three-Fold Flame Creation
Myth: 328
definition: 381

United States
Declaration of Independence: 294
Pledge of Liberation: 196
restoration of the Republic: 148
transformation: 149
Unte, Golden City of: 236
definition: 381
Uverno, Golden City of: 236
definition: 381

V

Vanderbank, John
Francis Bacon: 292
Van Gogh, Vincent
Aries View from the Wheat Fields: 344
The Sower with Setting Sun: 382
vegan diet
Three Standards: 281
Venus: 247
temples of: 313
Violet Flame: 143
Violet Flame: 281
Alchemizing Fire decree: 161
Alchemizing Fire technique: 161
Alchemy: 144
and the Sacred Fire: 76
appendix and instruction: 281
Ascension: 48, 93, 122, 192
calling forth the consuming fire: 281
definition: 381
Eight-sided Cell of Perfection: 170
for depression: 104
for problems: 39
Gold Ray, the next step: 95
groups of seven: 77
invocation at sunrise, sunset: 211
lineage of: 283
Lords of Venus: 33
origins: 143
practice: 76
practice for two to seven years to enter
Divine Service: 142
Spiritual Lineage: 211
the Law of Forgiveness: 53
Violet Light
qualities of: 110

Saint Pantaleon the Healer
Nicholas Roerich, 1916.

About Lori & Lenard Toye

Lori Toye is not a Prophet of doom and gloom. The fact that she became a Prophet at all is highly unlikely. Reared in a small Idaho farming community as a member of the conservative Missouri Synod Lutheran church, Lori had never heard of meditation, spiritual development, reincarnation, channeling, or clairvoyant sight.

Her unusual spiritual journey began in Washington State, when, as advertising manager of a weekly newspaper, she answered a request to pick up an ad for a local health food store. As she entered, a woman at the counter pointed a finger at her and said, "You have work to do for Master Saint Germain!"

The next several years were filled with spiritual enlightenment that introduced Lori, then only twenty-two years old, to the most exceptional and inspirational information she had ever encountered. Lori became a student of Ascended Master teachings.

Awakened one night by the luminous figure of Saint Germain at the foot of her bed, her work had begun. Later in the same year, an image of a map appeared in her dream. Four teachers clad in white robes were present, pointing out Earth Changes that would shape the future United States.

Five years later, faced with the stress of a painful divorce and rebuilding her life as a single mother, Lori attended spiritual meditation classes. While there, she shared her experience, and encouraged by friends, she began to explore the dream through daily meditation. The four Beings appeared again, and expressed a willingness to share the information. Over a six-month period, they gave over eighty sessions of material, including detailed information that would later become the I AM America Map.

Clearly she had to produce the map. The only means to finance it was to sell her house. She put her home up for sale, and in a depressed market, it sold the first day at full asking price.

She produced the map in 1989, rolled copies of them on her kitchen table, and sold them through word-of-mouth. She then launched a lecture tour of the Northwest and California. Hers was the first Earth Changes Map published, and many others have followed, but the rest is history.

From the tabloids to the *New York Times, The Washington Post*, television interviews in the U.S., London, and Europe, Lori's Mission was to honor the material she had received. The material is not hers, she stresses. It belongs to the Masters, and their loving, healing approach is disseminated through the I AM America Publishing Company operated by her husband and spiritual partner, Lenard Toye.

Lenard Toye, originally from Philadelphia, PA, was born into a family of professional contractors and builders, and has a remarkable singing voice. Lenard's compelling tenor voice replaced many of the greats at a moment's notice—Pavarotti and Domingo, including many performances throughout Europe. When he retired from music, he joined his family's business yet pursued his personal interests in alternative healing.

He attended *Barbara Brennan's School of Healing* to further develop the gift of auric vision. Working together with his wife Lori, they organized free classes of healing techniques and the channeled teachings. Their instructional pursuits led them to form the *School of the Four Pillars* which includes holistic and energy healing and Ascended Master Teachings. In 1995 and 1996 they sponsored the first Prophecy Conferences in Philadelphia and Phoenix, Arizona. His management and sales background has played a very important role in his partnership with his wife Lori and their publishing company. Other publications include three additional Prophecy maps, seventeen books, a video, and more than sixty audio tapes based on sessions with Master Teacher Saint Germain and other Ascended Masters.

Spiritual in nature, I AM America is not a church, religion, sect, or cult. There is no interest or intent in amassing followers or engaging in any activity other than what Lori and Lenard can do on their own to publicize the materials they have been entrusted with.

They have also been directed to build the first Golden City community. A very positive aspect of the vision is that all the maps include areas called, "Golden Cities." These places hold a high spiritual energy, and are where sustainable communities are to be built using solar energy alongside classical feng shui engineering and infrastructure. The first community, Wenima Village, is currently being planned for development.

Concerned that some might misinterpret the Maps' messages as doom and gloom and miss the metaphor for personal change, or not consider the spiritual teachings attached to the maps, Lori emphasizes that the Masters stressed that this was a Prophecy of choice. Prophecy allows for choice in making informed decisions and promotes the opportunity for cooperation and harmony. Lenard and Lori's vision for I AM America is to share the Ascended Masters' prophecies as spiritual warnings to heal and renew our lives.

Books and Maps by Lori Toye

Books:

NEW WORLD WISDOM SERIES: *Book One, Two, and Three*

FREEDOM STAR: *Prophecies that Heal Earth*

THE EVER PRESENT NOW: *A New Understanding of Consciousness and Prophecy*

I AM AMERICA ATLAS: *Based on the Maps, Prophecies, and Teachings of the Ascended Masters*

GOLDEN CITY SERIES
Book One: Points of Perception
Book Two: Light of Awakening
Book Three: Divine Destiny
Book Four: Sacred Energies of the Golden Cities
Book Five: Temples of Consciousness
Book Six: Awaken the Master Within

I AM AMERICA TRILOGY
Book One: A Teacher Appears
Book Two: Sisters of the Flame
Book Three: Fields of Light

I AM AMERICA COLLECTION
Building the Seamless Garment: Revealing the Secret Teachings of Ascension and the Golden Cities

Maps:

I AM America Map
Freedom Star World Map
United States 6-Map Scenario
United States Golden City Map

I AM AMERICA PUBLISHING & DISTRIBUTING
P.O. Box 2511, Payson, Arizona, 85547, USA. (928) 978-6435
I AM America Online Bookstore:
www.iamamerica.com
For More Information:
www.loritoye.com

About I AM America

I AM America is an educational and publishing foundation dedicated to disseminating the Ascended Masters' message of Earth Changes Prophecy and Spiritual Teachings for self-development. Our office is run by the husband and wife team of Lenard and Lori Toye who hand-roll maps, package, and mail information and products with a small staff. Our first publication was the I AM America Map, which was published in September 1989. Since then we have published three more Prophecy maps, thirteen books, and numerous recordings based on the channeled sessions with the Spiritual Teachers.

We are not a church, a religion, a sect, or cult and are not interested in amassing followers or members. Nor do we have any affiliation with a church, religion, political group, or government of any kind. We are not a college or university, research facility, or a mystery school. El Morya told us that the best way to see ourselves is as, "Cosmic Beings, having a human experience."

In 1994, we asked Saint Germain, "How do you see our work at I AM America?" and he answered, "I AM America is to be a clearinghouse for the new humanity." Grabbing a dictionary, we quickly learned that the term "clearinghouse" refers to "an organization or unit within an organization that functions as a central agency for collecting, organizing, storing, and disseminating documents, usually within a specific academic discipline or field." So inarguably, we are this too. But in uncomplicated terms, we publish and share spiritually transformational information because at I AM America there is no doubt that, "A Change of Heart can Change the World."

With Violet Flame Blessings,
Lori & Lenard Toye

For more information or to visit our online bookstore, go to:
www.iamamerica.com
www.loritoye.com

To receive a catalog by mail, please write to:
I AM America
P.O. Box 2511
Payson, AZ 85547

our next evolution ...

Points of Perception

Prophecies and Teachings of Saint Germain

Light of Awakening

Prophecies and Teachings of the Ascended Masters

Golden City Series

The Science of the Golden Cities and the Ascension Process

1. **POINTS OF PERCEPTION:** *Prophecies and Teachings from Saint Germain*

2. **LIGHT OF AWAKENING:** *Prophecies and Teachings from the Ascended Masters*

Divine Destiny

Prophecies and Teachings of the Ascended Masters

Sacred Energies

of the Golden Cities

3. **DIVINE DESTINY:** *Prophecies and Teachings from the Ascended Masters*

4. **SACRED ENERGIES:** *Of the Golden Cities*

5. **TEMPLES OF CONSCIOUSNESS:** *Ascended Master Teaching of the Golden Cities*

6. **AWAKEN THE MASTER WITHIN:** *Golden Age Teaching of Saint Germain*

Temples of Consciousness

Ascended Master Teachings of the Golden Cities

Awaken the Master Within

Golden Age Teachings of Saint Germain

loritoye.com
iamamerica.com

I AM America Trilogy

The contemporary Spiritual Journey

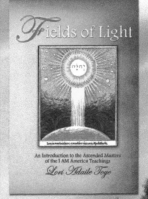

A Teacher Appears	Sisters of the Flame	Fields of Light
ISBN: 9781800050446	ISBN: 9781800050262	ISBN: 9781800050613
254 pages	216 pages	310 pages

This series of insightful books, written by the creator of the acclaimed *I AM America Maps* shares a fresh and personal viewpoint of the contemporary spiritual journey. Lori Toye was just twenty-two years old when she first encountered Ascended Master teaching. The *I AM America Trilogy* takes us back to the beginning of her experiences with her spiritual teachers and includes insights that have never been disclosed in any previous books or writings. In "A Teacher Appears," learn how true wisdom and the inner teacher is within all of us. "Sisters of the Flame," continues an initiatory passage into the feminine with the Cellular Awakening. "Fields of Light," explains how to integrate and Master our spiritual light through soul-transcending teachings of Ascension. Lori's personal story is interwoven throughout the I AM America Trilogy in a rich tapestry of spiritual techniques, universal wisdom, and knowledge gained through a life-changing spiritual journey.

CPSIA information can be obtained
at www.ICGtesting.com
Printed in the USA
LVHW071925170723
751787LV00001B/4

9 781880 050330